THE MYSTERY OF OVEREND AND GURNEY

Also by Geoffrey Elliott

From Siberia, with Love, Methuen, 2004
I Spy: The Secret Life of a British Agent, Little, Brown, 1997

(with Harold Shukman)
Secret Classrooms: An Untold Story of the Cold War,
St Ermin's Press, 2002

THE MYSTERY OF OVEREND AND GURNEY

A Financial Scandal in Victorian London

GEOFFREY ELLIOTT

Methuen

Published by Methuen 2006

10 9 8 7 6 5 4 3 2 1

Methuen & Co. Ltd
11–12 Buckingham Gate, London SW1E 6LB
www.methuen.co.uk

ISBN-10: 0 413 77573 9
ISBN-13: 978 0 413 77573 3

A CIP catalogue record for this book
is available from the British Library

Typeset by SX Composing DTP, Rayleigh, Essex
Printed and bound in Great Britain by
The Cromwell Press, Trowbridge, Wiltshire

This is for Timothy and Mari Beth

Alas, regardless of their doom,
The little victims play!
No sense have they of ills to come,
Nor care beyond today.

Thomas Gray, 'Ode on a Distant Prospect of Eton College', 1747

Contents

Acknowledgements

Thanks are due to Joanna Clark of The Library of The Religious Society of Friends; Jessie Campbell of Barclays Group Archives; Sarah Millard, Jennie Mountain and Kath Begley at the Bank of England Archives; Michael T. Burke of Galway City Council for sight of Father Daly's portrait; Tim Collins for a tour of the Father's landscape; the staff of The Guildhall Library for help with the illustrations and pointing me in the direction of the Shareholders List; Chris Wheal, for his always diligent research support; Mark Gamsa, Angus Cundey of Henry Poole and Son; John Hellyer, historian of West Ham United; Marianne Welch of the University of Western Ontario Law Library; The London Library; Jonathan Evans of the Royal London Hospital Archives and Museum; Sandra Gee of The Royal Household; Ioannis Leptokaridis, EFG Scholar at St Antony's College, Oxford, and the College's Polly Friedhof; Caroline Showell, Librarian of The British Trust for Ornithology; Tony Blee, who over many years has never failed to find answers to arcane questions, and did so again here by tracing the origins of Gurney's Pitta; and Emily Hedges, for her help with the illustrations.

At a personal level my gratitude goes first and foremost to Fay Elliott, who travelled down many of these roads with me and was unfailing in her support. Ben Yarde-Buller provided helpful insights in an early draft of the text and, as it reached finality, I was deeply appreciative that Sir Adrian Cadbury took the time and trouble to read through it. Linda Osband provided careful editorial insights, which were most valuably augmented in the final stages by Methuen's Elizabeth Brennan. Any errors that remain are mine alone.

Illustrations

1. 'Black Friday', 10 may 1866 (© Mary Evans Picture Library)
2. Doré print of Ludgate Hill with a view of Saint Pauls Cathedral (© Mary Evens Picture Library)
3. Lombard Street (© Mary Evans Picture Library)
4. 'Samuel Gurney the Great' (© The Library of the Religious Society of Friends)
5. Elizabeth Fry, the famous Quaker reformer and sister of Samuel Gurney (© Mary Evans Picture Library)
6. The Gurney bank in Norwich, 1780. Cornerstone of the family's remarkable wealth (Private Collection)
7. Grove House School (© The Library of the Religious Society of Friends)
8. Henry Edmund Gurney (Private Collection)
9. John Henry Gurney. (© The Library of the Religious Society of Friends)
10. Greek novelist and entrepreneur, Stefanos Xenos (Private Collection)
11. The dapper and devious 'Baron' Albert Grant (Private Collection)
12. Father Peter Daly whose idea for a new transatlantic shipping line led to one of Overends' nastiest financial disasters (© Galway City Archives)
13. An architect's vision for the Galway deep harbour (© Timothy Collins)
14. Transatlantic ships in Nova Scotia (© Mary Evans Picture Library)
15. The Isle of Dogs, site of the last of Overends' major calamities (© Mary Evans Picture Library)

Chronology

1663	Child's Bank, Temple Bar, founded
1680	Hoare's Bank, Fleet Street, founded
1685	Snow's Bank, Strand, founded
1694	The Bank of England founded
1770	Gurney's Bank, Norwich, founded
1786	'Samuel Gurney the Great' born
1788	Joseph John Gurney born Peter Daly born
1802	Thomas Richardson, a London Bill broker's clerk, founds his own business
1805	Richardson is joined by his brother-in-law, John Overend, and Richardson & Overend Co. is founded
1807	Overend, Gurney & Co. founded following Gurney's investment in Richardson & Overend Co., John Overend leaves the business soon after
1821	Henry Gurney born Stefanos Xenos born

1823   Hudson Gurney born

1830   Albert Zachariah Gottheimer (later Grant) born, Dublin

1830s   William Fairbairn buys the Millwall Shipyard, later selling it to John Scott Russell

1850   The Galway Line proposal is sent to Whitehall by Father Peter Daly

1851   The Great Exhibition is held

1856   Samuel Gurney dies

1857   Greek & Oriental Steam Navigation Co. founded by Stefanos Xenos

1859   The Galway Line's *Argo* is lost when it runs aground off Newfoundland in May

1860   The mercantile Discount Co. goes out of business

         The Galway Line AGM held in London to angry protests from shareholders

1861   The Galway Line loses the Royal Mail subsidy

         John Scott Rusell becomes bankrupt and the Millwall Shipyard is taken over by Charles Mare

1863   Father Daly secures a promise from Lord Palmerston in February that the Galway Line may re-qualify for its Royal Mail subsidy if it demonstrates that it has reliable ships and a regular schedule

         The Galway Line begins trading again successfully in August

1864   The Galway Line's business finally winds up

Charles Mare leaves the Millwall Shipyard and, in April, Overend, Gurney & Co. decide to offer publish shares in the yard

1865   Overend, Gurney & Co. becomes a limited liability company, publishing a prospectus for the sale of shares to outside investors

1866   Railway contractors firm Watson, Overend & Co. fails in January, owing Overend, Gurney & Co. £1.5 million

Millwall Iron Works, Shipbuilding and Graving Dock Co. Ltd collapses in March following a costly and fruitless attempt to launch HMS *Northumberland*

The 'new' Gurney & Co. Bank, Norwich, founded on 23 April

Overend, Gurney & Co. suspends its trading activities on 10 May

Judgement appealed to the House of Lords in August

1868   Summonses served to Overends' directors to appear before the Lord Mayor of London on 1 January 1869

Father Peter Daly dies

1869   The Lord Mayor of London decrees on 26 January that there is enough evidence of fraud to commit the Overend & Gurney Co. directors John Gurney, Henry Gurney, Robert Birkbeck, Henry Ford Barclay, Harry Gordon and William Rennie to trial

In December all six of the Overend, Gurney & Co. directors are acquitted

1875   Samuel Gurney dies

1890   Albert Grant dies

John Henry Gurney dies

Dr Thom dies

1893   Henry Ford Barclay dies

The books are finally closed on Overend, Gurney & Co. Ltd

1895   Stefanos Xenos dies

1898   Charles Mare dies

1905   Henry Edmund Gurney dies

Introduction

May 1866. It would take two more daunting months for the last dripping lengths of telegraph cable to be hauled ashore like a harpooned sea serpent from the Atlantic deep at Heart's Content Bay in Newfoundland, permanently tying the Old World to the New.[1] So the news of the sudden death of Overend, Gurney & Co. Limited travelled the old-fashioned way, in a heavy canvas bag flung overboard to a waiting pilot boat from the deck of a steamer approaching Nova Scotia from Liverpool. From Nova Scotia a telegraph operator's nimble fingers clicked it out with an ebony and copper key in the dots and dashes of Samuel Morse's Code, which for twenty years now had been the staple of long-distance messaging. In the *New York Times'* office, the electrical signals were urgently translated into letters of the alphabet. As the story took shape, the newspaper's sub-editors, trained to turn even banking stories into high drama, distilled its essentials into the eye-popping headlines which would cascade down the left-hand side of next morning's front page:

'Terrible and Disastrous Financial Panic in London'
'Almost Total Suspension of Business in London, Liverpool and Other Commercial Centres'
'Failure of Many of The Largest Banking Houses in London'
'Lombard Street Blockaded By A Tumultuous and Terror-Stricken Mob'
'The Panic Without Parallel in the Financial History of England'

Except for those who made their living in the money and stock markets, the London firm whose shock collapse had triggered the headlines, was little known in the new United States. But London was the world's financial and trading capital, the deposits held by its banks three or four times greater than those of New York, and the merchants and bankers among the *New York Times'* readers were painfully aware that problems in London would hit them too.

Notwithstanding the firm's official name, the original and blameless Overend had departed long before the events in this story took place and the business was essentially under the control of several members of the East Anglian banking family of Gurney, rich and respectable Quakers. It is thus slightly unfair to shorten it to 'Overends'. However, as one of the financial markets' icons, it had also acquired its own nickname and that is how the City by and large referred to it. Much as The Bank of England had over time become 'The Old Lady', the Stock Exchange had been abbreviated to 'Change' and the array of Government securities which were the main investment medium of the time was shorthanded to 'The Funds', Overend's was known as 'The Corner House,' from the commanding position of its offices at the intersection of Lombard Street and Birchin Lane.

In Whitehall and the City of London, in banking firms across Britain, the name of Overend, Gurney & Co. had a special resonance. It was 'the bankers' bank', wholesaler of money, with a turnover second only to the Bank of England itself and double that of all its competitors combined. In the opinion of *The Times* in London, the bank was 'the greatest instrument of credit in the Kingdom'. It also resonated in a rather different way in the mainly middle-class homes of the country's emerging breed of gullible Stock Market investors. Only a few months before the bank's collapse the company's shares had been touted as a cornucopia of capital gains and dividends. Now they were not just a loss but carried, as we shall see, a heavy liability for their owners. The collapse shocked England not just by its suddenness and immensity, a tidal wave sweeping all values and certainties down the drains of the City streets, but because the firm's partners were prominent heirs to a Quaker banking tradition of shrewd probity. How could they of all people have been brought down; and in the process ruined not just themselves but many thousands of others?

This book tells the story of how in just three years, from 1859 to 1862, while it was still a private firm, the principal partners of Overend, Gurney & Co., seduced by the speculative mania of the times, set their highly respected and profitable Quaker banking firm slithering down the road to ruin by taking a series of ever more foolish business and financial risks. In the three years which followed, even as red-ink evidence of their folly spilled over the margins of their ledgers, they deluded themselves day after day that things would come right and that they could keep the rumbling mountain of 'junk' debt they had kept concealed from the world from erupting into a volcano.

In 1865, in a spasm of desperation, they took their final gamble, an attempt to stave off collapse by raising fresh capital through the sale of shares to investors lured by a prospectus that, even by the lax standards of the day, was short on hard facts and long on soft promises. Instead of deliverance, less than twelve months later this foolish and, by today's harsher standards, fraudulent throw of the dice brought disaster and disgrace and sparked off a wild panic in financial markets, which went into the history books as 'Black Friday'.

Space and lack of information mean that we cannot look at each of their bad deals, though it would be fascinating to know more about some of the smaller lunacies that crop up in The Corner House books. What were they doing advancing money to Mr Garraway's plantations in Dominica[2] or to the three-times bankrupt fraudster David Leopold Lewis, promoter of the London & Hamburg Bank and the Cork and Youghal Railway, whose career was described by a judge as 'a romance of a most inexplicable character'? What induced them to finance a railway line across the wilds of Ulster from Portadown to Omagh, via a 'front man', one John Edward Campbell Koch, a Bayswater metal merchant, a venture in which they lost several millions in today's values? We shall sadly never know what strange dealings lay behind the tantalisingly brief tale, told by one of the contemporary chroniclers of the

Overends story, about 'the two fugitives, George Sedgwick and Charles Gray, and their adventures at Neufchatel with Madame Formachon when Mr James Beard . . . was tracking them with detectives and . . . the display of daggers and revolvers made by these gentlemen at Naples'.

But the conclusion to be drawn, whether from these sideshows or from the major calamities which we shall be looking at, is always the same. The Corner House died because this band of about-to-be bankrupt bankers did business 'in a manner so reckless and foolish', in the crisp condemnation of Walter Bagehot, editor of *The Economist*, 'that one would think a child who had lent money in the City of London would have lent it better'. He might well have added that, having lent it and seen problems emerge, they insouciantly poured good money after bad. As we shall see when we pick over the bones of the Greek & Oriental Steam Navigation Company, the failed Gaelic dream of the Galway Line and the misadventures at Millwall Iron Works, they lived to the letter the harsh biblical forecast that, 'As a dog returneth to his vomit, so a fool returneth to his folly.'

Making money and, even more, losing it in large amounts are always subjects of morbid fascination, but this story is about much more than that. It is a story about mid-Victorian England, a country at the pinnacle of its power, with the City of London as the Empire's financial centre of gravity, a country bursting with energy and technological inventiveness, which went hand in hand with speculation and the creation and destruction of fortunes.

The financial drama is played out against a rich, almost surreal landscape: the wooden beams sunk into a muddy slope which are all that remain of a bankrupt shipyard on London's Isle of Dogs; the Georgian façade of what was once Ireland's biggest hotel; a small church on the road out of Galway to Oughterard; a fine Adam house a few doors along from the London Library in St James's Square; the pigeon-splattered statues of British worthies which stand incongruously under the neon cinema hoardings of Leicester Square; even, several statute miles and many social light years to the north, the West Ham United Football Club ground, once part of an idyllic

Gurney family estate in what, well into the nineteenth century, was still London's countryside.

Silhouetted against this landscape are the cast of characters who give life to the story, headed by the principal Overend partners, Henry Edmund Gurney, David Ward Chapman, Robert Birkbeck, and later in the story, the bird-watching banker John Henry Gurney. Much in evidence too is the equivocal Edward Watkin Edwards, accountant, Inner Temple barrister, Bankruptcy Court official and Garrick Club stalwart. Edwards was a 'fixer' in whom the partners placed, some said misplaced, a great deal of confidence and who was vilified after the debacle as the firm's *éminence grise*. We will also meet the Greek novelist and Black Sea tramp-steamer operator Stefanos Xenos; the flashy and unscrupulous 'bucket shop' share promoter 'Baron' Grant – born Albert Gottheimer – on whom Anthony Trollope drew for some of the traits of his fictional swindler, Augustus Melmotte, in *The Way We Live Now*, as well as Father Peter Daly, a uniquely Irish combination of charismatic parish priest and wheeler-dealer (Trollope biographer Richard Mullen conjectures that the author may actually have met Daly and drawn on him for one of his Irish characters); and the racehorse owner and twice-bankrupt shipbuilder Charles Mare. The relentless Aberdonian Adam Thom, once a 'hanging judge' in Canada, stalks onto the stage in the drama's closing scenes, bent on vengeance. As the story ends, we even catch a brief and macabre glimpse of Sir Basil Zaharoff as a young Balkan hustler, long before his twentieth-century apotheosis as a mystery-shrouded international arms dealer.

Threaded through the whole tale is the complex web of relation-ships between Overends and The Bank of England. The Bank, though still privately owned by City interests, was already central to the funding of the Government and the money markets of London, controlling short-term interest rates and the exchange rate between sterling and gold bullion. Crucially it also served, as we shall see, as the 'lender of last resort' when, as happened periodically, the money supply in the City ran low and Overends and other market operators needed to turn commercial debts into cash at short notice. At the same time however the Bank was also a major competitor in

Overends' core business, and their relationship had at times been difficult. Though not yet armed with the power of suasion, supervision and sanction over British banks which it would build up over the next decades, the Bank was nonetheless powerful enough to decide whether Overends lived or died when 'Black Friday' dawned, a power that it exercised with the professional dexterity and 'careful, calm deliberation', that were to become its hallmarks.

Many of those connected with Overends were from families prominent in the Society of Friends, or 'Quakers'. One of the most interesting aspects of the story will be the challenge to understand why men of unblemished reputation, brought up in a faith whose teachings had many warnings about 'the deceitfulness of riches' and the danger of 'pushing forward in the pursuit of greatness, upon hazardous attempts which have too often issued in the fall and ruin of themselves and families, the reproach of the Society and great loss to others,' could have gone so badly astray. How could men taught to be honest and truthful in word and deed have put their names to a share prospectus singularly short on truth? Quakers, as we shall see, had made an extraordinarily important contribution to British mercantile, industrial and social progress, out of all proportion to the Society's minuscule membership. Many had become hugely rich in the process, but without sacrificing their integrity and only very rarely diluting their prudence. Why then did The Corner House partners fail so miserably? Their failure could well have destroyed not just the reputation but also the fortunes of the Gurney family bank in Norwich, cornerstone of the family's remarkable wealth, whose history, partners and business were inextricably linked with those of Overends'. Or 'almost inextricably' that it did neither is perhaps another example of Quaker shrewdness since, as we shall see later, thanks to an adroit family shuffle, there later emerged from the firestorm a main constituent of one of Britain's largest banks.

For many years after the débâcle, the affair generated publicity, legal actions and parliamentary debates, culminating in a dramatic criminal trial. It has been cited in various financial histories, but this is the first time the full story has been laid out with the benefit of hitherto unexplored archival material and other untapped sources, and the strands of a complicated web drawn together.

In taking a fresh look, we have the benefit of the correspondence files of Gurney's Norwich bank, especially John Henry Gurney's letters to his partners there in the immediate aftermath of the collapse. We also have the treasure trove of history meticulously collected and collated in the Library of the Society of Friends in London, which includes family correspondence – the eighteenth- and nineteenth-century black ink and blue notepaper equivalent of weblogs – recording every thought, journey and feeling. There are the laconic Minutes of the Bank of England and even a few shreds from the files of the Bank's solicitors, Freshfields. There are yards – literally – of coverage in *The Times*, *The Economist*, the *Pall Mall Gazette* and the banking journals, and the volley of pamphlets launched by angry Overends' shareholders. The *New York Times* gives us an interesting perspective on how the affair and London itself were seen in the infant United States. Even Karl Marx and Friedrich Engels have some observations for us.

The affair's crescendo, the much-publicised criminal 'Trial of the Directors', attracted so much attention that the summing up was published as a hardcover booklet. Among the story's unexpected features is that the trial did not flow from a prosecution launched with the full weight of the official legal system as we now know it, but crowned a private campaign by an aggrieved investor represented by a barrister whose paranoid incompetence makes 'Rumpole of the Bailey' look like a strong candidate for Lord Chief Justice. We also have the colourful insights, especially into Overends' dramatis personae, in the privately printed memoirs of the mercurial Stefanos Xenos, a quintessential Greek cocktail of charm, passion and recklessness with whom the quintessentially English Gurneys tangled to their great mutual disadvantage. Like several of our cast, Xenos (pronounced 'Ksenos', which means 'stranger' or 'foreigner' in Greek and is part of our own linguistic currency as the root of 'Xenophobia') was a study in contrasts. On the one hand, he was an impulsive, cash-strapped entrepreneur who took risks with other people's money; but he also turns out to have been rather more – a novelist with dashing good looks, widely read in his day, the publisher of a newspaper which was as polemical as he was, a highly cultured man remembered in textbooks on Greek political history and literature, and even the subject in recent years of a comprehensive Greek-language biography.

Though the story is fascinating as living proof of the sixteenth-century adage that 'a fool and his money are soon parted', it is ultimately the extraordinary mix of people and places, a mix no novelist would attempt to put on paper, which gives it its special flavour.

1

History Repeats Itself

As Karl Marx – who saw the Overends crisis unfold at first hand – once noted, history does repeat itself, '. . . the first time as tragedy, the second as farce'. I was struck, when I first began to put the pieces of the Overends puzzle together, that in its business essence and the human frailties which drove apparently sensible and honest men to behave, or misbehave, in the way they did, the failure of The Corner House has much in common with financial implosions before and since. These include the twentieth-century financial panics that were a formative part of my own unsentimental education during years spent white-water rafting through the rapids of the City of London and the windy canyons of Wall Street. In medieval times Italian bankers such as the Medicis and Frescobaldis got themselves into terminal difficulty by lending money which was not theirs, money left on deposit with them by trusting clients, to British monarchs who could not or would not pay. Even though the royal debts turned out to be worth no more than the parchment scrolls on which they were so carefully recorded, the bankers' liability to repay their clients was real and pressing. In essence that was the root of Overends' problem. The world had advanced and Overends' loans were made against the contemporary icons of ships and railways rather than to finance bloody sorties against the French or the Scots. But they too were financed with money deposited with The Corner House, money which was liable to be withdrawn, and indeed was, at very short notice, when depositors lost confidence. To use a couple of banking clichés, 'borrowing short to lend long' is a major risk; when the risk becomes reality there follows as night follows day 'a run on the bank'. So it was with Overends and so too in my own experience.

Money messes always start the same way, when judgement is fuddled by greed, ambition and overweening self-confidence. Then when problems arise, there follows an obstinate refusal to admit mistakes or the imminence of disaster, the Micawberish delusion that something will turn up to save the day. The slippery slope down which men under pressure descend from optimistic glossing over of the truth to downright mendacity, and the naïveté of investors large and small, stoked by a headline-hungry press and preyed on by unscrupulous market operators, was just as evident in my own world as in Overends' day. I started my business life in the 1960s working for a pair of no-nonsense brothers from South Africa, lending money to cash-strapped entrepreneurs in scruffy industrial estates up and down Britain. When the economy lurched into one of its periodic fits of depression, trade plummeted and loans could not be repaid. A surprising number of the businessmen we dealt with, pillars of the local Rotary and golf clubs who would never have thought of themselves as in any way crooked, lied and doctored their accounts, diverting assets to their wives' names and cash to the Bahamas without turning a hair. Back in Victorian times, the influential *Bankers' Magazine* had highlighted the same characteristics, pointing its pen at 'that class who abound in all trading communities whose needs, difficulties, recklessness and unscrupulousness shade down so finely through all the gradations from embarrassment to downright roguery'.

Ten years later I witnessed the so-called 'Secondary Banking Crisis' of the 1970s from the understated elegance of a City merchant bank, whose founding partners were émigrés from 1930s' Germany. The depression years and the cancerous inflation of the Weimar Republic had taught them harsh but valuable lessons about human frailty, the whiplash of the markets and what could happen even to the soundest banks. The firm remained largely detached, cynical spectators as the new wave of banking *condottiere* rolled into the City in their Rolls-Royces. Convinced, like Overends, that they had the Midas touch, they made the same mistake of locking too much short-term money in long-term assets. In the nineteenth-century it was ships and railways. In the 1970s it was property:

blocks of London flats to be 'broken up' and sold at a massive profit to their hapless tenants; decrepit greyhound racing and speedway tracks supposedly ripe for redevelopment as shopping centres; and crumbling mills in the North to be crushed by the wrecker's ball into sites for 'executive homes'. The inevitable crisis came when the property bubble burst and those assets became unsellable, even worthless, and the depositors (which in this case included many bigger banks, who should have known better but who could not resist joining the madcap revels in return for juicy interest rates) started to clamour for their money back. No amount of denial and 'spin' could avert calamity.

To call even a partial roll of what became known as the 'fringe banks' who rose to transient glory in those interesting and irrationally exhuberant times, is to evoke wry memories: Burston & Texas Commerce Bank, Cannon Street Acceptances, Cedar Holdings, Dalton Barton, David Samuel Trust, First National Finance, Keyser Ullman, London & County Banking, Slater Walker, Triumph Investment Trust and many others, their once highflying chairmen now reduced to anonymous 'walking wounded', stumbling shell-shocked past the burly pink-jacketed hall porters through the high double doors of the Bank of England, to plead in the Governor's Parlour for transfusions of money rather than blood.

There are especially powerful echoes of Overends in the story of one of the more poignant crises of the 1970s, the near-collapse and government bailout of the 'Crown Agents for Oversea Governments and Administrations'. Set up in 1837, the Agents were almost as venerable, their history reflected in the archaic spelling of 'Oversea'. Like Overends, they had a reputation for conservatism and an unimpeachable credit standing, boosted in the Agents' case by the confidence-enhancing legal view that they were 'an emanation of the Crown'. Like Overends too, the Agents were private, with no outside shareholders to be kept informed or to question what was going on. They were unregulated, inbred and naïve. They too were increasingly concerned that their mainstream business, in this case providing a range of worthwhile services to many of the former outposts of Empire, was not generating enough income and that they needed to find new ways to make money. They too fell prey to shrewder operators who sensed their vulnerability. And in yet another parallel, when the London press first began to probe their activities, the Agents too were described as 'the biggest force in the City's money markets after the Bank of England'.

Overends' predilection was ships; the Agents, children of their time, joined the lemming-like leap into property. They were much helped by the property developers and their West End hangers-on who circled the skies above the Agents' Millbank offices like suntanned and manicured vultures. Their 'too good to refuse' offerings included: a deal to buy Manchester Central Station; finger-burning entanglements with speculative developers across the UK; stakes in other marginal finance houses; a joint venture with the Australian Anglican Church, the late Felix Fenston and the socialite Prince Radziwill to develop 'glebe lands' in a Sydney suburb; a disastrous entanglement with one compulsive borrower whose eventual failure earned him the newspaper accolade of 'Britain's Biggest Bankrupt.'

After it inevitably all went wrong, the Agents' misfortunes were laid out in clinical and compelling detail in an official report which in yet another echo of Overends described their banking forays as 'folly and euphoria'.[3]

When later I was seduced into working on Wall Street – 'just for a handful of silver he left us' – I stood close, at some moments too close for comfort, to the epicentre of the volcanic eruption in the financial markets: the 'crash' in October 1987, which was rapidly dubbed 'Black Monday'. I doubt that those doing the dubbing recalled or cared that they were reprising Overends' original 'Black Friday'. The experience gave me a uniquely personal perspective from which to try to understand the panic all those years earlier when Overends went under; the 'malignant fear', the bewilderment of 'not knowing who was sound and who was not', and the feeling of being 'disconcerted beyond example' that had gripped the Victorian City in 1866 were just as sweatily palpable on Wall Street in 1987. Bankers, brokers, investors, the television 'talking heads', everyone felt that they were in the grip of incomprehensible and irresistible forces for what seemed like forever but was really only a few days, days filled with bad news, worse news, terrible news and government platitudes. When the Black Death scythed across medieval Europe, pious peasants prayed to their local saints for mercy; on 'Black Monday', terrified brokers, traders and dealers beseeched the market's own pope, the chairman of the US Federal Reserve Bank, to intercede with the Almighty. Maybe he did, but reliable legend has it that what actually turned the mood around was not divine intervention: a canny trader spotted that by steadily buying a few million dollars' worth of an obscure Chicago-traded option on the Dow Jones Industrial Average as he sensed the panic was beginning to ebb, he could use the power of leverage inherent in options to turn the Average back in a positive direction. He earned the gratitude of his colleagues and a mouth-watering bonus. Today he would probably be led off the trading floor in handcuffs, accused of market rigging.

We can even find a parallel between Wall Street and the Overends' era. Stefanos Xenos' account of his dealings with Overends is called 'Depredations', with Overends cast in the role of The Predators. At the height of its fame the Wall Street firm of Drexel Burnham, which prided itself on inventing the 'junk bond' market but which, like many other financial inventors, fell from grace in a welter of litigation and criminal charges, put on orgiastic get-togethers in lush resorts for its coterie of risk-blind investors and tightrope-walking borrowers, many of whom tapped the Drexel-manipulated market to finance grandiose takeovers. The press swiftly nicknamed this annual homage to the God of Greed, 'The Predator's Ball'.

2

Paper Promises

Money, the lifeblood of Overends' business, is at the heart of our story. So before we tell it, we have to decide how best to translate Victorian-era values into figures which have any meaning today. Football goals, cricket scores, racing results – 'Coracle won by a short head' – have the same weight now as they did 150 years ago; money, on the other hand, has been clipped, debased and inflated, especially in the years since the Second World War. What are these Victorian gold sovereigns and crisp white banknotes worth in today's money?

Addressing the point some years ago in his mellifluous biography of Gladstone, the late Lord Jenkins took the view that, 'If this is to be done simply, it must also be done crudely, and the best rule I have been able to devise is to multiply all 19th century values by a factor of fifty . . . This obviously leaves jagged edges.'

In some cases these are more like gaping holes. For most readers house prices are perhaps the biggest complication; in Southern England, they must have multiplied well over a hundredfold since the 1950s alone. The art market, tugged up and down by changes in taste as well as inflation, is even more of an aberration. In 1855, Constable's *The Lock* was sold for £630 and in 1860 a Canaletto fetched £360; both figures would today be multiplied several hundredfold. The beggarly wages paid to Victorian factory, mill and mine workers, farmhands and domestic servants, minimal taxation, lack of a medical or social infrastructure, stark regional contrasts in living standards, indeed the absence then of today's all-encompassing nanny state and its army of bureaucrats, all conspire to make the comparison even more of a 'guesstimate'. A much higher multiplication factor can also be justified; the UK's Office of

National Statistics recently suggested that Victorian prices should be multiplied by eighty, but eighty is a hard number to keep juggling as one reads, and the practical choice would therefore seem to lie between 100 and Lord Jenkin's Fifty Factor. Since, as he suggests, the latter 'produces results which rarely defy commonsense', housing apart, we will follow his example.

Even without these conversions to modern value, Overends was 'big business'. Unlike the 'fringe banks' or the 'cowboys' of Wall Street, Overends mattered so much when it was alive and even more so when it died because it was at the heart of the Victorian system for financing trade and industry across Britain and the Empire, a system which rested on a prosaic but infinitely flexible financial instrument, the Bill of Exchange. In the City of London's money markets, which were themselves the financial centre of the world, only the Bank of England outranked Overends in the volume of Bills passing though its hands (in 1860 turnover was some £170 million, a huge sum even before conversion to modern values), business that year after year had generated large profits for its family partners.

In our age of seamless international capital markets and global banks, in which keyboard strokes send billions of dollars, yen, euros and pounds bleeping across the world along fibre-optic highways each second of the day, the Bill is now largely just a bank clerk's memory to be found only in financial history books along with black Underwood typewriters, carbon paper, Roneo stencils, the clattering Telex machine, the hand-cranked calculator, starched shirt collars, bowler hats and the 3/– vouchers doled out to clerical staff to buy themselves a decent midday meal.[4] A medieval creation sometimes attributed to Jewish merchants in Florence, the Bill, by Victorian times, had evolved into the world's most widely used financial instrument. It was ponderously and precisely defined by English law as 'an unconditional order in writing, addressed by one person to another, signed by the person giving it, requiring the person to whom it is addressed to pay on demand or at a fixed or determinable future date a sum certain in money to or to the order of a specified person or to bearer.' Translated into everyday language, it is in effect a business to business post-dated cheque, with the supreme virtue of being 'negotiable', in other words freely transferable from one party or bank to another with no more than a scrawled signature, a piece of paper almost as good as cash.

Victorian London was the capital of the British Empire and the banks, brokers, merchants and insurance underwriters clustered in its ancient City around the Bank of England, the Mansion House and the Stock Exchange, the financial hub of the ten million Imperial square miles which were coloured red on every schoolroom wall map. The colonial governors, gunboats, administrators and red-coated soldiers ruled over lands which had seemingly infinite resources of raw materials, and were ripe markets for British exports – ships, textiles, machinery, railway engines and lines, pots, pans, boilers and bicycles. But the wheels of trade could only turn if they were lubricated with money. The 'global bank' had yet to be conceived and within Britain the nationwide networks of joint stock banks, with branches on every High Street, were still only an emerging and rather suspect phenomenon. In the capital itself, only London & County and London & Westminster, with eight and six branches respectively, stood out in a trade register of some sixty banks, most of which were still single-office private partnerships.

So the cotton spinner, the woollen mill, the coal mine, the iron works, the corn merchant, the brewer, the tanner, the tea, rubber and coffee planters and merchants, the railway contractor, all used Bills to settle their debts. But the Bill itself was just a piece of high quality white paper, usually nine inches long and five inches wide, embossed with impressive black curlicues. To fulfil its function, to allow the firm which held it to convert it into cash, there had to be a market: traders who made their living buying (or 'discounting', in the trade jargon) the Bills from firms who needed the money to keep their own businesses going, and either holding them for a small profit margin or, as was or more often the case, selling them on to country banks and others with surplus cash to put to work at attractive rates of interest. Over the centuries a small group of mainly private firms, and the Bank of England itself, had developed the art of trading Bills into an informal grouping centred in and around Lombard Street, which became known as 'the discount market', in which Overends was far and away the largest of the private participants. It was thus technically not so much a bank, which dealt with the tiresome public, but rather a 'discount house'. To modern ears the term conjures up the image of a factory outlet store or a warehouse stacked with Romanian refrigerators and end-of-range sofas upholstered in uncut moquette. Until the 1970s their role was, in effect, that of the tiny aperture through which the sand of cash and credit flowed from one bowl of the financial hourglass to the other. With much influence on short-term interest rates and money flows, the discount houses became an essential part of what made London work as a financial centre; an agglomeration of nimble-witted gentlemanly risk-takers which a later City grandee praised as 'that essential link and cog in the machine . . . a side of business peculiar to the City of London . . . without which the City would never have reached the position of international eminence which it undoubtedly has reached'.

Overends would not have become the pre-eminent discount house if those who ran it had not had a flair, even a genius, for the business. But its dominant role was much reinforced by its umbilical ties of blood, kinship, interlocking partnerships and daily business dealings with Gurney's Bank in Norwich, one of Britain's premier private firms. The Gurneys, as we will see, were pillars of the Quaker establishment, which meant that they, and through them the London firm, had close ties to a tight-knit clan of bankers, brewers and manufacturers across the country. The Gurney name stood for honesty, principle and 'almost proverbial' wealth, in the words of the *Bankers' Magazine*. It was trusted without reservation and the lustre of its name shone not just from Norwich down to Lombard Street, but countrywide, especially where there were Quaker communities.

Like any bank, Overends made its money on the 'spread' between what it paid its depositors and what it earned on its Bill assets. Because of its history and connections, the deposits flowed to it mainly from country banks, many also Quaker owned, in the South and East. Similar to Gurney's in Norwich operating from elegant Georgian town houses close by the local cathedral, they took in the money generated by harvests, agricultural rents and the profits of merchants, haberdashers, professional men, silversmiths and cabinet makers. Though their needs changed with the seasons and the success or failure of each harvest, these country banks usually had more deposited with them than they could prudently lend out again locally. The surplus had to be put to work, and what better home for it than Overends, who became virtuous money-launderers, and whose buying and selling of industry's Bills recycled this 'country' money to finance the growing industries of the North and West and the mining areas. They became 'the bankers' bank', the heart which pumped the British credit bloodstream. However, being at the heart of things means that heart failure can have nasty repercussions.

To be sure, as in any large banking operation, there were minor blips when even solid firms hit a bad patch and went broke, leaving Bills unpaid, or 'dishonoured' in the jargon. But long years in the business and an information network of trusted Quaker bankers and businessmen across the country had given Overends a justified reputation for being able to sniff out most potential bad apples. Nuances from their correspondence files show the subtle distinctions they made between 'Good bills purporting no particular let down, and not running in lines of danger yet probably not impregnable', 'very nice people – highly respectable', 'sound and bona fide', shading down to 'quite respectable', 'we would not count them strong' and the almost medicinal 'we recommend you take them only in small amounts'.

But if the ease with which Bills could be traded through the discount market was their supreme virtue, the supreme risk, and the essence of the tragedy that we will see unfold, was the ease with which an age-old system based on trust, began to be subverted. Assumptions that behind each Bill lay a genuine trade deal which would generate cash to pay it off, gave way to that always lethal combination of unscrupulous intermediaries and investors greedy for higher returns. Bills were created to finance the speculative building of ships and railways, Bills which could be repaid after ninety days only by renewing them on faith and for a sizeable fee, rather than out of any real trade. Companies could and did connive to draw virtually fictitious Bills on one another for 'accommodation', hoping that something would turn up to pay them off; a parent company could similarly get a subsidiary to put its name to a Bill, the technique known as 'pig on pork'.

It was Overends' willingness, its pathetic eagerness, after almost half a century of highly profitable dealing in 'traditional' Bills, to traffic in this early version of the junk bond market, to lock up short-term deposits in dubious debts which at best were long-term and increasingly turned out to be worthless, which is at the heart of its collapse. That collapse, with millions of pounds owed to banks around Britain, and businessmen wanting to sell Bills left without their main outlet for raising cash, risked gutting the London money market. Making the distress far worse was the huge black hole of liability which suddenly yawned in front of the luckless share-holders, sucked in just a year before. It was, in meteorological terms, 'the perfect storm'.

Using Lord Jenkin's Fifty Factor, the crude financial scorecard of Overends' bizarre self-immolation is that they went into liquidation owing, directly and indirectly, close to £900 million in today's values. Though after several acrimonious and litigious years the creditors got their money back, with interest, the new public shareholders lost the equivalent of £175 million almost before the ink on their share certificates had had time to dry. The losses of the firm's partners and their families are harder to calculate, but were probably in today's terms not far short of £100 million. The many lawyers who descended upon the carcass ended up – as always – on the right side, paying for their grandchildren's and probably great-grandchildren's education out of the steady stream of fees.

We shall try to stay with the highlights of the story rather than the minutiae of the figures, mindful of the weary comment of a judge hearing one of the many legal cases which followed in the years ahead: 'The figures seemed to dance about in a sort of mazy labyrinth, out of which there was no possibility of extricating oneself . . . there was no need to go into the wearisome details of accounts and arithmetic.' Who are we to disagree?

3

Halcyon Days

Though the Overends' story has the same mix of all too human ingredients as so many other manias, panics and crashes before and since, we need to look at it against the backcloth of its time, an embarrassing stain on the rich velvet that is the texture of mid-Victorian Britain, now properly recognised as a golden age of power, relative peace, growing prosperity, social progress and, above all, dazzling technological advances. It was a secure country, protected by the world's most powerful Navy, ruled over by a diminutive, iron-willed Queen at the apex of an evolving system of democracy which while a long way from all encompassing or perfect had kept the nation largely free from the revolutions, mob violence and blood-letting which were the hallmarks of much of recent Continental history. Napoleon and the centuries-old French threat had been removed, and Prussia was only just flexing its muscles on the way to becoming the next menace. British foreign secretaries, who travelled rarely and spoke to the press even less, were free to preoccupy themselves with maintaining the post-Waterloo 'balance of power' in Europe and juggling the heavy burdens which were the price of being the world's superpower. The issues of the day were often classed by newspaper leader writers and later historians as 'Questions', with a meaningful capital letter. There was the Eastern Question (whose unsatisfactory answer was the Crimean War in 1854), the Question of Greece, the Italian Question, the Indian Question and its attendant Mutiny, the Luxembourg Question, the Question of Canada, and the not unrelated complexities of relations with the new, unsteady America and Britain's often ambivalent position in the latter's Civil War.[5] There was even the Schleswig-Holstein Question, a matter so arcane that, as Lord

Palmerston is claimed to have remarked, only three people really knew its answer: the Prince Consort, who was dead; a Foreign Office clerk, who had vanished; and Palmerston himself, who had forgotten it. At home successive whiskered, well-born Cabinets wrestled with what Thomas Carlyle termed 'The Condition Of England Question', as the Chartist movement struggled to widen the voting franchise and redress many other social evils. They also faced the Land Question, the Catholic Question, and, year in and year out, the already bomb-punctuated Irish Question; as early as 1864, riots were reported from Belfast's Shankhill Road, already a sectarian fault line.

The golden years from 1815 to 1870 have been classified by historians as the Age of Reform. Within that span others have seen the 1860s as a particular watershed, when the country passed from its phase of 'Industrialisation' to a period of 'Economic Maturity'. Put in less academic terms the period of our story is one of huge change, and the various ways in which that change made itself felt – in ships and shipping which are at the heart of the story, in Quaker disciplines, in family generations and in the financial markets – add texture to the tapestry of our narrative.

Even 'change' does not do full justice to the extraordinary vitality of the Victorian age. British industry and society were being transformed at breathtaking speed – a speed which shatters any stereotypes of our forebears as dull, Dundreary-whiskered men and prim, whalebone-corseted ladies reading the Bible in front of a succulent aspidistra in its Spode jardinière, the backs of their armchairs protected by lace antimacassars from the men's greasy hair pomade, the entire family stuck in the aspic of a hidebound and hypocritical society. Certainly Victorians could be dull, but they were also human – greedy, speculative and ambitious in the finest twenty-first-century style with a strong whiff of sensuality. Brothels pandered to a full range of tastes (flagellation prominent among them) and wallets. Prostitutes promenaded proudly along Regent Street at high noon and the dealers, many of them women, in pokey Holywell Street (demolished, sadly, to make way for Aldwych), sold more pornographic books and etchings in the 1860s than the whole of what is left of the Soho 'dirty book trade' does today. Sensuality and brutality were also hallmarks of another, sometimes exaggerated, aspect of that icon of the Victorian age – the British public school. In tune with the contemporary drive for change, a generation of thrusting and visionary headmasters such as Arnold of Rugby transformed ancient foundations in sleepy market towns into educational and above all character-building 'factories', whose pupils were trained to rule the Empire. Unfortunately, while public schools laid great emphasis on the value of manly outdoor team sports, they could not eradicate more furtive indoor activities of the kind rather unfairly identified with the British character. In 1861, the future Lord Derby noted that his father had been summoned to a meeting of his fellow governors at Wellington College, itself a mid-Victorian creation, to discuss the expulsion of a son of General Ridley for 'indecent practices which have spread widely though the school . . . it is said that these practices are increasing rapidly in the great schools and that from Eton especially many boys have been removed in consequence.' All in all through their yearning to change things, to invent things, to make things better and to do great public works the Victorians personified the poet John Milton's description in *Areopagitica* of his fellow countrymen as a people 'of a quick, ingenious and piercing spirit, acute to invent'.

Today we are convinced that nothing can be more exciting and often bewildering than the changes we see around us. But much of that change, however amazing – whether in travel, communications or medicine – is in one way or another an evolution; the text message and e-mail from the hand-delivered telegram by way of the telex, as just one example. For the Victorians, the railway was not just an evolution from the horse-drawn carriage but an entirely new phenomenon, which in half a lifetime had transformed their countryside and thrown open the horizons of their lives. It was a triumphant marriage of technology and raw capitalism, which the historian Sir Llewellyn Woodward saw as 'the greatest physical achievement carried out by the human race within a comparatively short time'.[6] The railways were made possible by the ingenious harnessing of steam, which was then applied to industrial machinery and printing presses. Coupled with lowering of taxes on advertising and paper and the new distribution channels opened by the railway, these in turn gave birth to the first mass circulation newspapers.

The electric telegraph, which flashed the news of Overends' death across Britain and much of Europe, and which after a remarkable feat of engineering and endurance would soon span the Atlantic, was new rather than an evolution, as were coal gas and, eventually, electric lighting, chloroform and antiseptics, photography and even a postal service, which was cheaper and infinitely better than that of the twenty-first century. Also, more relevant for our story, with steam came yet another change: new, iron-built ships to carry more people further and faster, shrinking and thus changing the known world.

Its people felt that Victorian Britain, supported by its history and its wealth, was entitled to call itself 'Great'. The *New York Times*' London correspondent, 'Monadnock', did not agree. Though Britain had once been able to hold 'the empire of the seas' and dictate the balance of power, 'all that is among the departed glories' of a nation past its tipping point. 'It is now a question of self-preservation and national existence,' Monadnock told his readers in a perceptive forerunner of an American statesman's jibe in 1962, close on a century later, that Britain had 'lost an empire and not yet found a role'.

Despite his griping, London was still the world's wealthiest as well as its largest city and the hub of much of the world's trade, which was carried across the oceans in British-built and British-owned merchant vessels from British ports, the greatest of which was London. The trade was financed by Bills of Exchange and the cargoes insured by Lloyds. British investors put their money – whose value rested on gold, not the bank-note printing presses – into bonds from Portugal to Peru, and Ecuador to Egypt, and were mildly relieved at a small rise in the price of Mexican debt, reflecting 'the further favourable news regarding the defeat of the bands who . . . seek to perpetuate the brigandage of which the country has been the prey for nearly half a century'. On the same page as it reported money market dealings, *The Times* carried daily accounts of the state of the yarn trade in Manchester, steam coal sales from Cardiff to the West Indies and Mediterranean (for ships' boilers rather than heating), hosiery manufacture in Leicester, demand for 'lace edgings and silk mechlins' in Nottingham, and the prices realised in Mincing Lane for Necranzie rice, Penang sugar and 'palish mixed to good ordinary, even brownish' coffee beans from Brazil. Trading in linseed oil, hops, wheat, butter, potatoes and even spirits were all carefully monitored. That 'the French Government has taken 70,000 gallons of rum from a Liverpool firm' was noted with chauvinistic pride. Many great English novelists flourished; great painters were scarcer, however, depending on one's appetite for the Pre-Raphaelites.

Just why Napoleon dismissed Britain as a 'nation of shopkeepers' is unclear; maybe he was just suffering from the despondency and spleen of exile. However, though industry and commerce had mushroomed, the official Census for the year of Prince Albert's death in 1861 still found the agricultural sector to be 'the great central productive class of the country', employing over two million people. Agriculture meant land and there were 30,000 'landed proprietors and landed gentlemen', from dukes with many thousands of acres, lesser nobles 'born to hunt and vote and raise the price of corn', down to rural squires and yeoman farmers with their smaller but equally treasured properties. As the landowners and their guests trotted through their estates, 'there were gates to fly open . . . a general touching of hats, with the delightful consciousness that speed where you would, the horizon scarce limited the possession of your host.'

After gazing grandly round the Cabinet Room from his Foreign Secretary's seat in a Disraeli-led administration, Lord Derby confided to his diary that there were three groups of ministers. First, the large landowners – the Duke of Richmond, the Marquis of Salisbury, the Earl of Carnarvon and Derby himself (with some 62,000 acres), plus Lord John Manners as heir to the Rutland estates. Four ministers had 'middle-sized holdings', defined by Derby as between 11,000 and 50,000 acres, while the rest, Disraeli included, had little or nothing by comparison.

Though as part of the pace of change industrial fumes from St Helens already bothered Derby's Lancashire estate, most village and country life was still much as it had been for centuries. An 1861 survey in the hamlet of Catton, three miles outside Norwich, showed that it was home to fifty 'agricultural labourers', earning about 10/– a week, eighty-six domestic servants, twenty-one gardeners, eleven dressmakers, seven carpenters, six brick makers and four laundresses. Many of those in this list, with its echoes of 'The Twelve Days of Christmas', were no doubt employed in and about the local 'big houses' of which the largest was Catton Hall, one of the Gurney family estates.

The Times' hunting correspondent, confident that his readers were well up enough in the sporting argot of Surtees not to need a glossary, telegraphed from Leicester that 'The Quorn had a capital thing of fifty minutes on Friday; the next day Mr Tailley had a clipper from Tilton Wood and the Duke a fast forty minutes on Monday.' However, it wasn't all pink jackets, top boots, country-house jollies and discreet flirtation. It was not until May 1868 that the British public saw its last ultimate reality show, a public hanging. The usual crowd of cheery, jeering ghouls gathered outside Newgate Prison to watch as the Public Hangman, William Calcraft, 'a repulsive sight . . . with a white beard, a black skullcap and broadcloth jacket', deftly slipped the noose over the hooded head of Michael Barrett, an Irish Republican convicted for his part in a murderous bomb attack on Clerkenwell Jail. Calcraft, who was also the prison's official flogger, was paid a guinea for each execution.

In the revolutionary view of the world, which in the 1840s had rocked Europe and shaken but not stirred Britain, to an extent, in 1848, the bourgeoisie were growing richer at the expense of the masses toiling in the mines and mills. On a wider canvas, countless millions of black-, brown- and yellow-skinned subjects of the Empire felt the condescension and arbitrariness of pith-helmeted colonial satraps and the rifle butts of British redcoats. All good caricatures contain some lines of truth. The Victorian poor lived miserably and died too young in rotten housing with no social infrastructure. But changing Britain to change lives for the better was an integral part of the Age of Reform, even though to those affected the pace of change must have seemed pitiably slow.

In between the swamp of poverty and disease, and the prosperity of the middle classes, there lay another layer, not without its own miseries. In 1865, as a random example, *The Times* reported a verdict of suicide on twenty-one-year-old Rosa Hobson, a housemaid whose sodden body was found in the New River in Highbury, a major source of London's drinking water. It had been there for some days. Her employer, a senior clerk at the Bank of England, had found her 'very inefficient, which caused him to speak to her sharply'. She ran away, wearing 'a dark linsey dress, a black cloth jacket and a black velvet bonnet trimmed with white lace', but was brought back by a solicitous friend, despite Rosa's sobs that 'there is more work than I can do'. On Boxing Day she left the house again, this time without her bonnet or shawl, wrapped only in her apron. The inquest heard that she had left a note saying, 'Dear Mistress, I am sorry to run away again but I cannot help it – I shall wander about till I die.' She had a shilling in her pocket.

The *New York Times*' curmudgeonly 'Monadnock' would have had little sympathy. He reported in June that 'servants in England have grown independent, saucy, scheming, rapacious, immoral and not infrequently the associates of thieves and burglars'.

At the other end of the social spectrum a group signing itself 'Ladies Who Walk in Belgravia' also moaned about the lower classes, complaining in a letter to *The Times* that they had 'cheerfully submitted to men, women and children civilly begging for money, food, and clothes,' but because there were too few policemen around, 'the Irish and Welsh have begun bullying us in Eaton Place, cursing us in Halkin Street, and stoning us in Belgrave Square.'

Government had not yet begun its century-long pervasive encroachment into all aspects of business and private life. The Victorian financial marketplace, the snake pit in which Overends and the coterie of shabby hangers-on who were part of its downfall lived, moved and had their being, was the epitome of free-market capitalism: grubby, greedy, unregulated, unsupervised and unashamed. In his autobiography, Trollope wrote of those mid-Victorian years as a time of 'dishonesty magnificent in its proportions and climbing into high places'.

Writing in the 1930s in his *History of the London Discount Market*, W. T. C. King looked back on the years which frame our story as a period marked by 'financial abuses which for sheer recklessness and audacity have hardly been surpassed by the worst scandals of recent years'.

Nevertheless, twenty-first-century readers should not be too ready to condemn out of hand the behaviour of those who operated in the markets a century and a half ago. If not refracted through the prism of hindsight, it is seen through the eyes of bandwagon-jumping politicians and witch-hunting regulators inventing new principles of market rectitude, not least to justify the budgets of the organizations created to police them. Ways of doing business which today would bring down shrill public censure, conviction by headline and harsh punishment on the heads of those allegedly involved, would not have been crimes even ten years ago. Mid-Victorian England had little in the way of corporate law, only the hazy outlines of a police force with a bull's-eye lantern and a truncheon apiece, and no computers, no Fraud Squad and no Crown Prosecution Service. Even the creation of the Metropolitan Police in 1829 had been greeted by grumbles that the move was just the first step towards emulating the despised French and Prussians, whose society was pervaded by networks of informers and secret agents; a development, according to *The Times*, 'for the purpose of arbitrary aggression upon the liberties of the people'. Indeed, one feature of the age at once surprising and, looked at through today's eyes, deeply depressing, is just how small the central state machinery actually was. As K. Theodore Hoppen has pointed out in *The Mid-Victorian Generation*, in 1846 the aggregate salary bill for all public departments was a trifling £750,000; the Foreign Office had a staff of eighty-five and the Treasury, excluding the department which dealt with army payrolls and supplies, just 105.

The financial markets were far from unique in falling well short of today's prudish standards. When we look at the loose way the Victorian Bankruptcy Court ran, for instance, we have to remember that though times were indeed changing, the standards of public life were not what they are – or at least are held up to be – today. Until

1871, rich young men seeking to become army officers could still get into the better regiments and then advance their careers by buying commissions and further promotions. Though early Civil Service reforms had been introduced in 1855, it was not until 1871 that competitive examinations were made the norm. Like all well-meant reforms facing entrenched opposition, neither of those changes worked in quite the way intended. The abolition of the Army purchase system helped prevent rich idiots from being elevated to a position from which they could blindly consign the Light Brigade to its doom, but did little or nothing to make the better regiments less of a preserve for aristocratic 'chinless wonders'. Likewise, while the reforms of Civil Service recruitment (not adopted by the snobbish Foreign Office for many more years) meant that it was more difficult for mavericks and misfits to get administrative posts through political or family patronage, they were clearly not designed to create a level social playing field. On the contrary, examinations were structured so as to present hurdles only Oxford and Cambridge graduates with a classical education could expect to clear.

Reform of the electoral system, a central plank of the Chartist movement, was also under way but democracy was still rough-hewn. Elections were often determined by whichever local magnate owned or controlled the 'rotten borough', and even in supposedly 'open' seats bribery, pressure or cajolery from London were heavily deployed. Even if their squire had been squared, local electors expected to be generously treated as the price of casting their votes.

'Public houses are open to all comers, whole communities wallow in drunkenness. The money comes up from nobody knows where, and the corruption of the people who sell themselves to one side or the other, or both, is disgraceful,' 'Monadnock' growled, as if he had never seen one of New York's own roistering and utterly corrupt elections.

The brazen 'Baron' Grant, who appears later in fuller colour, won the parliamentary seat of Kidderminster in 1865 by funding a theatre and, so it was claimed, buying at top prices the surplus stocks of several local carpet merchants. That he was later unseated for this glad-handing, egregious even by the standards of the time, does not detract from the point.

The press, too, was eminently biddable; Lord Stanley, later Lord Derby, frequently mentions in his diary Conservative efforts to buy control of various newspapers and journals, as well as a plan he had hatched in 1851 for the improvement of what today would be called the Conservative Party's 'media image'. Each member of the Cabinet agreed to contribute 2 per cent of his official salary to a fund for 'supporting the press'. Sadly, 'though we found the money, we never found writers and part of the sum thus raised was returned.'

They were probably not offering enough to compete with the City. Marmaduke Sampson, the first Money Market commentator of *The Times*, was so often seen to be using his column to puff the share issues sponsored by the bouncing Baron Grant and foreign bond offerings of more eminent London merchant bankers, that he was nicknamed 'The Jew's Harp'. Cynics and jealous colleagues wondered where he got the money to buy the palatial Hampton Court House, built in 1757 by the 2nd Earl of Halifax, let alone add a picture gallery and a ballroom. Grant's later claim that he had given Sampson money to compensate for market tips Grant had given him, which had failed, were received with justified skepticism.

Reform was even wafting along the darkened and draughty corridors of Windsor Castle where by 1862, the early years of our story, Queen Victoria had shut herself off from the world, wrapped in her widow's weeds, grieving for her beloved Prince Albert. Her grief did not temper her predilection for the attempted exercise of monarchical rights to dictate to her Ministers in a style reminiscent of earlier centuries. But successive Prime Ministers and Foreign Secretaries had learned to deal with her by flattery, bombast or simply pretending to accede to her whims. She was inching or being inched towards Bagehot's definition of the Sovereign's powers as limited to 'the right to be consulted, the right to encourage and the right to warn'. It is safe to say, though, that she would definitely not have been amused at his conclusion that 'The Queen must sign her own death warrant if the two Houses [of Parliament] unanimously send it up to her.' By 1865, as the Overends' pot was close to boiling over, her invisibility was grating on her subjects; one newspaper grumbled that, 'She has lost a husband but there is no reason the nation should not have a Sovereign.' A mischievous fly poster is even said to have plastered handbills on the Buckingham Palace garden walls announcing:

THESE EXTENSIVE PREMISES TO BE LET OR SOLD,
THE LATE OCCUPANT HAVING RETIRED FROM BUSINESS.

4

The Smoke, the Wealth, the Din

This then was Overend's Britain. What about London itself, the metropolis where they made their money even if the partners were rich enough to live in areas insulated from its more unpleasant manifestations? It may have been the capital of a new 'Roman Empire', but it was filthier, noisier and not much healthier than ancient Rome itself. It was still as much a site of factories and workshops as the seat of the Court, government and the *beau monde* of fashion. London employed 15 per cent of the British manufacturing workforce, while one in four was in the various service industries. An early bid to clean up the capital through the Metropolitan Nuisances Act of 1844 had pushed many of the nastiest polluters out to the eastern edges and into the Isle of Dogs (setting for one of the biggest losses in our tale of woe). Nonetheless, the mid-Victorian map of London shows a landscape punctuated by potteries, paper, flour, timber and even silk mills, and factories churning out everything from the still essential candles, to turpentine, starch and heavy steam boilers. On the site by Vauxhall Bridge where the Ziggurat of the Secret Intelligence Service now broods over its empire of illusion, a large gin distillery bubbled profitably.

To the post-millennial eye, perhaps the most striking feature of mid-nineteenth-century London is its size; not its vastness, but rather, like the machinery of government, how small it was. This rich, powerful and still pestilential city was ringed until as late as 1863 by a necklace of 140 tollgates installed centuries before. To the north, cattle chewed the cud in Islington, while Cricklewood and Golders Green were hamlets wrapped in fields through which country lanes still meandered, even though in the distance the rumble of the railways was making itself heard ever more loudly. In amongst leafy squares and crescents built to emulate the fashionable façades of Bath, the proud bourgeois residents of Ladbroke Grove would see fingerposts showing the pathways to the farms of Notting Hill Barn and Portobello. The Victorian passenger bouncing westwards in a hansom cab along the Cromwell Road would trot through the 'market gardens' which began just 100 yards past the Natural History Museum and ran all the way to Earls Court; at the junction with Gloucester Road, Cromwell Road itself petered out into the rural-sounding Red Field Lane. A contemporary writer described Sloane, Thurloe, Trevor and Edwardes Squares, today integral and expensive features of the London landscape, as 'portentous, parvenu-like [and] suburban'. Further west still, Fulham was a landscape bucolic enough to have prompted Constable to reach for his palette and brushes; the majesty of the Bishop's Palace was surrounded by fields, cottages, grander riverside homes, bosky pathways and water meadows.

None of this would last long in the face of the commercial and social imperatives of the Victorian Age of Change. 'Projectors', as developers were known, ancient families 'long on land but short on cash', speculators, surveyors who were the outriders of the over-ground and underground railways, civil engineers, bridge builders and their City financiers were already rubbing their hands over the profits to come from the next waves of demolition, excavation and the submersion of all those market gardens under a tidal wave of bricks, mortar and stucco. New bridges were being cantilevered across the Thames by Irish navvies like the beachheads of a Hibernian invasion force. From Paddington to Farringdon Road, a short walk from the City itself, navvies and steam-powered machines were an invading army, smashing down buildings, digging up roads and excavating deep trenches to create London's first underground railway. Other lines would soon follow, adding to the mercenary mayhem. Old marketplaces, street after street of working-class homes, crooked alleys and folk memories fell to the pounding of Irish sledgehammers as the railways sliced their routes into the centre. Their terminal stations – first King's Cross and Paddington in the 1850s, then Victoria in 1860, followed by Charing Cross, and later Broad Street, Cannon Street and Ludgate Hill – outdid each other in architectural grandeur and more so in the luxurious hotels which were often twinned with them. Was Holborn Hill too steep for the lumbering dray horses? An energetic committee decided to throw a massive viaduct across it. Were the eight handsome stone arches of Blackfriars Bridge too narrow for the stream of river traffic? Contractors rushed to knock it down and build a new one. Was London's air too foetid and pungent as centuries of filth clogged its medieval drains? Yet again Victorian engineers acted with boldness. Along the north bank of the Thames at Westminster wooden bulkheads, cofferdams and mountains of wet soil heralded the building of the Embankment and the excavation of London's first and badly needed sewage system. Were streets dangerously dark and eyes over-strained by candlelight? The answer was gas, piped under pavements and into wealthier homes and clubs from the huge iron holders, later known as 'gasometers', which stored the new lighting 'wonder fuel' and would soon sprout like Triffids around the London skyline. Did the prevailing spirit of religious revival mean that the soul needed new space as much as business or traffic? The answer was to create more and more elaborate places of worship. In Gavin Stamp's estimation, the 1840s to the 1870s was 'the greatest period of church building in Britain since the Middle Ages'.

The *Illustrated London News* commented in a mix of admiration and nostalgia, that 'we are excavating through strata of civilisation in the execution of these great changes. By scientific application of Titanic character and machinery of automatic power our engineers and contractors are enabled to effect this change with such rapidity as to remind us . . . "Here Today and Gone Tomorrow".'

Lyn Nead, from whose valuable study of the period, *Victorian Babylon*, the quotation above is taken, also prints an illustration from the same magazine that highlights just how tenaciously intermingled the old was with the new, even in 1864. Captioned 'A Block in Park Lane', it is an allegory of urban chaos and social strata of a different sort. Traffic is at a standstill. A dowageresque figure, forerunner perhaps of Oscar Wilde's Lady Bracknell, gazes with studied indifference from her open landau, with a coachman and groom on the front bench. A businessman running late for a meeting berates the driver of his hansom cab, and a cross-section of the London public watches stoically from the open benches of a horse-drawn 'knifeboard' bus. A costermonger tries in vain to tug his donkey and cart through the blockage. On the pavement a top-hatted gentleman of evident *gravitas*, a banker, even, tries not to take much notice, though the lady clinging to his arm is clearly edgy and their daughter or granddaughter is much alarmed. The cause of it all is the ancient country clashing with the heart of town: Park Lane blocked by a pungent, noisy, mixed herd of sheep and cows being driven to some nearby market for sale or slaughter. Though probably exaggerated by the artist for effect, scenes like this would not have struck our characters as out of the ordinary as they went about their lives.

Victorian London was a city of coal, which meant smoke, smuts and choking fogs, the 'London Particular' that turned morning into night for days at a time and left pedestrians wheezing, scarves clutched to their mouths. The nineteenth-century Quaker meteorologist Luke Howard, who gave clouds their names, described a midday City fog that was 'as dense as we ever recollect to have known it. Lamps and candles were lighted in all shops and offices and the carriages in the street dare not exceed a foot pace. At the same time five miles from town the atmosphere was clear and unclouded with a brilliant sun.'

Rubbish, or 'dust' (hence today's 'dustman'), was carted off to huge man-made hillocks of the city's waste, like the pyramid of filth, ancient and modern, just behind what is now King's Cross Station. As the topcoat swirled into the sky with each eddy of wind, the stench of boiling bones and the rotting leavings of a thousand households made noses run and eyes water. Though there was a major push under way to give London a proper drainage and sewage system, the Thames, into which most of the City's waste oozed down ancient gullies, was so polluted that the summer stench in 1858 lead to 'great talk' of moving Parliament somewhere less noxious. The medical journal, *The Lancet*, reinforced 'Monadnock's' picture with the warning that many of London's poor had no running water. They stored what they could in 'tubs, jars and barrels . . . in overcrowded and unclean living rooms or in extremely filthy yards'. The consequences were 'filthy houses and filthy habits . . . personal degradation and neglect'. To the east of the East End itself lay the Isle of Dogs, setting for part of our story, a carcinogenic concentration of poison and filth-spewing industrial plants. Closer to the City's heart (some may have doubted whether it had one), the eight-storey City Flour Mills, the world's largest, towered above the warehouses and the new gasholder, its steam-powered millstones filling the surrounding air with a fine yeasty dust. Across the river on the south bank, more factories belched smoke and dirt as they turned out porcelain toilets, lead shot and complex iron castings.

Victorians lived in the shadow of epidemics of cholera, typhoid, diphtheria and smallpox, and accepted with equanimity, as the will of God, the appallingly high rate of death in childbirth. The poor lived in the shadow of death day by day. The City clerks and partners were less at risk, but still spent their evenings cooped up in houses whose heavy curtains had to be drawn to seal off the draughts from ill-fitting windows and doors. Rooms were heated for much of the year by coal fires and bathed in the weak, yellowish light of paraffin lamps, or the eye-straining glare of the hissing gas mantles which home owners were readier to accept after the new House of Commons had been fitted with gas lighting in 1852 and had not blown up. Fires and flames threw off smoke and greedily sucked in the oxygen, making nagging headaches a feature of family life along with chilblains and constipation. Victorians who could afford it were hearty eaters. In the 1850s, London's Leadenhall Market sold an annual 1,266,000 chickens, 45,000 geese, 84,500 partridge and 680,000 rabbits, not to mention a slightly upsetting tally of 213,000 larks (many netted on the downs of Dunstable), all of it a fairytale diet for most of the urban poor, scraping by on a diet of bread, potatoes, herrings and offal.

Physical statistics about Britain in the period are opaque. By and large, only army and naval recruits, prisoners or others passing through institutional hands were measured with any method, and the figures will therefore have been skewed towards the less well off. Nonetheless, the figures do seem to demonstrate that the mid-Victorian British male was 3 per cent shorter and weighed less than even fifty years later, with children in particular classified as 'Stunted and Wasted' (a technical term rather than writer's hyperbole).

Middle- and upper-class men, women and children sweated gently under a burden of layers of clothes that were seldom cleaned and carried the stench of food, tobacco and the streets; they bathed with less frequency than might nowadays be thought socially desirable; they slept in rooms whose walls shimmered with the deadly fumes of lead-based paints, and whose porcelain commodes tucked under the bed gave off an eye-watering cloud of ammonia. The medicines they took with gusto when they fell mildly ill were all too often concoctions such as 'Mrs Winslow's Soothing Syrup' or 'Parker's Tonic for Coughs, Consumption and Asthma', little more than placebos whose positive effects were achieved largely through the inclusion of generous levels of opium. The 'Nell Gwyn Ancient Chalybeate Cold Spring Bath' in Exmouth Street claimed that its constantly flowing water loaded with sulphur, iron and magnesia was 'useful in nervous disorders, colds, loss of appetite, indigestion, weakness of constitution'. It is doubtful that the '6*d* Cold Plunge' drew many customers from City banking parlours or did much more than transmit skin ailments from one suppurating splasher to the next.

Index entries in biographies of Disraeli as well as Gladstone make the point. The two iconic figures of British politics, men of enormous Victorian vitality, battled in the case of Disraeli with 'Exhaustion, asthma, affection in throat, bleeding gums, Bright's disease, bronchial asthma, bronchitis, catarrh, depression, gout, indigestion, liver, influenza, nephritis, tinnitus and uraemia', as well as a youthful dose of venereal disease. Gladstone was a hardier type than his dandified but deadly protagonist, thinking nothing of cross-country and cross-mountain walks that would daunt a twenty-first-century SAS trooper, and into old age chopped down trees on a scale modern environmentalists would deplore.[7] His index entries include erysipelas, strain and exhaustion, bronchitis, gastric attacks (despite the discipline – perhaps rather tedious for his dinner partners – of chewing each mouthful of food thirty-two times), lumbago, gumboil, pneumonia, insomnia, tonsillitis, laryngeal catarrh, influenza, cataract, and the finally fatal cancer of the cheek, as well as a host of 'unspecified complaints and ageing infirmities'. Even so the Grand Old Man of British politics conceded that in giving birth to their children in that largely pre-anaesthetic age, his wife Catherine had 'undergone six times as much bodily pain as I have undergone in my whole life'.

Karl Marx was suffering just as much as Gladstone. His letters to his friend and financial backer Friedrich Engels sometimes have less about the state of the world than the state of his toothache, rheumatism, boils, carbuncles and liver, none of which can have been much helped by his doctor's prescription of arsenic as the medicine of choice. (Engels' solicitous advice that, to be effective, the poisonous brew had to be taken for at least three months was almost in the category of killing with kindness.)

Senior City clerks lived in fresher air, commuting in from Sydenham, Shooters Hill or other fast spreading suburbs into London's cathedral-like main railway stations. The snapshot we have in his wife's memoirs of George Brightwen, one of Overends' managers, is characteristic. He earned £500 a year, married an intelligent and artistic woman, and had a ten-day honeymoon in Dieppe and Paris. They settled in Shaftesbury Villa, Stamford Hill, and were proud of their two sitting rooms and two live-in maids, two dogs, an aquarium and a beehive. Though he was from a Quaker family related to the Gurneys, Brightwen was a churchgoer and one of the founders of Stanmore Cricket Club, and had the good sense or luck to leave The Corner House well before the time of troubles.

As the *Illustrated London News*' sketch showed, though the underground was riding to the rescue, commuters, delivery men and town dwellers alike still relied on the plodding horse. Buses, carts, hansom cabs and private carriages added to both the filth and the pungency, especially at the height of summer, with a background din which, though less in decibels than today's motorised rumble, must still have bruised the ear. Most streets were unevenly paved with small wood blocks, which amplified the clatter of hooves and the rumble of iron-rimmed wheels. On stretches where the newly developed 'macadam' coating had been laid, even a light shower turned it to yellow slime. Yellow too must have been the City's tint at night as lamplighters made their rounds, popping into life with their torches the gas lamps mounted on iron pillars along the streets, creating pools of light and dark, menacing or romantically mysterious depending on the stroller's imagination.

5

Men Only

In 1857, Trollope saw the financial heart of London, the 'Square Mile' along whose lanes and alleys the Overends' partners could have walked blindfold, as 'the weary City, where men go daily to look for money but find none; where every heart is eaten up by an accursed famishing for gold; where dark, gloomy banks come thick on each other, like the black, ugly apertures to the realms below in a mining district, each of them a separate pit mouth into hell.' Well over a century earlier Joseph Addison, co-founder of the *Spectator*, had taken an equally bilious view of the look on City men's faces: 'You see a deep attention and a certain feeble sharpness in every countenance; they look attentive but their thoughts are engaged on mean purposes.'

Despite the grandeur of the three-acre site of Sir John Soane's blank-fronted Bank of England, the crazy quilt of streets and alleys, the financial heart of the City within a city, still had some of the 'feel' of the medieval maze in which the goldsmiths from Lombardy had started up a banking business, by issuing notes against gold and valuables left with them for safekeeping by wealthy London families. Medics among Venetian and Florentine merchants had also set up shop there in the Middle Ages, sparking an early display of the usual British chauvinistic revulsion against foreign traders, 'who in their galleys bring in apes and jades, nifles and trifles, and all manners of chaffer, and carry away the lifeblood of England, her precious wool'. Birchin Lane, on whose corner Overends sat, had been the thirteenth-century 'Berchervereslane', or 'Lane of the Beard Cutters'. Two or three centuries as the City's second-hand clothes' market led naturally, some might think, to its evolution into a banker's burrow. In the eighteenth century, it had been home to the

Sword Blade Company, itself a forerunner of the South Sea Company and an early attempt to break the monopoly of the infant Bank of England.

Like surrounding London, the ancient City was being hacked and hammered in the cause of progress and change. Almost every street had its cat's cradles of wooden scaffolding, bridging gaps where old buildings had been yanked out like decayed teeth to make way for new, regardless of their historical or architectural merit. Its ancient boundaries were being penetrated by the new railways leading to the grand cast iron, granite, and glass – roofed stations that were the new commuter landing grounds – Farringdon, Cannon Street, Broad Street and Ludgate Hill.

The City was far from the parks and greenery of central London and heading east just a few hundred yards a casual stroller would find himself nervous and out of place in the slums, home, as the *New York Times*' 'Monadnock' told his readers, to a 'crowded, filthy, drunken, half-starved population of several hundred thousand'. In the country at large there were 116,000 'lazy, filthy, abandoned vagabonds', who 'will not dig and who are not in the least ashamed to beg or steal either'. They were 'fit only for the stocks and the whipping post'.[8]

Cheapside, the traffic-clogged main artery to the flinty heart of the City from the West End (a mid-century survey counted 11,000 vehicles of all sorts moving along it each day between 9 a.m. and 9 p.m.), was lined with hosiers and shirt makers, tailors and tobacconists, as well as jewellers tempting the City man with gold fob watches, 'Albert' chains to attach them to buttonholed lapels, signet rings and scarf pins.

Though only a couple of hundred yards to the north, London Wall might have been a hundred miles from the City the Gurneys knew. There were a few shipping and merchant firms at its eastern end, but most of it was still a nest of coffee shops and lodging houses, and artisans making anything from shirt fronts to church hassocks. Basinghall Street, seat of the Bankruptcy Court, was a study in contrasts. The addresses close to the Bank of England housed larger trading firms, solicitors and accountants; even 'Edwin Levy, Private

Detective'. Just a few yards to the north, where it ran into London Wall, clustered dealers in 'Otto of Roses', gloves, 'Berlin wool', whalebone, 'bonnet shapes' and 'Lemon bergamot'. Even Lombard Street, already the address of choice of the more substantial banks, still found room for the offices of three gunpowder manufacturers. Though by 1864 Barclay & Co. had built a four-storey head office in the style of a miniaturised Medici palazzo in Lombard Street, most private bankers felt that their customers were more impressed by an office with 'an air of shabbiness, almost of dinginess', which was certainly true of Overends. The clerks clearly had the worst of it. One of them who worked in a bank close to Overends, where conditions must have been much the same, wrote anonymously to the *Bankers' Magazine* to highlight 'the foul atmosphere the clerks are compelled to breathe in consequence of so many persons being congregated together in such an ill ventilated place'. Victorian bank clerks had a long working week: 9 a.m. until 7 or 8 p.m. and all day Saturday, until 1867 when Saturday closing was brought back to 3 p.m.[9] There were occasional distractions. Arthur Mills, senior partner of the private bankers Glyn, Mills & Co., had a great fondness for wind-up mechanical toys and encouraged street peddlers to set them rattling across the pavements outside his firm's offices. Overends' clerks must have enjoyed the fun too since their Birchin Lane building was next door.

The better paid clerks and managers lunched at one of the City taverns or chop houses, on liver and bacon, veal and ham, or Welsh Rarebit, helped on their way by mugs of stout and rounded off with cheese and celery or gooseberry pie. Those feeling better off could take a stroll for turtle soup and 'fixings' – a glass of Madeira and an oyster patty – at the Ship and Turtle in Leadenhall Street, Birch's in Cornhill or Baker's Chop House in Change Alley, before going back to close the banking day and tot up for the partners' private ledger how much money the firm had made, or, in Overends' dying years, lost.

The City was a man's world. Women were only to be seen at the start and end of the working day, when the chirping, flirting Cockney and immigrant seamstresses flocked in and out of the millinery and dress factories on its fringes. There were no female secretaries or receptionists and no telephonists (there were no telephones, only the electric telegraph. It would be another ten years before even the early versions of the typewriter began to be seen and heard in offices).

Our story is thus a man's story, sadly lacking in heroines or even the women's angle. Novelists had the licence to give life and voice to the women who supported their heroes and villains, and were often badly let down by them. Here, though, the ladies stay unseen and unheard in West Ham, Walthamstow, Norfolk and Brighton. When not getting ready to give birth, or recovering from it, they engaged in a genteel minuet of running their households and 'calling' on neighbours, interspersed with decorous visits to the theatre and, in London, the opera, concerts and art galleries. The raucous music halls were out of bounds for the middle and upper classes other than as handy places for men on the loose to pick up even looser women. On Sundays and maybe in the week too, the ladies went to church or, in the case of most of our Quaker characters, the Meeting House. In London and the major cities, they could shop; drapers such as John Lewis and Derry & Toms were beginning to expand into full-scale department stores, briefly upstaged when William Whitely opened his sprawling shop as a 'universal provider' in Queensway. To judge by the advertisements of the larger stores, silks, muslin and winter wools for dressmaking were much in demand, though a newspaper offer of '1,000 half price crinolines' in 1866 reinforces other evidence that, like ships and Society itself, fashion was crossing a watershed of its own and that women were replacing the full-hooped skirt with the rump-boosting 'bustle'. Quaker matrons frowned on such worldliness, but their daughters are bound to have checked themselves furtively in the mirror to see how they matched up to 'Miss Rachel's' definition of feminine charm in the *Illustrated London News*: 'youth, beauty, grace, golden tresses, ruby lips, pearly teeth and a soft peachlike complexion'.

The escalator of Victorian marriage ran from shops that offered bridal wear and 'underclothing for ladies about to be married', through others which specialised in maternity gear such as 'accouchement belts' to be worn during and after pregnancy, and hopefully much later (though death was a frequent visitor in Victorian England) to the London General Mourning Warehouse in Regent Street. There ladies could buy suitably sombre dresses and 'widow's weeds' in which to greet the undertaker and his escort of top-hatted 'mutes', while the lacquered black hearse drawn by plumed black horses waited patiently outside the front door for husband, parent or, all too often, child.

Although we do not see much of them, Overends' collapse hurt the women too. On the wives of the partners and of the many ruined shareholders, there descended a shroud of shame, the 'downsizing' of home and lifestyle, a forced dependence on others and the sibilant gossip of supposed friends. Financial ruin could do serious harm to marriages to which dowries and nuptial settlements were an essential buttress: as the later song says, 'What's love got to do with it?' Or as Trollope has Lady Carbury remark in *The Way We Live Now*, 'Love is like any other luxury. You have no right to it unless you can afford it.'

For a Victorian middle- or upper-class girl of marriageable age, a father's loss of money was seriously disfiguring, a fate far worse than the loss of youth and the ambush of middle age. We shall see later how some of the Gurneys agonised about just this problem as the stakes grew ever higher.

Xenos' account of his misfortunes makes only a few passing references to women in nearly 400 pages, one to his otherwise invisible wife and children, and one to a poor mother and her waifs singing for coins in a snowy street. He does allow himself the hint – we can almost see him twirling his moustache like the villain in a Victorian melodrama – that if he wasn't such a gentleman, he could have told us much more about 'Pretty Horsebreakers' and, in a rather characteristic throwaway reference to the legend of Odysseus' shipwreck, 'certain titled Calypsos at whose bidding some of our good City men entered the commercial lists and there fought the most desperate combats'.

Perhaps the most intriguing gap in our knowledge is about

women as investors and speculators. High-born ladies had dabbled up to their décolletage in the South Sea Bubble. Others had gambled their estates away at Regency Faro tables. From anecdotal and some empirical evidence, not least the target lists of the share-pushing sharks who styled themselves 'company promoters' and the records of The Corner House itself when it became a public company, we can surmise that in the financial field women were far from passive with minds and fortunes of their own. All the more at a time when, yet again, the lessons of the past had been forgotten or dismissed as irrelevant in this era of mighty change. The country was once more caught up with what Bagehot called 'the delirium of ancient gambling cooperated with the milder madness of modern over-trading', creating fertile ground for the over-confidence, euphoria, fraud and then, inevitably, despair which are the sub-headings of Overends' story.

6

'Not Slothful in Business'

'Delirium' was not, and is not, a word associated with Quakers. Who were they and why did many of them do so well? Why by painful contrast did those responsible for the débâcle of The Corner House fail so spectacularly? For a country which at least until recently liked to pride itself on its stability and tolerance, Britain's history is one of turbulence and intolerance, a long chronicle of warring monarchs and noble rivalries, civil war, regicide and revolution. Religion – its own history punctuated by persecution, Popish plots, the rack and thumbscrews, the barbequing of supposed heretics at the stake – is no exception. Protestantism, itself a constitutionally handy rejection of Rome, became Britain's Established religion; but that too gave birth to groups which for one reason or another could not accept central elements of the Church of England's doctrines or its authority. Among these Dissenting communities the Quakers have, over the centuries, probably attracted more suspicion, melding into envy, (initially grudging) admiration and fascination than any other.

Some, such as Baptists or Methodists, far outnumbered the Quakers and thrive mightily today. Some, like The Plymouth Brethren, were even more inward looking and austere. Some, such as The Countess of Huntingdon's Connection, The Ranters or The Muggletonians, were splinter groups finding their own way to dissent, from dissent.

Why the suspicion? In a nutshell because, in the eyes of nervous sixteenth- and seventeenth-century ecclesiastical authority and civil government, much of what the Quakers stood for was downright subversive. George Fox, their spiritual guiding light, had taught them that there is 'That of God in every man', a doctrine translated into a belief that Quakers should look for personal guidance from an Inner Light. It followed that since God can speak through, and be spoken to by, anyone, there was no need for appointed clergy, sacraments and structured worship. This and their difficulty finding Gospel authority for the concept of The Trinity, their reliance on the Gospels of the New Testament to the exclusion of the Old, their refusal to pay tithes, their simple exchange of marriage vows and their avoidance of baptism, all cut painfully against the grain of the Church of England and its congregations. In government eyes, Quakers were men and women who could not be relied on to know their place, toe the line and do what they were told was their duty. They were pacifists in a society that often waged war. They were stubborn, refusing to doff their hats to 'authority'. They had no time for the niceties of social degree and the complex British web of patronage and honours. As the Quaker-schooled twentieth-century historian A. J. P. Taylor summed it up, they were convinced that 'I am no better than anyone else and no one else is better than me.'

After the Restoration of Charles II, the authorities came down hard on Dissenters and made an oath of adherence to the Established religion, a touchstone of allegiance to the Crown. Quakers did not swear oaths, in part because they believed it was forbidden by the Bible, but also because for them there was only one Truth which did not need formal reaffirmation: 'Let your yes be yes, and your no be no.'

In a country which put, and still puts, much value on conformity, Quakers also raised suspicion by deliberately standing apart, in their beliefs and practices, in their often quaint language, and in the homespun austerity of their lives and the plainness of their dress: described by an early Gurney as 'holding out a flag which is intelligible to everyone and . . . unquestionably operates as a valuable help in protecting [young people] from worldly habits and follies. It represents a sober mind within.' The Society's insistence that Quakers should only marry Quakers perpetuated another barrier to assimilation and understanding. So too did education. Early Quakers had no comfortable place in Britain's Anglican public schools and were debarred from taking degrees at the principal universities since this would have required affirmation of the Church of England's '39 Articles'. Thus many Quaker men had been moulded outside the British mainstream in the Society's own schools and by its free-thinking teachers, unconfined by pedants and prelates, and, as we shall see, all the better for it.

Their commitment to peace meant that Quakers could not follow the Victorian paths of glory into an army career, or, standing as they did so apart from the Anglican Church, amble along the genteel career pathways from a country parsonage to a cathedral close, popularly said to be reserved for the 'fool of the family' amongst the upper classes. Thus many went straight from a Quaker home and school into practical learning as an apprentice in a Quaker family business, again intensifying the sense of a world apart.

As the years passed, British attitudes mellowed. The Quakers' benign steadiness under fire, their demonstrably happy family lives, their enlightened approach to the lives of the men and women who worked in their businesses, their financial success, their social commitment in fields such as the anti-slavery movement and prison reform and their charitable generosity converted suspicion into respect. The watertight door between Quakers and the wider community, the separate and singular education, the exclusion from other career streams, the channelling of energies, may tell us why there were so many Quakers in trade and industry. It does not, however, tell us why so many, the Gurneys among them, did so well. In 1800, when many of the businesses we list below began their growth, only one person in 500 was a Quaker. Thus, as Sir Adrian Cadbury has calculated, the foundations of a large percentage of Britain's industrial revolution were laid by just 0.2 per cent of the population.[10] In England, Darby set up the first iron works in Coalbrookdale while Huntsman's development of tempered steel placed the centre of gravity of the cutlery industry in Sheffield. Friends founded two of today's biggest British banks, Lloyds and Barclays, the latter a family firmly woven into the Gurney family fabric. The pharmaceutical manufacturer Allen & Hanbury, which started life as a chemist's shop in Plough Court, a few yards from Overends' offices, eventually grew into Glaxo. The Cadburys,

Rowntrees and Frys produced chocolates and cocoa infused with a strong social conscience and care for their workforce, though Joseph Rowntree's own 'still, silent voice' allowed him to indulge in what today would be regarded as rather aggressive 'industrial espionage' into his competitors' trade secrets and attempts at price fixing.

Britain's wealthier homes would have had a harder job keeping time without the clocks and watches of Tompion and Quare, and many lesser known local craftsmen made watches and complex marine chronometers. Londoners would have found it hard to keep themselves warm without the coal poured into their cellars by the Quaker merchants Charrington, some no doubt mined from the seams owned in the north-east by the Quaker Peases. Huntley & Palmer teamed up to deliver biscuits, as did Peak and Frean, though Carr's seem to have cornered the water biscuit market without partners. Hornimans' blended tea, starch and mustard came from Reckitt & Colman (another Norfolk enterprise), chemicals from Albright & Wilson, machinery from Ransome's, and most of the quinine which kept the Empire alive (though a French invention) was manufactured by Howards, the family firm of the cloud-defining Luke Howard. The efforts and the rather less than Friendly lack of concern for workers' health of Bryant & May gave us the humble, hugely profitable British match while giving hundreds of their girl workers the fatal 'Phossy Jaw'. Against this perhaps unfair example, however, we have to set the pioneering of many of the great Quaker manufacturers, who invested heavily in housing their workforces in 'model communities' like the Cadburys' Bournville. 'Persil', although a German invention, was introduced to British washtubs by the Warrington-based Quaker soap manufacturers Crossfields. Men and women who could afford them walked the streets in stout shoes made by C. & J. Clarke, Morlands of Glastonbury, or 'K of Kendal'. As the century moved on, walkers in major cities would be struck by the rise of new Gothic buildings that symbolised the civic pride and business confidence of the age. In London, they included the Natural History Museum, the red-brick, quasi-Flemish bulk of the Prudential Assurance Company's head office in Holborn, University College Hospital and the now vanished Hammersmith campus of St Paul's School. The centre of Manchester was reborn around its new Town Hall. Cambridge showed off the new Girton College, yet another Victorian symbol of emancipation, in this case of women students. This is just a partial list of work by the man many would have known as Britain's leading architect, Alfred Waterhouse. Fewer would have known or cared that he was a Quaker, schooled alongside some of the characters in our own story. His brother Edwin made his mark in a different way as co-founder of the accounting firm of Price, Waterhouse & Co.[11]

Quaker energy, imagination and community capital built bridges, canals and many of Britain's early railways, starting with the first track between Stockton and Darlington in the North-East of England, built to haul coal from local mines to the coast. It was known as 'The Quaker Line' as its major initial backers were the Pease family, who, as we have seen, had major coal-mining interests in the North-East. It provides a fine example of how Quakers came together, at least when the circumstances suited them. The Line was losing money. The Norwich Gurneys were among its lenders but had become disillusioned and, although one of their early London partners, Thomas Richardson, was an investor, in 1825 they demanded repayment of some of their loans. The Line's treasurer Jonathan Backhouse, from yet another Quaker banking family, spoke of its 'pecuniary embarrassments'. All changed in 1826, when Backhouse's sister-in-law, Emma Gurney, joint heir with his wife to a large part of the family fortune, married Joseph Pease. The Gurneys, the Line's chronicler writes, 'then became more under-standing', given not just money but enhanced standing in Whitehall circles. The Pease family's later involvement in the first days of electric power companies, major consumers of coal and coke, is less romantic but another demonstration of how one Quaker success often led to another. (Even after the industrial song the memory lingers on: Darlington Athletic Football Club still proudly carries the nickname 'The Quakers'.) Quaker engineers developed a device to fix rails to sleepers, and invented both the railway ticket and the machine which stamped it. Yet another Quaker conceived 'Bradshaw's Guide', the thick volume of timetables, fares and interchange stations which was an essential precursor to any British rail journey until the Second World War.

Though to a layman it seems a slight stretch of the moral elastic, brewing ale was acceptable. Spirits, however the Hogarthian scourge of the urban poor, were anathema under the Quaker's code. The Truman, Hanbury & Buxton brewery combined three Quaker family names. Another was Barclay, Perkins & Co. When the partners came to sign the deal to buy the Anchor Brewery for £135,000 from the estate of Dr Johnson's friend Henry Thrale, the Doctor, in attendance as one of Thrale's executors, spurred them on with the memorable sales pitch that, 'We are not here to sell a parcel of boilers and vats, but the potentiality of growing rich beyond the dreams of avarice.' Thrale's widow later declared almost as memorably and with evident relief, 'God Almighty sent us a knot of rich Quakers who bought the whole, and saved me and . . . Dr Johnson . . . from brewing ourselves into another bankruptcy.'

Another stretch of the elastic involved the successful Birmingham Quaker businessman and scientific thinker Samuel Galton, who had married a Barclay in 1777. He had inherited his father's gun-making business and by 1790, with the threat of revolution, war and invasion on the horizon, found himself targeted for disownment from the Society on the not unreasonable grounds that his business was incompatible with Quaker pacifist principles. His robust defence, replete with emphatic capital letters, that he had inherited rather than built the business, and that gun making was valuable to 'the purpose of DEFENSIVE war, to the Support of the CIVIL POWER, to the PREVENTION OF WAR and to the PRESERVATION OF PEACE', won the day.

From these examples – the Gurneys' Norwich bank is another, which we will look at in more detail in a moment – we can see that some eighteenth- and nineteenth-century Quakers were extremely successful. 'Some' is a salutary qualification. Because our story is about money and success we are looking at families and individuals who might be called, without discourtesy, the 'superstars' of the Society. It is too easy to forget that many more of the Society's members were a cross-section of middle-class England – shopkeepers, millers, maltsters, craftsmen, printers, clerks and farm workers.

The fascinating question here is why did so many members of such a small community who went into business do so well? Here it is hard to avoid catchwords, starting with 'Conscientiousness'. Faced with the challenge of making a living, they worked hard because they were brought up to be focused, prudent and responsible, and because they wrestled painfully with themselves to be sure that their decisions were right, not just for themselves and future generations but within the context of the Society's teachings. Also because they had no choice, no career alternative.

Education is the critical character former in any community; and for the Quakers it was 'something essential to our life as a Society', as historian Edward Grubb observed in the 1940s. A full picture of The Friends' network of schools, the largest of which, Ackworth, was opened in 1779, and is a network that continues to flourish today, is outside the scope of our study. Yet it is worth looking more closely at one of them, Grove House, since for fifty years from 1828 the thirty or so boys it took in each year were a roll call of most of the prominent Quaker families: Barclays, Lloyds, Gurneys, Foxes, Peases, Backhouses, Hanburys, Bevans and Allcards. Among them were several of The Corner House partners, and it may help to take at least a passing look at how they were moulded, even if it adds to the bewilderment that men in whom all the Quaker strengths were so firmly embedded could have behaved as they did.

Built around 1700 as a squire's manor in what for most of the nineteenth century was the country village of Tottenham, and for some years notorious as a roistering cockfighting ground straight out of *Tom Jones*, Grove House had none of the trappings of the mainstream public school. It was small; more like a 'crammer'. Instead of river-lapped, elm-fringed playing fields, it had a garden along whose mellow brick walls apricots grew in the summer. Instead of compulsory and competitive games of cricket, football and 'rugger', its boys played hockey in the garden if they wanted to, or, when it rained, a private version of Fives adapted to the architecture of their Playroom. Instead of doffing caps to a beetle-browed and feared headmaster with the power to have them bloodily birched, the boys addressed theirs by both names, 'Thomas Hutton', and he reciprocated. The School Register, one of the many treasures in the Society of Friends' library, is another demonstration of the Quakers' fascination, obsession even, with detail. It lists, as one might expect, the boys' date of birth and the dates and ages at which they entered and left the school. It also gives, as would be usual, their fathers' name and occupation and their mothers' maiden name. But in a column one might not normally have expected to see are given, in some cases, the names of the girls the pupils went on to marry. The female names in both lists are a sober recitation of Marys, Elizabeths, Rebeccas, Sarahs and Lucys, with the occasional flash of a Tabitha, Letitia or Grizell.

A sense of the School – a calm oasis, a focus on the practical and the real world, not 'overpoweringly Exhilarating and Romantic', as one Old Boy noted, but still a nice place to be – comes from the reminiscences of one of the pupils and even more from three issues of its magazine for 1850 and 1851 (appropriately for us a Gurney family memento also nestling in the Society's Library). The boys learned to use telescopes and micrometers, and wrote essays on mines, bridges, chemistry, astronomy, the compass, 'mechanisms', human physiology, and the flora and fauna of Norfolk. (Though Classics figured far less than in the grander schools, it is a salutary reminder of present-day standards that the Latin word games which fill some of the spaces would baffle a twenty-first-century classics graduate.)

In keeping with Quaker tenets, although the Scriptures were not central the contemplative and spiritual side was not ignored; one essay in the magazine is on 'Adversity', in which the boys were reminded of their heritage by a listing of the attendance numbers at various major Quaker Meetings across the country. After a visit to Ackworth in 1816, Joseph John Gurney had remonstrated that while the children seemed to him 'remarkably sheltered from evil', the emphasis on unseen guidance rather than the Scriptures meant that they were 'less positively led to God'.

What is far harder, in fact impossible, to recreate is the sense of history, the ethos of time and place, which would have been instilled into the Grove House boys in the early 1800s, just a quarter of a century away from the American War of Independence and Captain Cook's discovery of the world of the Pacific. Closer still was the French Revolution with its wild mixture of high principles, some of which Quakers might have sympathised with, and the baseness of regicide and savage bloodletting. While they grew to be men of the Victorian era, their parents' world and thus to an extent theirs as children, was that of George III, the Regency and George IV, and then William IV; Victoria did not succeed to the throne until 1837.

Though impossible to be sure, and easy to be artificially sentimental, one has the sense that Grove House was a place where no one was left out or left behind, no one beaten, bullied or ragged for being no good at games. Boys will be boys, but Grove House pupils thought seriously about themselves and their behaviour without being priggish. Because university was not an option, they stayed on the Quaker path and went into their fathers' or a relation's business, and in what may have been another ingredient of success, learning it from the ground up without the swagger, airs and graces that came with thinking of oneself as 'the young master'. Their schooling must have helped them look at how factories and businesses worked with a practical rather than a patrician eye. A well-cared-for workforce meant steadier production. Getting things done by consensus rather than dictation made for easier industrial relations.

The talent and opportunity for good communications, or in today's language 'networking', is another element of Quaker commercial success. As Quakers pushed their businesses forward, customers, suppliers, guidance, capital and if necessary admonition (even though it might sometimes be regarded as intrusive) were freely available through the Society's fine-tuned communications system. Passed to and fro were comments, news and views distilled from a torrent of letter writing, Society circulars and the verbal reports of the indefatigable Quaker travellers, whose caravans never seemed to rest. In the words of an anonymous essayist in 1859 quoted by Elizabeth Isichei in her careful study *Victorian Quakers*, the Friends 'remain the special object of their own concern, a family of interest . . . a society for combined action, self protection and public relations'. The social penalty of failure in a Quaker enterprise could be harsh, a factor which no doubt made businessmen even more cautious and attentive. Elizabeth Gurney, sister of Samuel, the man who built The Corner House into a powerhouse (and who strides onto our pages later), took the surname by which she is far better known when she married Joseph Fry. When Joseph's 'bank' – a typical nineteenth-century City combination of tea and coffee merchants and banking – had a rocky time in 1812, a delegation of heavyweight Gurneys, Samuel among them, descended on London to straighten out the mess and, in her words, 'do what is needful for us'. The firm survived, but did not escape another crisis in 1828 caused by a wave of South American debt defaults, when desperate country bankers rushed into town to haul their London connections out of church on a Sunday morning 'clamouring for gold', according to Disraeli, a man who knew all about the perils of speculation. The Quaker community, demonstrating a most un-Friendly propensity for thin-lipped gossip and sanctimoniousness, began to mutter that funds from the Fry bank had been diverted to Elizabeth's charitable works and to maintain an extravagant standard of living. Though another Gurney posse managed to save the tea and coffee business for future Fry generations, the Society launched an investigation. Her brother, the pious Joseph John Gurney, felt with a singular lack of family loyalty that 'painful justice' was required. Six months later Joseph Fry was formally disowned by the Society for causing 'a great and lamentable loss . . . and a reproach upon our Christian profession'. When Elizabeth sent word to East Anglia a few months later that she wanted to visit local Friends, she was told that she would not be welcome. She even had difficulty getting her son into a Quaker school.

It was hard, probably impossible, for an early Victorian Quaker businessman to escape the sharp eye of the community. The Society's Meetings for Worship, one midweek and two on Sunday, which were their quietist equivalent of church services, were the spiritual heart of a complex structure of monthly and quarterly local and regional assemblies. These culminated in the London Yearly Meeting – the

Quaker 'parliament', to use another term to which Victorian Friends might have taken objection – at which organisation, finance, doctrine, discipline and personal behaviour were debated. In a notable exception to what we have come to mean by 'democratic', Quakers did not vote; there was no stark 'majority versus minority'. Decisions were reached by consensus, the 'sense of the meeting' as deftly drafted and put to the assembly by the presiding Clerk. If no agreed 'sense' emerged, the issue would be deferred for discussion at the next gathering, or with a characteristically British touch, referred to an ad hoc committee for more scrutiny. By today's standards the emphasis on meetings may have been overdone. In 1851, British Quakers had 346 'preparative', eighty-six monthly and twenty-four quarterly meetings, quite apart from a parallel stream of gatherings for women, ministers and Elders. However, we can see that overlain on such a relatively small community, they had enormous value in pragmatic business terms and in bolstering the sense of togetherness against the world, being somehow 'special'.

The Quaker businessman never haggled; he named a fair price and stuck to it, a tactic which his competitors found annoying but to which customers responded with loyalty. But naming the price also required a practical eye for cost and for book keeping; as the story unfolds, we will see that some of our non-Quaker protagonists had a flair for conceiving grandiose projects of whose costs they remained in blissful ignorance until it was too late. It was not only in business. The architectural historian Gavin Stamp reflects something of the same point, and indeed other Quaker traits, when he describes Alfred Waterhouse as a 'practical, commercial and prolific architect', whose approach to his work was one of 'a hard, no-nonsense rationalism, if not bloody-mindedness'.

'Trust' is another compass-bearing on our map of understanding. Quakers were, and indeed still are, encouraged to examine themselves to make sure that they maintain 'strict integrity' in all their dealings, to avoid speculation, and to be 'personally scrupulous and responsible in the use of money entrusted to you'. Outsiders knew that a Quaker's word was his bond, all the more important if the Quaker was a banker.

Quaker business tended to be steady and constant since it made and dealt in, by and large, the plainer things that an expanding consumer society would go on needing and wanting – chocolate, tea, biscuits, shoes, wool, mustard, agricultural machinery, medicines, pots and pans, beer and even money. None were products susceptible to swings of fashion or rapid technological change.

Nor should we underestimate the value of keeping control firmly within the family. The Quaker businesses which have left their names and mark on the historical page and the public memory, were all built up steadily over the long term, helped by judicious and non-controversial mergers and acquisitions rather than by glittering Stock Exchange coups. Their survival and the powerful ongoing role of so many of the founding families were helped by a canny approach to inheritance. Unlike the traditional British pattern, in which the bulk of the assets in an estate passed to the eldest son, Quakers handed on their wealth through careful allocations designed to make sure that no incompetent or wastrel heir could dissipate the family fortune inside a single generation. A neat distinction drawn in one of the major firms saw the early generations' capital divided into Ordinary Shares, which had the risk and rewards associated with equity and went to the male heirs, while the girls had equal allocations of Preference Shares, which produced a fixed dividend and would not fluctuate in value as profits inevitably rose and fell. Thus the apocryphal North Country warning about mill-owning families who went 'from clogs to clogs in three generations' rarely applied in the Quaker world.

The family ties forged by intermarriage and sometimes shared calculation of mutual parental advantage (by no means an exclusively Quaker trait in eighteenth- and nineteenth-century Britain) were critical. Maybe they were the most important aspect of all. Up till the time of our story, intermarriage was encouraged, or forced on families by one of the harsher rules of Quaker discipline which dictated that any man or woman who married 'out' of the Society was liable to be 'disowned', removed from membership, sent, in historian James Walvin's words, 'into spiritual exile'. Not only that, their children were also barred from membership and thus also from access to Quaker schools. After years of earnest debate, the rule, deep-rooted in a biblical injunction against being 'Yoked with Unbelievers', was abandoned in 1860. But this was not before it had done much to weave tightly the fabric of success on the one hand, whilst on the other, to mix the metaphor, sown the seeds which over time left the Society 'weakened not only in numbers but also in spirit and energy'; the rule had been the cause of between one third and half of all 'disownments' from the Society.

Those in our story had been born, raised and taken wives themselves under the shadow of the marriage rule. It is thus little wonder that in the partners' list of The Corner House, of Gurney's bank and of most other Quaker businesses, there were connections via a web of brothers, sisters, in-laws, first, second and third cousins. The same names pop up in different permutations, a geodesic dome of relationships even a skilled genealogist would find it a challenge to unravel. As just one example, an early Gurney, Joseph, who died in 1830, had a Backhouse, a Birkbeck, a Barclay and a Pease as his four sons-in-law. The ties helped bind the community even more tightly. They helped in business too. Bankers need to put their money to work with borrowers who are likely to repay. The strong Quaker presence in banking cannot have been a hindrance when Friends and families, vouched for as hard working and ambitious by personal acquaintance, by links of blood or marriage or the Society's grapevine, needed finance for business ventures. Over the centuries these ties were certainly of great benefit to the growth both of the Gurneys' Norwich bank and to Overends.

Also, in those early Victorian years the Quakers, by setting themselves apart, had not yet been lured into the silky web of the British class system with its niceties and inhibitions. This left them freer to act as they and their Friends believed to be right, with no concern for what the wider world thought. The Trollopian subtleties of social standing were not for them and, though this would change with time, they were deaf to the siren call of the country's honours system. Barred by their belief from taking oaths, Quakers did not become lawyers. When disputes arose Quaker businessmen looked to conciliation and informal arbitration rather than litigation, a constant striving for amicable resolution to discord which must also have made it easier to manage relations with their workers. Their free-thinking practical education made for liberated and enquiring minds. They were technologists more than scientists. The Quakers were ready to challenge existing methods and to innovate. It was a group of Quaker investors – most of them from the same group of families who had invested in the Stockton and Darlington Railway – which transformed Middlesborough from a hamlet of 154 people in the 1830s to an industrial landscape of blast furnaces and docks, with a population ten years later of 6,000.

In fairness, not every commentator rose in applause at Quaker success. More than one early nineteenth-century critic attributes it simply to 'avarice' or 'a money getting spirit'. One wrote: 'Wealth is pursued with systematic purpose and all the powers of the mind are bent to serve that end.' The comment ignores the extraordinary Quaker spirit, of which the Gurneys were but one example, of open-handed and open-hearted philanthropy in such a broad and ecumenical range of local and national causes. Kinder souls remarked on the Quakers' determination, verging on obstinacy, their gravity, calmness and self-control, and, suggesting that the compulsion to marry in did indeed produce good results, their 'unusual capacity for domestic tranquillity'. Another writer encapsulated the mid-nineteenth-century Quaker as a 'good hearted, placid, rich man whose profession is to do good'.

It is hard to imagine a Quaker boasting as did Sir Richard Arkwright, who began as a barber and grew hugely rich in the late eighteenth century from adroit use of new technology in his spinning mills, that if he lived long enough he could pay off the entire national debt. Writing about the development of British industry in the late eighteenth and early nineteenth century, Steven Watson describes how the 'great nineteenth-century virtues of thrift, family solidarity and great self-confidence were hammered out in the new towns along with the nineteenth-century vices of hardness, narrowness and self-satisfaction'. By and large, the Quaker men of business seem to have been able to capitalise on those virtues without falling prey to the vices, save perhaps from time to time for the latter.

The mill-owning philanthropist Robert Owen, a founder of modern socialism, was in some ways as enlightened in his attitude to his hands at New Lanark as any Quaker businessman, providing them with model homes, schooling and a community structure. But, as Watson points out (and here again we may discern a distinction between paternalistic Quaker owners like the Cadburys and their harder-boiled business peers), in ruling the lives of his employees Owen was 'as dictatorial as any hard-fisted mill boss . . . creating a closed society under benevolent despotism'.

To the amateur eye, squinting back through the distortions of time and culture, the hazy overall impression is of the Quakers drawing their strength from being 'a family of families'; and by and large of 'happy families, [which] resemble one another', though Tolstoy did not have Quakers in mind when he wrote this in *Anna Karenina*. It was a family whose nucleus and commonality were belief, a family which was determined, strict, harsh even. A family that was prying and interfering, but a family which was quiet, caring and tight-knit, and which saw nothing wrong in worldly success and helping others to attain it, within its self-set limits of what constituted proper behaviour. This family, like any other, had its faults, biases, rich uncles, scatty aunts and the occasional black sheep, but it was a family very much of its time, 'all for one, one for all,' today a fast vanishing if not already extinct template.

It was a family which 'kept itself to itself', watched by its neighbours with wary respect. In that sense even though the British pointed jealous fingers at both communities for their alleged keenness on wealth, there was a difference between the way many thought about Quakers on the one hand and the Jewish community on the other. When Trollope's Georgiana Longestaffe told her parents, steeped in alluvial British prejudice but so short of money that they ought to have leaped at the prospect of any wealthy son-in-law, that the rich Jewish banker Ezekiel Breghert had asked her to marry him, their reflex reaction was one of alliterative horror. The idea was 'disgusting, degrading, disgraceful'. Had she announced that her suitor was a wealthy Quaker Bill broker, they would probably have been no more than momentarily perplexed and then started to calculate how much to mulct him for in her marriage settlement.

In the teeth of this unthinking and commonplace hostility it was interesting to find a mid-Victorian comment tucked away in a book about London which, though not without a slightly snide touch, sets out a view of the ties that bound the Jewish community which is not that different from what we have sought to tease out about Quakers. Writing in 1844 one W. S. West remarked that 'the associations of boyhood, the influence of religion, the dislike to quit[*sic*] a society of which they are members, all conspire to keep the Jewish community – rich as well as poor – united. A sense of interest strengthens the bond. The clannish spirit kept alive in the tribe enables the wealthier members to command in their often daring speculations the assistance of the modest funds of their less wealthy brethren. . .'

We should leave the last word with the Quakers themselves, to be found in the seventy-seven panels of crewel embroidery which seek to convey the Society's insights and experiences, and which are the centrepiece of the Meeting House at Kendal. Panel D6, 'Quaker Merchants', is captioned with a quotation from St Paul's Epistle to the Romans: 'Not slothful in business: fervent in spirit: serving the Lord.' The Quaker men of business succeeded, the panel suggests, because they were 'diligent in the management of their trades & affairs. Keeping their word & promises, they gained credit in the country.'

7

The House That Samuel Built

Whatever the complex reasons for the Quakers' success, the question for us is why in Overends' case the Inner Light was a light that failed. Whether or not they were still fully committed members of the Society, the main players in the Overends' drama had been steered from birth, by example and teaching, down the flinty path of truth, honest dealing and plain speaking, and pointed firmly away from the snares of speculation and the world's glittering temptations. Most of them had been to Grove House School. What happened? Part of the answer, elaborated later, is our now familiar theme of 'change'. Britain was gripped by the excitement of change. Quakerism, as we have seen, was also changing, relaxing its rules, its membership falling, some of its families inching inexorably closer to the British mainstream as they became ever wealthier. The Corner House too was changing.

The Gurneys were wealthy Quakers, men and women of integrity, piety, honesty and culture, their fortune spun from wool and much multiplied in the business of banking. Some in the family claimed that, like Norwich Castle, it could trace its roots back to the Norman conquest and the 'Gournays' who had arrived in the Conqueror's entourage, though that may have been a gloss designed to impress an aristocratic family into which a later Gurney boy wanted to marry.

Gurney's Bank was founded in Norwich in 1770, and its origins and a sense of its standing were recorded in an 1838 'Circular To Bankers', the influential journal that country bankers relied on to assess the credit reputation of their peers:

The collecting of yarns from the numerous scattered

manufacturers of the East of England and holding them in stock to supply those who were weaving them into various textures was a very lucrative business and we deliberately question whether the Gurneys did not at one time derive from it an annual income greater than is obtained by any bank in the Island of Great Britain excepting not more than fifty or sixty out of the whole thousand. In the course of dealing with the worsted spinners for their yarn the family began to supply them with cash to pay the wages of labour and enable them to carry on their operations in business.

'Various textures' is a rather dry way to describe Norfolk fabrics with such splendid names as challis, *mousseline de laine*, paramatta cloth, a cotton and worsted mix called 'Palestine', bandana, *gris de Naples* and Norwich shawl. 'Worsted' itself is said to take its name from a Norfolk village now called Worstead. It is hard to imagine today that in sixteenth-century England, as Penry Williams has pointed out, sheep outnumbered humans by two or three to one, and that in 1700 Norwich was the second largest city in the country after London. In 1724, Daniel Defoe reported that its townsfolk 'dwell in their garrets at their looms, in their combing shops and their twisting mills'. By 1780, Norwich's textile industry made it the country's largest manufacturing centre, even though until the railway arrived in 1834 it took longer to reach London by boat than it did Amsterdam.

'Polite and commercial', a description used by the great jurist William Blackstone about his fellow countrymen and taken by Paul Langford as the title for his sweeping study of eighteenth-century England (a book, coincidentally, printed in Norfolk), suits the Gurneys well. They lived comfortably, as befitted wealthy bankers, but conservatively, without the 'flashiness' of new money or the Whiggish hauteur of the old, but also without some of the starker constraints of Quakerism. Their houses, for instance, had pictures and framed prints on the walls – much frowned on as ostentatious in strait-laced Society circles – and some of their daughters were even allowed to paint. Nevertheless, their beliefs permeated their lives.

The essence of what it meant to have to balance God and Mammon is caught in the words of the venerated Quaker leader and theologian Joseph John Gurney (1788–1847), who combined a passion for Bible scholarship with a serious view of his responsibilities as a banker: 'I wish to complete the Psalms, attending a little to Syriac and Chaldee as I go along. After that to read Solomon, to make myself the master of the Jewish laws and translate the Yad Hachazekah of Maimonides,' he confided to his personal journal. But business came first. 'I suppose my leading outward object in life may be said to be the [Norwich] Bank. While I am a banker the Bank must be attended to. It is obviously the religious duty of a trustee to so large an amount to be diligent in watching his trust.' When he braved the Atlantic on an evangelical mission to America, Joseph John even asked his partners to cut his share of the Norwich bank's profits by a third to compensate for his absence from work.

In keeping with a fundamental Quaker precept, the Gurneys were unflinchingly generous philanthropists, their names appearing all over East Anglian and East London local histories, heading the lists of subscribers in financing hospitals from King's Lynn to the East End of London, churches, schools, drinking fountains and working men's cottages. But they were never dull. Notwithstanding early Quaker disapproval of the frivolity of singing, dancing, painting and the theatre (William Penn once asked rhetorically, 'What poems, romances, comedies and the like did the Apostles and Saints make or use to pass away their time withal?'), early Gurneys supported the Theatre Royal in Norwich and were members of the Norwich Society of Artists founded by the talented local watercolourist John Crome. In later years family members were part of the circle around Harriet Martineau, the brilliant writer on economics and early campaigner for women's rights, herself also from a weaving family.

The inscription on an engraved portrait of an eighteenth-century Gurney sums it up well:

> See plainness here with decency combined,
> And looks sedate, which speak a furnished mind.

Indeed, that the engraving or the later portrait of Samuel Gurney even exist suggests again that the Gurneys were less constrained than some of their brethren.

Though the Gurneys had their roots in Norwich rather than the City, they fitted well Bagehot's definition of the London private banker: 'He was supposed to represent, and often did represent, a certain union of pecuniary sagacity and educated refinement which was scarcely to be found in any other part of society.'[12]

But what led men who were the personification of 'pecuniary sagacity' to branch out from the cobble-stoned charms and comfortable certitudes of Norwich, a city ancient even by the time William the Conqueror arrived to build its castle, to the City of London's narrow streets, where risk lurked in the fog round every corner? The Depression-era American hold-up man, Willie Sutton, knew the answer. Asked why he robbed banks, he joked, 'Because that's where the money is.' Put less frivolously, in modern business jargon, for the Gurneys it was a sensible diversification.

The Gurney generations had built a fine banking business in East Anglia. With branches in Fakenham, King's Lynn, Yarmouth, Wisbech, Aylsham and Bury St Edmunds, they could be said to be 'the' bank of East Anglia.[13]

Everything and every place have their season. Norwich had once been larger than Newcastle and had ranked in size and vitality only behind Bristol and Plymouth among the provincial centres. However, in the industrial age it was 'too far from coal and too near to London' to hold its ground. Lancashire textile mills may have been 'dark and satanic', but their pool of sweated and child labour made them efficient and hugely profitable. They drove the small Norfolk weavers out of business; domestic looms of the sort Silas Marner operated became museum pieces. But by then the Gurney fortune was well secured and, like all good fortunes should, went on multiplying comfortably as East Anglia's agricultural, milling, shoe and boot making, packing and starch industries threw off new streams of cash for the bankers to put to profitable use. The opportunity in the early 1800s to spread their wings to London, into a specialised area of banking they knew well, made business sense.

The Gurneys knew about money; they also knew about Bills of Exchange and the profits to be made from them. The small firm in which they invested eight years before the Battle of Waterloo was a dealer (or broker, as they were known) in Bills, which would grow successfully and emerge as the discount house of Overend, Gurney & Co., and met the Quaker criteria. The prospects were good, the business was not speculative, the men involved were known to the Gurneys and the risks were essentially those of the bankers' trade, risks the Gurneys understood well. Thomas Richardson, a London Bill brokers' clerk, had set up on his own in 1802, at the age of thirty-one. It helped that Richardson was a Quaker, from a family which, though not wealthy, was related by marriage to the coal-mining, railway-backing Peases, whose business origins like the Gurneys had been in the cloth trade. As the Gurney family knew and trusted him, he was given the lion's share of its Norwich bank's Bill business – both buying and selling – in London. In 1805, he was joined by his brother-in-law, the Yorkshireman John Overend, and with a large investment from Norwich in 1807 Richardson, Overend & Co. became Overend, Gurney & Co. Overend left the firm soon after the Gurneys invested, but in a twist worthy of a Jacobean drama his ghost will return to transfix The Corner House, like the Spirit of Christmas Past, just before the roof falls in. Richardson also moved on to prosper in insurance and invest in the best Quaker tradition. He headed the investor group which transformed Middlesborough and in 1841 he put up most of the cost of the nearby seventy-four-acre Ayton estate to provide 'practical education' for children whose parents had married 'out' of the faith, to whom the Society's own schools were chillingly closed.

For the Gurneys it was a good time to be in the business of financing business. With the American war finished, and the end of the struggle against the French in sight, British trade and industry had many advantages – ships and railways, new industries such as iron and new trading markets across the world, all of which relied on Bills for their working capital. Interest rates were also low and less volatile, making it easier for firms like Overends to 'lock in' a profit between what they paid for their deposits and what they earned on the Bills they bought.

For the greater part of its life Overend & Gurney was another nineteenth-century Quaker success story. That success is largely attributable to the character and talents of one man, Samuel Gurney, born in 1786. In the Quaker tradition, he started work with his relatives, the Frys, at the age of fourteen, and though in one sense he plays no part in our story, his death – the loss of a tough, shrewd patriarch – can be seen as symbolic of the shift in Overend's fortunes, when business started to tip from good to bad.

In a backhanded accolade, Karl Marx referred to Samuel Gurney as 'the first-rate expert, the esteemed, crafty Quaker' and, writing years later, Bagehot differentiated the patriarch from his son of the same name as 'Samuel Gurney the Great'.

Samuel's sister Elizabeth, six years his elder, who married the unlucky Joseph Fry, was far more direct than crafty. Equally strong-willed, she might also deserve the adjective 'Great' for her social conscience and her crusade to improve Britain's prison conditions, especially for women. She and her sisters had shocked Norwich's Goat Lane Meeting House. To the horror of the 'plain Quakers'[14] to whom any display or decoration were anathema, they wore bright clothes and even, as Elizabeth once noted proudly in her diary, 'purple boots with scarlet laces'. Those in the community who recalled that an early Gurney had spent three years in Norwich jail for his beliefs, would have pursed their lips in disapproval. As she grew up, Elizabeth too turned in the 'plain' direction, which may have lessened community anxiety, though some in the Gurney family were less enthusiastic about her new-found zeal. Another brother, the gentle philanthropist Daniel Gurney, took particular exception to her preaching, a Quaker practice pithily dismissed by Dr Johnson on another occasion as 'like a dog walking on its hind legs. It is not done well but you are surprised to find it done at all.' Daniel, so set against his sister preaching that he fell out with his local Meeting for allowing it, even forbade Elizabeth to read the Scriptures aloud in his house. In the closing pages of our story, poor Daniel has more to worry about than women reading the Bible in his drawing room.

Samuel Gurney understood the difference between a good Bill and a bad one, the fragility of credit and reputation, and that money was like mercury, hard to scoop up in one's hand and apt always to slip through even the tightest fingers. When brought the news sometime in the 1850s that the firm had been hit with a sizeable loss, he is said to have told his partners, 'Well, I'm glad to hear of it. It will be a good lesson to you young men and will teach you the uncertainty of riches.'

In the City, he stood out from the crowd, Quaker from top to toe. The City's upper echelons came to work in black frock coats and glossy top hats. Samuel, by contrast, wore a brown broadcloth coat, gaiters, squared-toed shoes and a low hat with a broad brim of white beaver, which he would wear inside and outside the office, removing it at home or in Meetings 'in the sight of God'. His business letters were addressed to 'Esteemed Friend' or 'Respected Friend' – the first rather more formal, suggesting an inflexible decision was about to be expressed, the second implying to those who understood the nuance that there was some room for discussion. They were studded with 'Thee's and 'Thine's, and dated either in numerals or as 'First Month', 'Second Month' and so on to avoid writing down days and months named after pagan gods. (Bradshaw stuck to the same principle in the early editions of his Railway Guide.) Samuel ran the firm with a shrewd eye to risk; clerks were suddenly switched from one ledger to another to nip any attempt at fraud in the bud. He was understandably a touch less benign than at home; he was remembered as 'brusque' (doubtless a reflection of the Quaker belief in the efficacy of few but plain words) though still 'beaming with cheerfulness'. His authority and Quaker principles shine through in a family memory of an incident in the 1840s, when Overends uncovered a forgery, then an offence which could end with the perpetrator swinging from the gallows. Summoning the guilty man to the partners' room, Samuel told him: 'We have thee under our power. By the law, we must hang thee. But we will not do that.' He opened a private door which led directly to Birchin Lane and said, 'Be off to the Continent and beware of ever returning.' There is much more that could be said about this remarkable family, but this is enough to show that Samuel, like all the early Gurneys, was a 'solid citizen', devout, principled and strong minded.

Samuel and his partners were often called in to give their advice and views to parliamentary committees trying to fathom the inscrutable workings of the financial markets, and made frequent appearances with City delegations to the Chancellor of the Exchequer. One probably apocryphal story has it that when Gladstone sought Samuel Gurney's private counsel on an early budget, the sage of Birchin Lane told him, 'One thing I will venture to urge. Whatever thy plan is, let it be simple,' a nineteenth-century admonition which, retranslated as 'Keep it simple, stupid,' has found its way into twenty-first-century political wisdom. There was clear blue water between the Bill discounters, whose trade was essentially domestic, and the internationally-oriented banking houses of their time – Rothschild, Baring, Huth, Hambro, D'Erlanger, Goldschmidt and Schroeder – the future 'Merchant Banks' with their trade and family connections around the world. Their business comprised raising loans for foreign governments (not infrequently of dubious stability and probity) and ambitious railway and construction projects, helping Britain to buy control of the Suez Canal and the United States to finance the purchase of Louisiana. This allowed the banks' partners to acquire peerages and over-decorated art-filled mansions in the Home Counties, far from the madding crowd. It is impossible, for instance, to imagine Samuel Gurney discussing with Disraeli, with the same sophisticated confidence as Lionel de Rothschild, the credit standing of Spain in the London bond market or the effect on bullion prices of political manoeuvres by the Tsar. In fact, Samuel is unlikely to have had any views on Spain or Russia at all; though his Quaker concerns, did lead him to worry about human suffering in the wider world, his single-minded business focus was mainly on the London money markets and English business credit.

However, there were bridges over the blue water. Samuel Gurney was one of the five first presidents of Alliance Assurance, when Nathan Rothschild created it in 1824, to open the insurance market to Jews and Quakers; Francis Baring was another.

Rothschild also raised the loan in 1835 used to compensate the slave owners and thus hasten the demise of the slave system, that flagship Quaker cause.

Nonetheless, in contrast to much of that banking *haute monde*, while some of our cast had expensive London homes, and the Gurneys' Catton Hall and Runcton estates in Norfolk were set in rolling acres and manicured lawns, they would certainly not have seen themselves as 'landed gentry'. Samuel Gurney's own estate was at Upton Park, in what is now West Ham, where Rothschild was a dinner guest. Several Gurneys and Barclays made their homes in Walthamstow, now part of the metropolitan sprawl with few nuggets of the past remaining, but in its Victorian heyday 'one of the largest and handsomest suburban villages near the metropolis . . . surrounded by beautiful and romantic woodland scenery [with] many large and handsome villas with tasteful pleasure grounds mostly occupied by wealthy merchants'. It was not far, it may be noted, from Grove House School.

Upton Park was Samuel Gurney's ark, over which he presided like a benign Noah, metaphorically pulling up the ramp to cut off the world outside and surrounding himself with his nine children, over forty grandchildren and a menagerie of kangaroos, peacocks, dogs, cows, horses and a donkey named 'Cordova'. The only evidence of lush living was in the gardens; the 3,400 species of tropical plants in his conservatory ran the Botanical Gardens at Kew a close second.

To encourage hard work and thrift, he persuaded his daughters to keep an account of what they were owed for homework and household chores they undertook:

> Reading, 30 pages at ½*d* a page,
> Peeling an apple, 1*d*,
> For lighting a fire 1*d*.

The City was never far away in any sense, and he had been known to embarrass his family by leaving a wedding party well before it finished, muttering that he had to get back to his desk. As an obituary noted, 'It was a remarkable sight to witness him plunge day by day into the vortex of City business and return home to his own domestic hearth without any trace of a Mammon-loving spirit.' Or as a Quaker contemporary wrote in rather more Old Testament language, 'He is the only man I know who has passed through the burning fiery furnace without the smell of it in some way hanging round his garments.' There was at least one day when he came home smelling of smoke, after he had been persuaded to try out a new 'steam engine' designed for road use, and rather improbably called a 'whisky'. The experiment does not seem to have been repeated; it seems probable, though we have no evidence, that the contraption was one patented by the unrelated Goldsworthy Gurney, a Cornish engineer.

Samuel stretched himself far beyond business, family and even Britain, summed up by a contemporary as an 'enlightened patriarch'. His support for the early growth of Liberia, the state created for and by freed American slaves is exemplified in another anecdote, showing him at his generous, decisive and discreet best. When Liberia's President Roberts came to London in 1849, he was asked at a reception what more could be done to help Liberia and stifle the transatlantic slave trade still being actively pursued out of the mouth of the River Lofa. He suggested Liberia should buy up the area between the capital Monrovia and neighbouring Sierra Leone, so it controlled the slavers' hinterland and the Gallenas 'slave factory'. Though it was a swathe several hundred miles long at a cost of only £2,000, it was a sum which the fledgling state could not afford. Gurney immediately offered to pay half adding that if the British Government would not come up with the balance he would pay it or find 'friends' to do so. The next day President Roberts called at The Corner House – a visitor rather out of the normal run of bill discounters and money brokers – where Samuel handed him his personal draft for £1,000. A few days later Samuel told a Liberian sympathiser that 'arrangements had been made' for the balance. It cannot now be found in the atlas, but there is somewhere a small settlement near Gallenas originally named in his honour. Closer to home, an obelisk was erected in his memory outside Stratford Town

Hall. All in all he was a man who lived his life well and, in the spirit of George Fox's 1656 injunction, had 'come to walk cheerfully over the world, answering that of God in every one'.

Thirty years after the events in this story, a City commentator with a short memory dismissed the discount business as 'mechanical and blind', whose managers needed 'to do nothing except shut one's eyes and buy Bills in the belief that the average value of short term money will always leave a profit on business so done'. This oversimplifies hugely the inherent risks even in the mainstream Bill business. However careful Samuel, his partners and their managers might be, there were bound to be bad debts among the thousands of Bills that flowed through their hands, and though the firm earned good money, its profit margins on each transaction were tiny. So, as in any bank, the risk of loss was a serious one.

But there was another, perhaps even greater risk: Overends relied on deposits to fuel their business, money drawn in by confidence that in Samuel the depositors had 'a safe pair of hands', and reinforced by a sense that behind him stood the fabled Gurney wealth and connections. These deposits had a short fuse; many could be withdrawn – 'called', to use another term of the banker's art – within the space of the 10 a.m. to 3 p.m. banking day, and money lodged for seven days or more was a long-term blessing. Though some depositors were part of the wider Gurney 'connection' and thus more or less to be counted on, much of the money came from unsentimental operators looking for the best return they could get with safety. Safety was paramount. If news of a serious loss got out, it could leave a black mark on Overends' reputation. One or two black marks were part of a banker's life. Too many and the reputation became tarnished and the deposits would gravitate elsewhere. Even without that, The Corner House faced hour by hour what bankers call 'liquidity risk': what would happen if external events anywhere from Birmingham to Bombay drove the market into panic, or money dried up because of shifts in the international exchange rate or the price of gold, wars or rumours of war.

Samuel Gurney and indeed many later generations would have stared in blank incomprehension if some bright-eyed twentieth-century financial analyst had asked them what their strategy was for dealing with 'the worst case scenario'. But in their stomachs that is just what they were always ready for. Their first line of defence was to keep enough liquid capital, enough cash, to meet most reasonable expectations of what would happen in times of stress. However, unlike banks, who paid their customers nothing for the balance they kept on their current accounts, the discount houses paid interest on all their deposits, so could not afford to keep much in the way of idle balances. The principle protection was to hold only high quality assets, Bills with the best names, paper which when money was short elsewhere could be sold to other banks or, as a last resort, to the Bank of England itself. The problem was that a money crunch could hit other banks too, and the Bank was, as we shall see, an institution whose conflicting roles in the City were to cause deep problems. This too is part of the text of our tale.

The Corner House weathered many storms in the years of Samuel Gurney's stewardship – bad debts, market crises that led to a run on their deposits – but Samuel steered through them all and the business flourished. By the 1850s, it was discounting £70 million of Bills a year and, after paying its senior partners handsome salaries, generating profits for its owners of around £200,000 a year, which, multiplied by fifty, put it squarely in the category of 'a nice little earner'. Even after a lifetime of generous giving, when Samuel died in 1856, his estate, together with earlier settlements on his family, still added up in today's terms to over £50 million.

Some have argued that the firm began to slide even before Samuel Gurney died, after he had stepped back from the business, tracing the first hairline crack in the firm's apparently impregnable façade back to a prosaic cargo of zinc ingots, known in the trade as 'spelter'. In 1853, Samuel's nephew David Barclay Chapman was next in seniority in the firm to the patriarch himself and was actually running the business day to day. He was from a Quaker banking family in the North-East, related needless to say by marriage to several Barclays and Gurneys.

Overends had discounted £200,000 of Bills for a metal-trading firm against the security of stocks of spelter, stored together with some tin, iron and cochineal (then a widely traded speculative commodity) in a warehouse on Hagen's Sufferance Wharf; no novelist could have invented a name so evocative of dank Victorian docksides and the filth-flecked Thames. It was a routine banking deal, but if multiplied by our Fifty Factor it was 'serious money'. There was one problem: the documents of title were forged; the metal had already been pledged to another lender. Chapman found this out only too late, after The Corner House had parted with the money. He had two choices: to prosecute or cover up. It cannot have been an easy choice: when Samuel Gurney was faced with the fatal consequences of prosecuting the earlier forger, Quaker humanity prevailed over public duty and the man scuttled into oblivion across the Channel. To avoid embarrassing publicity about his initial error, Chapman made the wrong choice. He gave the fraudsters a second chance, the opportunity to come up with real collateral, and told them not to breathe a word about it. They scurried around, laid their hands on some genuine security at other creditors' expense, and to the outside world the relationship with Overends continued undisturbed. It was a relationship the traders talked up to their great advantage as they went on gulling other banks in what turned out to be an early version of a Ponzi scheme; new investors' money is used to pay off the old and the last suckers drawn in lose a great deal of money when, inevitably, it collapses.

Chapman was more seriously embarrassed when he was called as a witness at the fraudster's trial where he was censured by the judge for his attempt to hush the fraud up and, as a result, 'inflicting injury upon other parties'. Samuel Gurney was already fading; in his prime, his fabled 'nose' would surely have twitched early enough to stop the deal before it became a problem. The discount market historian W. T. C. King believed that the débâcle had 'undoubtedly' hastened Samuel's death. While that may be so, the sad fact is that Samuel had been devastated by the long, drawn-out illness and painful death of his wife Elizabeth. He had leased Villa Saissi in Nice on the French Riviera to try to recover his health, but died in Paris on his way back to England, in June 1856, aged seventy-one. He was buried not in the City or in some 'fashionable' cemetery but like his sister Elizabeth in the Quaker Burial Ground at Barking, at whose Meeting House he and his wife were married. Quaker records speak of 'an immense concourse' of mourners.

8

A New Generation

Chapman took over, but not for long. The cover up had cost him his reputation for plain dealing; bankers, never especially charitably minded, are at their most unforgiving when they feel cheated by one of their own. Behind his back they called him 'Gurney's liar' and, in politer City correspondence, 'a man who wants for steadiness of character'.

One City history suggests that he was forced out of the firm after two years, but as he had reached the respectable retiring age of sixty this may be an unjustified extrapolation. He took with him his capital of £250,000. Since he had also been sharing in the sizeable profits each year, this, multiplied by fifty, is another indication of the wealth the firm created for its owners and adds to the mystery of why they put this at risk. He was still enough of an Establishment figure to be called on to give evidence that year to a House of Lords' committee looking into what had gone wrong in the last market crisis and the role of the Bank of England, particularly the awkward combination under one architecturally impressive roof of public duty and commercial profit motive.

Like many City firms of the time, Overends had active partners, who took a salary and probably the first slice of the profits, and money partners, who might take a passing interest in what was going on but who were far more concerned about their annual share-out. All however bore the same unlimited personal liability for the firm's obligations.

Active or sleeping, they were all cut from fancier cloth than old Samuel. By the time of our story some had moved away from Quaker tenets, and all had abandoned Quaker dress, part of an attenuation in the fervour and discipline of Quakerism which we shall look at later as one of the many possible factors behind their fall from grace. These were the men whom Bagehot accused of being guilty of a degree of folly which 'surpassed the usual limit of imaginable incapacity. In a short time they substituted ruin for prosperity and changed opulence into insolvency.'

With Samuel gone and David Barclay Chapman retired, the active partners in The Corner House in its time of troubles were Samuel Gurney's eldest son, Henry Edmund Gurney, Barclay Chapman's son, David Ward Chapman, and John Birkbeck, who was married to Henry's sister. For a time there was also Arthur Chapman, Ward Chapman's brother, then in his twenties.[15] The most vivid pen portraits of the partners were painted by the dilettante ship owner Stefanos Xenos and suggest his keen novelist's eye, though they are sometimes contradictory and he bore a heavy grudge, since he blamed The Corner House for his failure. The photograph we have of Henry Gurney (see illustrations) is misleading; it was taken twenty years after our story, though it hints at the arrogance or aloofness of Xenos' pen portrait. Born in 1821, putting him in his ambitious and experienced late thirties when The Corner House problems began, Henry Gurney was as prolific as the rest of the extended family. His wife brought eight children into the world between 1849 and 1864. Xenos portrayed him as 'Inclined to corpulency . . . his countenance indicated both goodness of heart and strength of intellect . . . His hair was fair, his eyes well shaped, and kindly in expression.' On the other hand, he was 'somewhat pompous and dictatorial in nature' ('dictatorial' also crops up in a family letter of the time), a trait exacerbated by his deafness. He carried a brass ear trumpet and always talked, even on private matters, at the top of his voice, reminding us of Queen Victoria's objection that Gladstone 'addresses me as though I were a public meeting'. A hint of steel comes in an account of a conversation Xenos had when he and The Corner House were both in difficulty and the Greek became aggressive. 'We can chop you, friend, in a few minutes,' Gurney growled back, sounding more like Bob Hoskins in *The Long Good Friday* than a respectable banker. On the other hand, he often bailed out Quaker businesses facing failure and Xenos saw him as 'incapable of uttering an untruth or playing a double game', a man of 'a high moral and intellectual cast'.

Xenos' views are borne out by the records of the Society of Friends, which, although admittedly unlikely to be hostile to the bearer of a distinguished name, portray 'a Christian gentleman of much beauty of character; his kindness and sympathy were freely given to his friends especially to those in trouble and in need of help'. Xenos tells us that the 'boyish looking' Birkbeck was a man of 'great talent, prudence and high morality'. He loved his work and took part in all concerns of the firm.' Endowed with great self-possession, he had in Xenos' view saved the firm several times from the 'labyrinth of shoals' on which his partners and their 'precious favourites' had nearly wrecked it. In the end, he failed.

Xenos clearly did not like Arthur Chapman, 'a fair-complexioned, boyish-looking young man . . . not a particle of hair shaded his downy cheek. Had he chosen to dress like a girl he, like the Chevalier de Faublas, might have passed as the femme de chambre of the Marquise de B—.'[16]

The epicene Arthur – Xenos tells us he lisped – was arrogant to staff and 'cavalier' to customers, and his role in the firm was soon confined to countersigning cheques, a job he did for a year and a half before being eased out of the door with an annuity.

By contrast Xenos and history, the latter feeding on the former, have painted David Ward Chapman as the weak link. On the one hand, he was 'one of the handsomest Englishmen I have ever seen . . . of middle height and perfectly well made. He dressed with the correct taste of a City man . . . He was not a financial genius but he possessed talent and experience.' Less positively, he was 'fond of flattery and as he could command the market he always had an abundant supply . . . he was surrounded by a troupe of sycophants – all clever fellows who knew how to trim their sails according to the weather'. Above all, he was 'arrogant in the supreme degree'.

Chapman led a flashy and expensive life, out of keeping for someone from a Quaker background (though it was claimed dismissively that he was actually a 'crossbreed').

The five-storeyed Chapman house, its top pediment decorated

with swags of plaster flowers and scallops, was part of a new and expensive development in Prince's Gate in Kensington, directly overlooking Kensington Gore and the green acres of Hyde Park.[17] The high and spacious drawing room opened on to a veranda from which graceful steps led down to the communal gardens at the back. Chapman kept a string of ten horses in a nearby mews stable and with his family and friends would take Sunday canters in Rotten Row, where everyone who was anyone in London congregated to see and be seen. Xenos thought that Chapman was 'as extravagant as The Prodigal Son' in his private life, which was 'a round of pleasure', entertaining lavishly or being entertained almost every evening. Chapman spent his weekends at his home in Brighton, since the days of the priapic Prince Regent a town whose sea air had always had a rather louche tang. Was this a man who, even if he were a 'crossbreed', should have been taught in childhood by the Quakers' 'Minutes and Advices' to their communities to beware of the 'pride, covetousness and hastening to be rich which are pernicious and growing evils'?

In fairness, if his address were the only reason for blaming him, we would have to acquit him. In Norfolk, the Gurneys lived on sizeable estates, and the great designer Humphrey Repton had landscaped the 230 acres surrounding John Gurney's Catton Hall. Also in London, just a few doors along from Chapman at 25 Prince's Gate, lived one of the firm's inactive partners, Samuel Gurney Jr, who seems to have been thought not quite up to the cut and thrust of The Corner House. He spent much of his time on other business interests (some of them like the Atlantic cable, and the plant which produced the thousands of miles of the cable's waterproof coating, eventually quite successful), philanthropy and as Liberal MP for Penryn and Falmouth. He told his constituents there that he was 'a member of the Society of Friends and conscientiously respects the rights of conscience of all religions and denominations'.

Then there was the home of Hudson Gurney in St James's Square, in between Pall Mall and Jermyn Street. In the mid-1860s, before London's social centre of gravity moved to Belgravia to be closer to Buckingham Palace, it was a rather grander address than the slightly arriviste Prince's Gate and was also home to dukes, earls, prime ministers, bishops and a fine cross section of Burke's Peerage entries. Hudson Gurney had the largest piece of the family fortune, which had been inherited from his mother, a Barclay, and boosted by the money brought to the marriage by his wife Margaret Barclay Allardice. Born in 1823, he had been disowned by the Norwich Quakers for subscribing to a fund for a militia to defend East Anglia against a rumoured French invasion. He was probably too far out of the Quaker mould to have survived long in the Society anyway. He lived lavishly at No. 11, behind a Robert Adam frontage, wore 'pink shirts and ornamental boots' (an echo of the rebellious young Elizabeth Fry) and pretended to regret the 'tireless entertaining' he had to do when he came to London to become an MP – seventy-six dinner parties and a ball in 160 days. That did not stand in the way of his election as a Fellow of the Royal Society of Arts, where he told a friend his real ambition was 'to write one good poem'.

When he died in 1864, he left the house and his sizeable fortune of £1 million to his cousin John Henry Gurney, son of Joseph John the Bible scholar, a partner in Overends and a man already wealthy from his share of the Norwich bank. John Henry Gurney had been a deftly dutiful son, as his letters home show. When Joseph John, himself the author of a tract with the uncompromising title 'Water is Best', asked him to promise to become a teetotaller, John wrote back tactfully that, 'I will abstain from customary use as thou wishest me to do, and if out, will endeavour to take it carefully.' But hedging his bets, he did not want to behave in a way 'which attracts attention or brings me personally forward'.

His father also fretted about John mixing with the high-living Hudson and his Society friends in St James's Square, prompting John to reassure him that, 'I seldom go there or anywhere else when I can with civility refuse; I still find something irksome in being thrown much with people of more polished habits than my own.' He could be firm too; although it deeply upset his pious father, who had only a short time to live, John could not be deterred from his decision to move away from the Quaker mainstream towards the Evangelical wing of the Anglican Church.

Until 1861, John Henry Gurney, whose mother was a Birkbeck and who had married into the Hanbury pharmaceutical family, had played little part in Overends' affairs. He spent most of his time in Norfolk, attending to the bank's business and, working diligently as president of the Norwich Museum and, from 1857, as Liberal MP for King's Lynn, which he represented in peaceful coexistence with the Tory Member, the future Lord Derby. The contrast between the earnest banker and the patrician was summed up in their approach to the 1857 election: Gurney canvassed from house to house, while the Tory grandee limited himself to calling on half a dozen of the constituency's leading men. (Though they were opposed politically, by one of those pleasant coincidences with which wealth glosses life, the Derby's London home was also in St James's Square.) Gurney was a philanthropist and an avid and widely respected ornithologist, corresponding with Charles Darwin and others on the breeding habits of pheasants, mallards and pintails and crafting learned monographs. *Catalogue of the Birds of Prey (Acciptors and Striges) with the Number of Specimens in the Norwich Museum, Early Annals of Ornithology* and *A List of the Diurnal Birds of Prey* have been regularly reissued over the years. When he did come to London, it was to pursue his intellectual interests or put in an appearance at the House of Commons, and by the time he sniffed the problems in The Corner House and became more actively involved it was too late; this was a pity since his letters show him to have been a shrewd banker. It was also a pity that after old Samuel died, neither the money partners nor the wider family, whose fortunes and reputations were also at stake, gave the new generation in Lombard Street the same cautious counsel as the senior Medicis delivered to their younger partners in London in 1469: 'avoid great undertakings' and remember that the policy of the less active partners is 'to preserve their wealth and credit rather than enrich themselves by risky ventures'. The active partners in The Corner House were therefore the men responsible for running the business and taking the decisions.

Xenos makes several references to the sycophants, favourites and 'designing men' who paid court to the active partners. He is not specific, but it is clear that one of those uppermost in his mind was

Edward Watkin Edwards. Edwards, quickly and conveniently for all, came to be portrayed as 'the villain of the piece', the man who insinuated himself into The Corner House by a corrupt bargain with the high-living David Ward Chapman, whose greed and bad judgement then brought it down. With a few nudges from the defence team at the later trial, history has extrapolated from Edwards' undoubted venality to brand him as the man who started the rot by bringing in the dubious deals in the first place. We are looking back nearly a century and a half, so the truth will be elusive. It is certainly stranger than any fiction, but it is far from clear that history's sweeping condemnation of Edwards is correct.

Edwards' story starts and finishes abruptly. The first trace is not until 1844, when he was called to the Bar in his early thirties. After his public humiliation in 1869, he vanishes. The only physical evidence we have is his signature in the leather-bound, copper-clasped register of admissions at the Middle Temple, a broadside of grandiose loops and whorls suggesting even then a man brimming with self-confidence. From 1850 to 1852, he was in partnership with the prominent accountant William Turquand (another distinguished accountant, William Deloitte, was one of the signatories of the £100 Bond that Edwards had to post at his Inn of Court as security for any unpaid dining-hall bills). Edwards then took over from his ageing father, described as a 'gentleman' but a 'grave invalid' with a home in London's Woburn Square, the sinecure of Official Assignee of the Bankruptcy Court – that grim last resting place for an ever growing number of orphans of the speculative storm. The Official Assignee's job was to try to find solutions or new owners for the assets of failed businesses so that their creditors could get some of their money back.[18]

Not a glimmer of the Age of Reform had yet penetrated the echoing galleries of the Court, then in Basinghall Street between Guildhall and Moorgate, built in 1820 to a design by William Fowler. Nepotism and patronage were rife, all the more since the Assignees' positions provided plenty of opportunity to profit from the misfortunes of others. *The Times* Index for 1860, as a random barometer, lists over 1,800 reports of bankruptcy petitions. Though many will have been the failure of small traders and shopkeepers, the aggregate amount of assets and money passing through the Assignees' hands must have been sizeable. The job was hardly arduous; after a leisurely start, the Assignees' working day finished at 4 p.m. and they took ten weeks' holiday a year. The Assignees paid the Court 'rent, rates and taxes' for their offices, the clerks they employed, postage and even 'Housekeeper, Gas, Firing and Repairs', and kept whatever fees they could collect. Though there was supposed to be an official scale, there was no effective audit, and the Assignees had a strong incentive to make things complicated and to mulct fees and commissions wherever they could. Yet again Trollope precedes us, with his picture of John Vavasor in *Can You Forgive Her?* – an unsuccessful barrister who had found a sinecure as 'an assistant commissioner in some office which had to do with insolvents', drawing a handsome salary for what amounted to one day's work a week and 'signing his name to accounts which he never read and at which he was never supposed to look'.

Two parliamentary committees fretted about the opportunities the system offered for inefficiency, conflicts of interest and outright fraud. In the 1850s, one had examined, with no evident result, 'What more effectual means can be adopted for obtaining a more effective check on the accounts of the Official Assignees and for preventing the misapplication of funds coming into their hands.'

Edwards himself gave evidence to a later committee.[19] Though this was before the Overends' scandal broke, he was probed, to no great effect, about the issue of taking fees from several parties to a transaction, a practice which was soon to be at the heart of the allegations against him, perhaps because rumours had already begun to circulate. Someone on the committee may well also have heard around London, comments like the one Edwards made to Xenos: 'My mission is to become a very rich man; I see that on every side I make money and that from every side money comes to me.'

His ability to lope smoothly through the City's undergrowth was no doubt helped by his style. As Xenos writes, he had a 'pleasing appearance, placid countenance, and cool temper, of not only gentlemanly but fascinating manner, and soft and sweet of speech'.

It humanises Edwards slightly to know that he suffered from gout and, on doctor's orders, had to eschew claret in favour of the 'excellent' hock at his club, The Garrick (of which Trollope, among many other distinguished men of letters and lawyers, was also a member).

Edwards had a hand in each of The Corner House's worst deals, pocketing fees and commissions on all sides, though his account of his role is at odds with history's harsh portrayal of him as the man who actually brought the House down. We shall compare both versions, but in summary he claims that he was no more than what would today be called 'a company doctor', called in to try to keep the bad deals alive and away from the harsh and damaging publicity of the Bankruptcy Court.

The last character to round out our cast is in many ways the most fascinating. In his early years in the City and when, as we shall see below, he first encountered Xenos, Albert Gottheimer had yet to change his name to Grant, but for simplicity's sake we shall use it from this point on. He was a rogue and a symbol of everything that was rotten in the mid-Victorian financial world, which is why he was of such value to Trollope when painting the unforgettable portrait of Melmotte, his hangers on and his victims. Melmotte had much of Grant in him, but there was much more to Grant: charm for one thing, and a mind that was fine-edged rather than just low cunning. In particular, while Grant was short on scruple, there is no hint in the real man of the fictional Melmotte's coarseness and bullying; based on a fortunately brief acquaintance when I was in my impressionable twenties, a closer parallel with Melmotte might be the overbearing and over-reaching Robert Maxwell. Despite or perhaps because of that, Grant is among the more intriguing actors to step on to our stage. Given his hovering presence in the wings of each act, it was quite likely Grant who first spotted the susceptibility of The Corner House and set his acolytes the task of exploiting them, much as a small coterie of Mayfair men dangled business temptations in front of the naïve Crown Agents a century or so later.

Who was he and how did he manage to scramble so far up the greasy pole of business and society? Grant was born in Dublin in

1830 as Albert Zachariah Gottheimer, son of an immigrant Polish peddler (though the surname sounds more German than Slav), who later moved to London and did well enough as a wholesaler of dress trimmings to send Albert to school, rather improbably, in Paris. Or so Albert claimed; his later career suggests that he could be as economical with the truth as he was lavish in his spending.

As our story starts he is in his pushy mid-twenties. He had been a wine salesman until, as Xenos later teased, 'he discovered that discounting bills is more profitable than selling sherry'. From then on he is never far away, but with some of the characteristics of T. S. Eliot's mystery cat, Macavity:

'. . . You may meet him in a by-street, you may see him in the square,
But when a crime's discovered, then Macavity's not there!'

Later on he reappears sporting the Italian title of 'Baron', a flash company promoter in authentic Melmotte style. But for now he is the prime mover of the Mercantile Discount Company, whose real if shabby office was in Abchurch Lane, where Trollope sets Melmotte's much grander fictional place of business. We shall look in the next chapter at Mercantile's place in the seedy underworld of Victorian finance.

Staying for the moment with the men involved, and compounding the overall impression of shiftiness, Grant's main partner was Henry Barker, who, despite his anodyne Home Counties name, was, according to Xenos, one of 'the Barkers of Smyrna'. He was a man with a questionable past and a mixed future, who before joining up with Grant had been under such financial pressure that he had put his household furniture in his aunt's name to keep it out of the hands of the bailiffs. Xenos blames Barker for profiting from his own later misfortunes and can thus be excused for his less than flattering pen portrait of a man lacking 'the Anglo Saxon firmness of character and the Greek vivacity of intellect'. Instead, as an Englishman brought up in a Turkish culture (one source suggests the family name was originally 'Bargigh'), he had learned the skills of 'bowing, scraping, fawning and favouritism . . . they are neither English, Greeks nor Turks but a mixture of all. They can change the hue of their personality with a chameleon-like facility to suit emergencies . . .'

Grant's third partner was Josiah Erek, another name with perhaps a hint of Asia Minor. It is not too much of a stretch to imagine him fitting Trollope's autobiographical portrait of the Bill discounter who had once pursued him for debt: 'A little, clean, old man who always wore a high starched white cravat inside which he had a habit of twisting his chin as he uttered his caution . . . 'Now do be punctual, pray be punctual."

These then are our main players. There is no place in the plot for an institution: 'Enter the Bank of England, stage left', does not work. But to understand the story, we need also to say something about the Bank, which played a key role in what was about to unfold. Indeed, at the end it had the power of life and death over The Corner House. Like Hangman Calcraft, it did its duty and pulled the lever of the scaffold trapdoor.

9

A Powerful Neighbour

Samuel Gurney's relationship with the Bank of England could never have been easy. He was a proud competitor and at the same time at moments of market stress, when cash was short in Lombard Street, a none-too-humble borrower. As the new team took over the firm, the issue of the Bank's role, and whether this access to borrowing was a right or a privilege, was about to become a major bone of contention. All the evidence we have, most of it testimony given over the years by Samuel Gurney, his successor David Barclay Chapman and other partners to a series of parliamentary committees, shows that Overends saw the will-o'-the wisp nature of their deposit base as the biggest area of risk and managed their affairs with great prudence.

Still owned by private shareholders, the Bank of Engand had seen off the challenge to its monopoly from the Sword Blade Bank and its better known, hopelessly fraudulent offspring, the South Sea Company. 'The Old Lady', as the Bank was referred to by some, had weathered a series of later market crises to emerge as the Government's banker. As early as the 1820's the prominent Liberal politician William Husskison visualised it becoming 'the great steam engine of the State'.[20] It bore heavy responsibilities for keeping often hard-pressed and sometimes profligate political administrations financed, setting the lead on interest rates and managing the key exchange rate between sterling and gold. Whenever speculative currents began to swirl and the tide of folly burst its banks, a regular feature of nineteenth-century financial markets, the Bank's role became even more sensitive. As it made its hesitant progress towards the role of money market regulator and issuer of the country's currency, the responsibilities of the 'Central Bank' would soon become *de facto*. It was a role not defined by statute and initially exercisable only by the crude method of turning on and off the money tap it controlled as the ultimate source of cash, the 'lender of last resort' in modern parlance, to the discount houses.

If it restricted their ability to pledge their Bills with the Bank as security for loans, the supply of money to the broader market would be constrained, and speculative or inflationary risks controlled. Not surprisingly, this new demonstration that the Bank had muscles and could flex them sat badly with Overends and the other discount houses. It was not just that it threatened the liquidity and thus the lifeblood of their trade, but the threat came from an institution which, while seeking to impose its will on a free market, was at the same time a competitor. The Bank was in the commercial banking and discounting business, a business which, as an anonymous commentator wrote tartly, had been of great benefit to the Bank's City shareholders; 'the body of rich men whose most successful possession is The Bank of England, endowed with very considerable privileges and opportunities for money making in exchange for its services to the state'. He pointed out that Samuel Gurney, 'wealthy as any', was not among them. 'His house was too much in rivalry with one branch of the Bank of England's business for him to have more connection with it than was necessary.'

The Bank had branches in major provincial cities touting discreetly for business; in 1855, it even took over as its West End Branch Uxbridge House in Burlington Gardens, off Bond Street (now a high fashion retail store). It was also trying to extend its London monopoly by squeezing Overends' country banking clients out of the lucrative business of issuing banknotes.

Commercial banking – lending and discounting Bills – was an important and lucrative part of the Bank's business, though it was reluctant to pay interest on deposits from other banks and upheld its policy, until later in the 1850s, that any Bills it bought should be of short duration and bear 'two good London names'. (Another piece of market jargon meaning two banks or commercial firms of high credit standing based within the metropolis, such that most of the country banks' business went elsewhere, predominantly to Overends.)

At the same time, Overends and its peers were themselves dependent on the Bank, operating their business in the knowledge, based on half a century of City practice, that if money got 'tight' they could raise cash by selling Bills from their own holdings to the Bank's Discount Office, or taking a direct loan.[21]

Over the years these conflicts had strained relations several times, coming to a head again in April 1860, a few years after Samuel Gurney's death, when in a bid to tamp down speculative financing activity, the Bank virtually shut off the discount houses' right to fall back on the Discount Office and also raised its lending rate. This sparked one of the more bizarre episodes in City history, an exercise in rodomontade which suggests that, with Samuel gone, the firm was quickly showing signs of waning judgement and waxing arrogance. 'Real money', the amount of notes in circulation, was a far smaller but at the same time more potent factor for everyday business than it is today. To hit back at the Bank, Overends orchestrated a minor 'run' on the Bank's cash holdings. In what today would be called 'a concert party' with Barclays, Barnett, Hoares (another Quaker banking house), the Gurney family's Norwich bank and the Quaker stockbrokers Sheppards, Pelly & Allcard, they sent a series of uniformed messengers across to Threadneedle Street to withdraw from their various accounts in the space of a few hours no less than £2 million in £1,000 notes. Answering an urgent Question in the House of Commons, Chancellor Gladstone, a *laissez-faire* Liberal to his fingertips, was sympathetic to Overends and their right 'to act . . . so as to bring into view what may be considered a public evil and . . . promote a disposition to apply a remedy'. Gladstone was the Bank's political master and, although he took care not to come down finally on either side, his measured support for the aggressive Quakers might have been expected to resonate in Threadneedle Street. But emotions had run too high and the Bank would not back off. To heighten the melodrama, an anonymous letter postmarked 'London EC' arrived in the Bank's morning mail declaring, 'Overends can pull out every note you have – from actual knowledge the writer can inform you that with their own family assistance they can nurse seven millions.'

The Governor, Bonamy Dobree, went to see Gladstone, who then summoned Overends. At first they stood firm, putting it about in the City that if the Bank chose to change its stance, why should they leave large balances with it to be used to help the Bank compete with them in the discounting business. The notes would be returned if and when the Bank relaxed its policy. At the same time they prompted, and may even have authored, an anonymous article in the *Bankers' Magazine* with a slight hint of the olive branch. They recognised the Bank's right to 'have a proper control over their own resources' and were 'perfectly willing and even anxious to come to a businesslike arrangement with the national establishment'.

Overends blinked first, perhaps because others in the 'concert party' had come under political pressure. One of the London partners – we do not know who – told a Bank director that 'if it would be though[t] a conciliatory step, they would return the notes at once . . . They are sorry for what they have done.' Back the notes came, though they had been cut in half and kept in separate vaults so two raids would have been needed to retrieve them. Gladstone, ever a politician, thought the Bank had behaved well and come out 'the winners'. Another anonymous Bank director castigated Overends as 'the conspirators of the Bank notes' and 'those tricksters'.

Overends might have argued that they gave the Bank fair, if veiled, warning. Three years earlier, giving evidence to a select committee looking at the banking system and musing about the 'very violent pressure' created when notes were taken out of circulation, David Barclay Chapman had remarked that 'there is more than one capitalist who can withdraw from the circulating medium £1 million or £2 million of notes if they have an object to attain by it'. Karl Marx analysed his evidence in great detail in *Das Kapital*, though he let his academic mask slip when he stigmatised Chapman as 'the arch-usurer' and The Corner House as financiers who 'skim off the cream by ruthlessly exploiting the precarious state of business'. These were rather harsh words from a man whom an admiring American journalist interviewed in 'a drawing room which would have formed very comfortable quarters for a thriving stockbroker who had made his competence and was now beginning to make his fortune'.

This confrontation is another aspect of our theme of change. The well-understood boundaries and the comfortable dynamics of established relationships could no longer be taken for granted. The dawning realisation that their core business and even their survival in times of crisis were dependent on the actions and policies of the Bank, that strange hybrid of competitor and government instrument, may well have made Overends even more determined to push on further with their perilous journey. It would take them into the netherworld, where danger and the ghosts of bankrupt bankers lurked, in search of a new area of business which offered higher returns and which would be less dependent on market forces.

The temptations dangled before the new men were great. The thrill and promise of the new were in the air. Progress needed money, the love of which, we are told, has been at the root of all evil since money began. No nation was immune from wallowing in the trough of speculative mania; the Dutch went crazy over tulip bulbs. In Britain, supposedly conservative men and women lost fortunes in the South Sea Bubble, best known because it was the largest and the most brazenly corrupt in a string of fraudulent promotions at the time, from the Pearl Fishery Company, a 'Company to import a number of large jack asses from Spain,' to the Royal Academies Company, which had high though short-lived hopes of a lottery offering 2,000 prizewinners – assumed to be 'gentlemen' – classes in 'Latin, Greek, Hebrew, French, Spanish, conic sections, trigonometry, heraldry, japanning, fortification, book-keeping and the art of playing the theorbo,' which in those enlightened days few needed to be told was a bass lute.

Even if those manias were lost in the past, those in our story must have remembered the railway boom from the 1830s to its fevered peak and then headlong collapse in the late 1840s, speculation inflamed by the speculation of unscrupulous promoters. Though it had made some sizeable fortunes, it had caused others to melt away and burned many middle-class fingers. But those who do not learn from history are doomed to repeat it. The Corner House was no exception.

By the late 1850s excess was fashionable again; finance was the 'new black'. It was as if the Victorian world's power over matter, to transform landscapes, cities and lives, had created a new power over money too. The old rules were for olden times. A new generation spotted that the humble Bill was actually a solution for many needs. Much as the 1970s' 'fringe banks' had played 'follow my leader' into the property market, and in New York others later followed Drexel Burnham's carefree plunge towards the wilder shores of the junk bond market, so Victorian finance companies and fledgling 'discount houses' followed in the wake of Grant's Mercantile and ordered shiny brass nameplates for their newly rented City offices. They all promised their investors generous dividends, a promise which, though it was not sustained for long, meant that while alive they could only fulfil it by investing in high-interest 'junk Bills'. In the same way as it dawned on Drexel that companies did not have to be able to repay the bonds they so freely issued, which could always be refinanced for another large fee as long as there were enough avaricious and indiscriminate investors around, so Grant and his circle re-engineered the Bill. Out of the window, or rather down the drain, went the old-fashioned idea that they were supposed to be 'self liquidating', related to real trade. Investors with cash and an appetite for higher than usual interest rates, fuelled by their pressing need to meet their dividend promises, were not bothered about what lay behind each Bill, or some hoary principle which belonged to the age of Sir Robert Peel. If they could not be paid off when they fell due, it did not matter. Mercantile and its ilk assured them that they would be renewed as a matter of course, 'rolled over' in the jargon, and the stream of high income would continue unabated. They made similar promises to their borrowers, with the smooth caveat that each time the debt 'rolled', the borrower would be paid a fee, but what was a small fee between friends was a price well worth paying if it kept their business afloat. Like every other financial fashion, it grew too fast and too far. Fraud mushroomed, most visibly in the humdrum market for leather and hides. Lacking the support of any genuine trade, the merry-go-round of Bills, with Grant somewhere near the centre, came to a juddering halt in 1860, saddling the discount market and banking community, Overends amongst them, with losses of some £3 million. The game went on nonetheless. To quote *The Times*:

> . . . every contractor who wanted to make a railway or build a city, had only to go to a finance concern, pay them an enormous bonus and be furnished with what was called 'money' in the shape of Bills drawn by himself and accepted by the company. Of course these Bills were not to be paid until all the grand works in question were completed and had become bona fide property, although perhaps the prospect of that consummation might be at two, five, or ten years date. The reliance was that the Bills drawn at short periods of three or six months would be renewed indefinitely. So tempting was the lure for borrowers and investors, and so magnificent the apparent profit that at length the competition of the various [finance] companies was such as actually to induce contractors to invent schemes to favour them with this kind of business. Of course the contractors who as a general rule knew little about financial theories, found themselves in a golden age . . .

Anyone who lived through the Drexel era will find those words eerily evocative.

It was not just major construction projects and railways. Shipbuilding and shipowning, both essentially businesses crying out for longer-term capital, were brought into the new short-term scheme of things. One small finance house is said to have made a nice business out of tracking down men in the East End with European banking names such as Huth or Goldschmidt, paying them a few pounds to put their name on a Bill and then selling it as a high-quality obligation of that illustrious house. By the time the Bill fell due for payment, the East Ender was either untraceable or simply denied any intent to defraud, and the broker had set up under another name. The bankruptcy of a Scottish wholesaler revealed that it had a network of seventy-five agents, men of straw, who were paid fees to sign their names to Bills with no backing in real business.[22]

As the world changed, so the tone of The Corner House shifted with it. Reflecting the private bankers' sense that offices should not be ostentatious, compounded no doubt by Quaker frugality, Overends' premises did not advertise the firm's wealth. Unlike Albert Grant, for whom office 'flash' – marble staircases, French panelling, pageboys, lacquered carriages and glossy horses – was an essential tool of his trade, Overends did not need to sell themselves to the world. They were 'old money'.

Messengers brought the Bills, usually in what were called 'parcels', to the desk of its ground floor 'counting house', the details of each slip of paper meticulously noted in the ledgers by the ink-stained fingers of the clerks. A frosted glass door separated them from the inner sanctum, shared, as in all private banks of that era and by many well into the twentieth century, by the partners, who made the credit judgements on each Bill and fretted about interest rates. In his memoirs, Xenos remembered the partners' room as 'plainly, even meanly furnished' with five desks of little better than schoolroom standard, each defended by a breast-high partition.

Next door were two small rooms – one 'pretty respectable as regards light and furniture', the other 'almost as grim and dark as a ship's lazaret [the maritime term for a foetid below-decks sick bay] where the less important visitor had to kick his heels . . . for the best part of an hour whilst waiting for an audience, surrounded by half empty medicine bottles, brushes, combs, a towel stand and washing apparatus'. The 'medicine bottles' (no doubt sent over from the nearby Quaker-owned Plough Court pharmacy) remind us again of the poor health that was no respecter of rank.

Nonetheless, while the new men did not go in for sumptuous new offices, the atmosphere changed perceptibly, much as over a century later Drexel Burnham's glossy Beverly Hills office, the plateglass and chrome epicentre of the brave new junk bond universe of which they were the masters, struck visitors as markedly different from the deliberately understated, even slightly shabby executive suites of

Goldman Sachs or Morgan Stanley. Those who had flocked to Los Angeles seeking Drexel's backing, sat murmuring into their phones, watching and wondering as other supplicants came and went, waiting nervously for the five minutes they were allocated to 'make their pitch'.

In Samuel's days, 'businesslike' might have been a good adjective for The Corner House: the partners tucked away in the inner sanctum and the clerks in the counting house carefully calculating, dipping in their inkwells and scratching away under the General Manager's watchful eye. At the front counter, uniformed messengers – Waterloo veterans in the earlier time, then whiskery men who had survived the Crimea, interleaved with a few cheeky East End lads – strode in and out with parcels of Bills, each worth more than their families might dream of earning in several generations. In Samuel's day, he and other strict Quakers would have kept their hats on while at work. At the time of our story, the disciplines had relaxed and the partners' top hats would be neatly ranged in order of seniority on the mahogany shelf outside their room.

The new Corner House was very different, with echoes of the future Drexel. Xenos has left us a vivid account:

> No anteroom of any Minister in Christendom presents a greater number of expectants than was frequently to be found there between 10 in the morning till four in the afternoon. Persons of all grades from the high to the low were to be seen waiting for an audience or even a reply through a clerk. You saw there . . . those officious insignificant courtiers whose sole occupation is to circulate groundless rumours and calumnies.

He watched with amusement 'the sycophantic smile and slavish humility with which they approached a disengaged partner and commenced an undertoned gossip. You saw there the . . . crafty courtier. He approaches the great man with a cautious and insinuating air and suggests – merely throws out a hint about – a promising transaction but he does not venture to propose anything until he has sounded the great man's inclinations.' Then there was the 'court spy', who brought inside information 'that might either save the great house from loss or bring it profit'. Backing up this tawdry cast, like the chorus in *The Rake's Progress*, were 'the flocks of commonplace courtiers, brokers and panderers of all kinds, full of all sorts of schemes and propositions'. It was these 'schemes and propositions' that eventually brought the House down. For a while the paper soufflé rose delightfully for those profiting from the cooking, though the *New York Times* chauvinistically derided it as 'English finance', while to Marx it was nothing more or less than 'fictitious capital'. By the end of 1863, the *Bankers' Magazine* was regularly listing the shares of sixty-two, income-hungry, dividend-promising banking and finance companies, compared to twenty-two just three years earlier.

A rather similar picture could have been gleaned from the London press a little over a century later, when the 'secondary banking' and 'asset stripping' boom-and-bust saga played itself out in the familiar sequence, starting with euphoria and ending in finger pointing and shrill cries for retribution. By then the Bank had long established itself as undoubted master of the British banking system. It is a chastening reflection on the limits to mastery that this did not prevent the saga from unfolding.

10

Levant Dreams

As we said when we started down this long road, we do not know enough to be able to look at each Corner House folly, fascinating though some of them must have been as microcosms of the Victorian age. So we will take just the major messes of Stefanos Xenos' Greek & Oriental Shipping Line, the Galway Line and the Millwall Yard. The sum total of the losses incurred on these deals alone by the time Overends failed was £5.2 million, or around £250 million today, though the figure was bloated by the firm's practice, in denial to the bitter end, of continuing to add interest to the debts even though they were long since irrecoverable. Many had probably been virtually worthless from the first day they were carefully entered in the Overends' ledgers. In each of them, in often conflicting and shifting roles, we shall see Edwards, along with Grant and his sidekicks.

Xenos was not just a borrower whose tangled affairs ended as badly for him as they did for Overends. Anyone whose memoirs begin, 'In the year 1856 I was running a line of sailing vessels from London to the Levant and the Black Sea', an opening line with immediate appeal to incurable romantics, has to be larger than life. Their handsome, headstrong author, born in 1821, was also a prolific writer, one of whose books – *The Heroine of the Greek Revolution* – was among the most widely read Greek novels in the latter part of the nineteenth century. Adding an unusual dimension, this justifies the description of him by the bibliographer Chris Michaelides as 'one of the most fascinating figures of the Greek community of London in the nineteenth century'. He graduated from the Greek Military School, emerging not only a soldier but a young man widely read and fluent in several languages, as well as trained in engineering.

Though the difference between the gilded vestments and incense-scented *basso profundo* rites of the Greek Church and the plain tranquillity of the Friends could hardly be more marked, the Greek traders' 'diaspora' in London had much in common with the Quakers. They trusted only their 'own', which meant families not simply Greek but only from the same cities or Aegean islands. Their word was their bond, at least within their own community. Like the Quakers, they formed ad hoc business partnerships and alliances around their core banking or shipping businesses. They also had large families and in the nineteenth century rarely married 'out'. Indeed, many of the marriages were forged by money and business motives the old Quakers well understood, which had as much to do with considerations of family commercial advantage as love. The Greeks even had a word, 'endogamy', for this type of alliance; unlike the Quakers, they were not, and are not now, men of few words.

The tone of Xenos' memoirs, and especially some of his aggrieved, almost puzzled comments on how the London Greeks thought, operated and closed ranks, suggest that while he came from a good family, and the merchant community was willing to give him support by using his ships, they did not see him, nor did he see himself, as really 'one of them', even though he was related to the Ionides, one of the great Greek dynasties in London. He also claimed, perhaps extravagantly, to be descended on his mother's side from the last Emperor of Byzantium and, more likely, from Apostolo Zeno, the eighteenth-century Italian playwright. His mercurial personality, a touch of intellectual snobbery and his conviction that he was somehow above business, a man 'whose first love was not commerce and whom the political aspect of his own country had driven to England to engage in the labyrinthine complexities of trade', cannot have helped him fit into an essentially conservative, business-minded clan. Xenos claims here that it was Greek politics that drove him into exile. However, it was more precisely what falling victim to the vicious vagaries of Greek politics had done to his father, who had been accused of counterfeiting, dismissed from his post as Greek Consul in Smyrna (now Izmir after the Turks massacred its 150,000 Greek community in 1922) and sent to jail. Xenos campaigned tirelessly – even writing a book on the case – and eventually succeeded in having his father vindicated. His father however was now penniless and urged Stefanos to go to London and into business to restore the family fortunes.

Research by Zefyros Kaukalides for his biography of Xenos has suggested two other motives for the move: one prosaic, he was tagging along in the wake of two restless friends; the other more in keeping with Xenos' picaresque style, that he had to get away from Athens in a hurry after horsewhipping a German merchant who had insulted him.

Though written by a man with a cellar-full of axes to grind, Xenos' memories of life in and around The Corner House are written more with sorrow than spite. The tale he tells seems plausible, though Xenos presents a better picture of himself by beginning the narrative conveniently after the point at which his first foray into London business, a venture in shipping insurance, had come to grief. The memoirs are unusually detailed, a fact he attributes to his long ingrained discipline of taking notes of all his conversations, keeping a diary and retaining copies of all letters and documents.

It is clear looking back that Xenos was far too much of a passionate dilettante to survive long in any business, let alone the cutthroat world of shipping. There were diversions of time and energy in writing the novels and a diversion of money as well in publishing a lavishly illustrated guide to the 1851 Great Exhibition in Hyde Park. His major mistake, on several counts, was to launch on a lavish budget financed with borrowed money, a London-based newspaper, the *British Star*, to put across the British and European point of view to Greek communities in the Ottoman Empire to counter Russian influence in that part of the world. The mix of polemics and politics was doomed to fail. The Foreign Office was unhappy about his campaign against the German King Otto of Greece and the Ottoman court complained about his anti-Turkish line. Xenos even managed to bite the hand that fed him by attacking London's Greek merchants for the profits they were making by investing in the 'junk debt' of the bankrupt Sultan of Turkey, and thus helping keep alive Greece's ancient enemy. All in all an expensive run of 'own goals', Xenos was unfazed. He also spent a great deal of money, a little of it his, a lot of it borrowed from the London & Westminster Bank, to buy and lavishly redecorate Petersham Lodge. A substantial 'gentleman's residence' in what was then a rural setting straight out of a Constable landscape is still, even today, a quiet and desirable enclave despite the twenty-four-hour background rumble of traffic through the village's narrow centre. Whether Xenos found it all that quiet is doubtful; he was beset by money worries and his marriage to Harriette Leyman Thomas, niece of a bankrupt peer, whom he had met at the Chelsea Flower Show, was singularly miserable.

Though for all these reasons Xenos was seen by more down-to-earth Greek businessmen as a spendthrift maverick, community support and self-interest (he was undercutting the freight charges of British lines) in a style the Quakers would have found familiar meant that his shipping line was nevertheless supported by most of the leading Greek merchants who controlled the flow of 'Levant trade' to and around the Black Sea. His 1859 'Customer Circular' is an evocative roll call of the golden age of the Greek diaspora, sparkling with names such as Rodocanachi, Mavrogordato, Ralli, Valliano, Cassaveti, Cavafy and Negroponti.

His Levant fleet carried their cargoes of textiles to Constantinople, Odessa and around the Black Sea, and brought back grain, coal, sugar, alum and anything else his canny trader customers thought they could turn to profit. But Xenos was losing business to the faster steamships. So he first chartered steamers and then bought them outright. He set up the Greek & Oriental Steam Navigation Company in 1857 and bought as if no more ships would ever be built. From what modern US car dealers call 'the pre-owned' market came the *Admiral Kanaris* (unrelated to Hitler's intelligence chief, who anyway spelled his name with a 'C'), the *Asia*, the *Scotia*, the *Modern Greece* and, despite Xenos' feelings about its English community, the *Smyrna*. Xenos was just warming up. Shipyards on Teesside and the Clyde were soon clanging with work on the *Palikari*, the *George Olympius*, the *Amis*, the *Londos*, the *Petro Beys*, the *Colocotronis*, the *Riga Ferreos* and 'two small yachts'; one of the latter cruises into our story a little later.

Ships cost money. Xenos had none. However, this was the age of 'English finance', when nothing was impossible if someone involved in the deal had a good name, a pen to sign Bills and friends in the City who would take the paper and, in Xenos' words, 'melt it' into cash.

11

When Greek Meets Greek

The 'someone' was George Lascaridi, a fellow countryman of Xenos' who was then around forty. He had been born in a now untraceable city in Asia Minor, according to his family records, but now lived in London and took British citizenship in 1859. The 'City friends' were first Albert Grant and later The Corner House.

Lascaridi had two advantages. Firstly, his own good name: he belonged to another of those rich, secretive Greek merchant families with tentacles in London, Liverpool, Aleppo and Beirut. No one knew quite what their business was, or how much money they made, but as often happens and indeed was the case with Overends, its mystique was enough to convince most people that it was highly profitable.

Secondly, his wife Catherine Lascaridi, who had been born in Constantinople, was a member of the even wealthier London-based Ionides family to which Xenos was more distantly connected. Even though her family lawyers would have taken care to see that there was a firewall between George and the Ionides fortune, the mere fact of the relationship gave Lascaridi a higher credit standing than he deserved, since he too was a speculator on a scale that makes Xenos look positively conservative.

Xenos describes Lascaridi as a cocktail of dangerous contradictions, a 'bourgeois romantic'. On the one hand, he had a 'soft-heartedness which renders him unable to say no, even to those whom he knows are imposing on his kindness'. On the other, he found the family export and import trade 'monotonous', was 'extremely ambitious' and wanted 'to distinguish himself in the British metropolis by some act that would win the praise of the English people'. Though he had 'foresight, pluck and enterprising spirit', he veered between being 'fickle as the wind' and 'obstinate as a mule'. He did indeed leave his mark in London, but not in the way he had hoped. His catastrophic loss comes later in our story, but among his initial failures were a venture in Gibraltar to ship cloth to Morocco and Tunisia and a chain of 'French glove shops' and perfumeries in London's West End.

Unknown to Xenos, Lascaridi had also been tempted by the 'finance business' and was among the biggest investors in Mercantile Discount. One of Grant's early techniques was to invite, in as investors, entrepreneurs who needed money. They would collude with Barker, Erek and himself to create Bills, often for more than they needed and with no real commercial rationale, which Mercantile would discount with greedy and undiscriminating buyers. In a neat recycling move, part of the proceeds would then be used to subscribe for shares in Mercantile, boosting its capital and giving depositors 'confidence'.

When Xenos launched his Line, he had no capital. That did not deter him nor was it a problem for the Tyneside shipyards, which, hungry for business, were quite happy to give him up to two years' credit with little or no cash down, against Bills backed by the name and credit of the reputedly wealthy house of Lascaridi. Turning this paper into hard cash was no problem through the outstretched and obliging hands of Mercantile and Grant, though at a price: a usurious interest rate and a swingeing commission, the under-standing with Xenos and Lascaridi being that the Bills would be renewed, or 'rolled over', when they fell due, minus, of course, another large slice for Mercantile. There was no nonsense about their being 'self-liquidating'. Lascaridi's own 'price' for obliging Xenos in this way was a loose understanding that he would become a silent partner in the shipping business. Nothing was put on paper. Xenos and the shipbuilders would have done well to remember Virgil's ancient warning to 'fear Greeks bearing gifts'.

At the start all was well. Xenos had enough backing from the Greek trading community to provide a steady flow of cargo and he was making money on the side speculating in grain. But having made him momentarily happy, the gods decided to behave as the myth ordained that they would and set out to destroy him. As seen from the tranquillity of his Petersham home, none of it of course, was his fault. Trusted men he had sent out to the Levant and Danube ports were inefficient and dishonest. Lascaridi's associated firms in the Levant whom Xenos was compelled to use, including the splendidly titled 'Salik Pasha, Agent to the Sublime Porte', were overcharging him for coal or holding on to his cash. Cargoes were trapped in the ice-bound Balkan reaches of the Danube and the grain market crumbled as fast as it had risen. About the only profit he seems to have made was when first one and then a second of his ships sank and he collected on the insurance, a benefit bestowed by Providence on so many cash-strapped shipowners over the years. The *British Star* was expensive to run and Xenos' polemics managed the rare feat of alienating several constituencies at once. His critical sniping at the Greek merchants in London who had made money buying the high-interest debt of the despised and already tottering Ottoman Empire cost him business and Turkey persuaded the Foreign Office to cut off the *Star*'s access to subsidised distribution in the Ottoman Empire via the British diplomatic bag to Constantinople. Whitehall was also sensitive to criticism from Athens about the attacks on King Otto.

As Xenos tells us ruefully, 'to accept bills for £150,000 is only an affair of a few minutes: to provide for them is only a momentary concern, your credit is virgin, your property free, your business well organised and your enemies too insignificant to do you serious injury.' He was honest enough to leave us a full account of what happens when Fortune hides her face.

Those Bills so insouciantly accepted were soon to fall due. Xenos had no cash to meet them, but had relied on Lascaridi to put his pen as guarantor to a new stack of paper so that the debt could be smoothly rolled over. To his horror the shipyard told him that they had heard rumours that Lascaridi had brought himself to the edge of ruin by investing hugely in a shipping venture in Ireland, which was fast running on the rocks. So his guarantee was worthless. The Galway Line, which cost Overends much more than they were to lose with Xenos, comes next in our chronicle of woe, but for the moment we shall stay with Xenos, at his wits' end. When he confronted Lascaridi, the latter confirmed the rumour. Giving his partner the cold comfort of the cliché that 'the brave man proves his courage in difficulty', Lascardi sent Xenos off to Barker, who in turn introduced him to Grant. The original deal had been between Mercantile and the shipbuilder, so this was Xenos' first encounter with the nimble moneylender. Grant lent Xenos £3,000 for a week at a rate of interest which worked out to a scorching 173 per cent p.a. In an early display of his panache, Grant persuaded Xenos not just to spend some of the money he had borrowed to buy a few Mercantile shares, but even foisted off on him a cargo of ultramarine dye which Xenos shipped to Romania only to find that it was unsaleable. It was eventually dumped in the Danube; whether or not it turned the river blue for a brief but glorious moment is unrecorded.

The Grant loan was just a patch, a small spoonful of medicine for a seriously ailing Greek & Oriental. A desperate Xenos told Lascaridi that the only solution he could see was to call a meeting of his shipyard creditors and negotiate more time to pay. Lascaridi was horrified. He then confessed to Xenos that when he had backed him by guaranteeing the shipyard Bills, he had signed in the name of the family firm, Lascaridi & Co., but had not entered the obligation in its accounts, nor had he even told his partners. If the Bills could be replaced or renewed, and if he could have some more time, things could work out. However, if Xenos admitted that he was in effect bankrupt, Lascaridi would be ruined too, publicly and in the eyes of his family and partners in Constantinople and Marseilles. Worse than that, the house of cards, or better house of Bills, he had built in the Galway shipping venture would tumble too. [23] He promised to find another solution, and he did.

With hindsight Xenos might have done better to make a clean breast of things and renegotiate his shipyard debts. Instead, Barker came to his rescue and produced the first tranche of money from, of all improbable places, The Corner House. Barker would not have got past the doorman in most reputable banking houses. A Levantine loan shark was rather out of the mould of the average caller on those supposedly conservative Quaker bankers, and years of painful experience would lead most bankers to agree with a rueful sigh that lending to Greeks is a business best left to Greeks, especially when it comes to shipping. The most convincing reason is that Overends themselves had already fallen under Grant's seductive spell. They had been one of the firms involved, and had lost out heavily, in the leather market fraud in which Mercantile had been the centre of gravity, a mess Edwards had to try to clean up as Official Assignee. In all likelihood, even before their foray into 'financing', they had become a valuable outlet for Mercantile's junk Bills, and in the process had taken on Lascaridi's Bills for the Galway Line. Here was one of many points at which they made a terrible misjudgement. Instead of taking the loss and facing the publicity, they decided that if they helped Xenos, at a price, it would give Lascaridi and themselves breathing space. Instead they ended up suffocated.

The way the Xenos deal was set up suggests that Overends knew full well that they were doing business that others might question, and this was not the first rather off-colour transaction they had handled. Overends insisted that the name of Greek & Oriental was not to appear in their ledgers. Instead, they would advance the money to Barker, who would then pass it on; Xenos would likewise pay his trading receipts over to the man from Smyrna, who would lodge them with The Corner House. Much of the other junk ballast that eventually sunk Overends followed this early example of doing deals 'off the books' (in our own time widely favoured by now toppled corporate giants in gleaming skyscrapers in Houston and Memphis). Xenos' first loan of £20,000 via Barker was at a rate less usurious than Grant's, but still stiff. More importantly, it was only another 'quick fix'. In the first three months of 1860, he would be facing a blizzard of Bills, some £143,000, coming due for payment, which he could not possibly pay. Xenos decided on the direct approach and wrote at inordinate length to Henry Gurney (asking him to discuss it with David Ward Chapman; again, there is no mention of Edwards), making the case for a loan of £80,000. 'We had beaten opponents and driven them out of the way, causing perhaps a great deal of jealousy, and we had in reality a field of gold before us, when unfortunately and without my knowledge in the least, Mr. George Lascaridi mixed himself up in the Galway Company on an enormous scale . . .' Xenos offered The Corner House mortgages over his ships and a share of Greek & Oriental's profits. When Lascaridi became distracted, dishevelled and showing signs of growing strain, Xenos began to understand that the Galway venture was also failing.

It is only now that Edwards, the moonlighting Official Assignee whom Overends knew from the leather market imbroglio, appears on the Greek & Oriental scene, the timing supporting his later defence that he was the 'company doctor' not the originator of bad business. When The Corner House realised what a mess Xenos was in, they told him that Edwards would negotiate the deal on their behalf. Edwards quickly offered to wrap up most of Xenos' near-term obligations into a loan whose real interest rate – the bulk of it described as 'a bonus' – would have made Grant whistle with envy. It was an offer that Xenos simply could not refuse. Edwards was then appointed to act as The Corner House 'watchdog'. Xenos was outraged at having to pay him an annual fee of £500, all the more since Edwards offered little or nothing by way of advice or help. He was even more upset about the 'gifts' he claims he was induced to give Edwards, gifts we shall look at in more detail later. Loan followed loan, and interest on interest racked up to a degree that would have had those ancient clerical foes of usury boasting about how right they were.

Xenos soon found his entire fleet mortgaged and a sizeable slice of any profit he might make in the future pledged to Overends. Business did not improve. By that time Xenos owed Overends some £380,000, though the unhappy Greek claimed later that £230,000 of this staggering debt represented compounded interest, 'bonus' and commission.

Here Xenos' account takes on a tone familiar to any banker who has had to deal with a borrower with his back to the wall: 'My assets are worth far more than you give me credit for. It is not my fault.'[24] On Edwards' advice, Overends decided to sell the whole of Xenos' fleet. Strident objections persuaded Overends that they should sell only half of them, a decision even Xenos thought wrong-headed since it left Greek & Oriental still burdened with the smaller ships and any new owner struggling to meet the running costs of the larger ones.

Overends asked Barker and Edwards to try to find a buyer. No one in London would touch the fleet and they ended up in Hull. The City's mayor, Zachariah Pearson, who owned a small fleet of tramp steamers, was nearly persuaded to take over Xenos' ships with no down payment and two years' Bill-based credit, but he took fright, telling Xenos that he was signing 'my death warrant'. Henry Gurney, who was yet again much involved in the negotiations rather than being the remote figurehead his friends depicted later, soothed him down. 'Now, friend Pearson, what is the matter again? I will give you on the spot a cheque for £500 if you will sign the acceptances and complete the business today. Bois', he barked at his Chief Clerk, 'draw a cheque for £500 for Mr. Pearson.'

The reference to 'acceptances' tells the real story: Xenos was broke. A prudent banker would have written off what he owed as a bad debt. Yet again The Corner House did not. Whether it was Edwards' idea (he was much criticised later for demanding a commission from Pearson of £2,000 when he was supposed to be acting for Overends), or far more likely a collective misjudgement, they concluded that if Xenos' now valueless IOUs were replaced by Bills with Pearson's unsullied name attached and backed by the ships, the paper would take on a new lease of credit life and no one would be any the wiser. Meanwhile, the Lascaridi debt too had been juggled away from death and there was another breathing space.

Again they were sadly wrong. Pearson went into the briefly lucrative but risky business of running the Federal blockade during the American Civil War. As the *New York Times* later reported, with understandable pride, six of his ships were captured within one year, two on the same day. The 'tradition of Britannia ruling the waves doubtless occurred to him, and he did not dream that any Yankee would have impudence enough' to stop him. 'He has probably learned better by this time.'[25]

Xenos' other ships came back into Overends' hands. Though it is not clear what happened to them, it is unlikely to have been anything profitable.

Xenos had by then thrown in the towel. Overends paid him £2,500 for control of his tottering and shrunken company, released him from his debt and swatted him away. In an early example of the self-deluding book-keeping to which The Corner House was prone, though Xenos had been freed of the debt, it was still carried forward in the firm's books, with interest punctually accruing, even though no one was responsible for paying it, and no one did.

12

'Those in Peril on the Sea'

If Xenos was an unlikely customer for Quaker bankers, Peter Daly was even more so. An aggressive, self-promoting and entrepreneurial Roman Catholic parish priest, his dream of a new transatlantic shipping line ended as one of Overends' nastiest financial nightmares; a story which takes us from the uncharitable streets of the City of London to the ancient stone-arches and cobblestones of Galway, on Ireland's squally Atlantic coast, 130 miles from Dublin.

The Galway Line, as it became known, or to give it its main corporate title (typically for most Overends imbroglios, names changed with each shuffle of assets), The Atlantic Steam Navigation Company, and a subsidiary which it spawned, cost The Corner House at least £1.4 million – well over £50 million in today's values – and probably a great deal more.

Born in 1788 in a Galway farming family, Peter Daly studied for the priesthood at Maynooth seminary and in 1818 took over one of the Galway City parishes of St Nicholas, a conventional enough start to an unconventional career.

Like Victorian England, our image of early nineteenth-century Ireland has become fixed like an early black-and-white photograph as yet another stereotype; a famine-ravaged, priest-ridden wasteland, plundered by absentee landlords, its peasants torn between death and exile. Much of that is true. In 1856, Friedrich Engels, Marx's financial backer and intellectual collaborator, toured Ireland with his family. Writing to Marx, with their shared memories of central Europe much in mind, he portrayed a countryside peopled by 'Gendarmes, priests, lawyers, bureaucrats, lords of the manor in cheerful profusion and a total absence of any and every industry, so that one could barely conceive what all these parasitic plants live on, were there no counterpart in the wretchedness of the peasants'. The 'iron hand' of British rule was everywhere, Engels wrote, 'and it is in the constabulary, which is armed with carbine, bayonet and handcuffs, that the bibulous expression of your Prussian gendarme reaches its ultimate state of perfection'.

'I had never imagined that famine could be so tangibly real,' he wrote to Marx, blissfully unaware that the latter's twentieth-century disciples were to create famine and human misery on a scale Engels could not have conceived in his worst dreams:

> Whole villages are deserted . . . The fields are empty even of cattle; the countryside is a complete wilderness unwanted by anybody.
>
> Even the aristocracy are infected by this wretchedness. The landowners . . . are here completely down-at-heel. Their country seats are surrounded by huge and lovely parks but all around there is desolation and where the money is supposed to come from heaven only knows. These fellows are too funny for words: of mixed blood, for the most part tall, strong, handsome types, all with enormous moustaches under a vast Roman nose, they give themselves the bogus martial airs of a colonel *en retraite*, travel the country in search of every imaginable diversion and, on inquiry, prove to be as poor as church mice, up to their eyes in debt . . .

And yet the city of Galway itself, as seen through a Trades Directory compiled just a few years earlier, has the flavour of George Eliot's *Middlemarch*; an agglomeration of prosperous 'gentry' and merchants surrounded by silversmiths, surgeons, surveyors, tailors, milliners and architects, served by two newspapers, four banks and 'shops . . . abundantly stored with all those articles which taste or fashion may demand, or necessity require,' not forgetting 'Sarah Ralph, fishing tackle maker'. Only the thirty Public Houses hint that we are not in Hampshire any more. Trade had been its salvation. Kelp, oatmeal and lead were shipped to England, while creaking schooners brought timber from Danzig, glass, iron, lead and coal from Bristol and London, port from Oporto and hogsheads of wine from Bordeaux; Kirwan of the eponymous Château was a Galway man.

It was also a city undergoing an uniquely Irish change in the balance of civic power. The Church of Ireland, Anglican mirror of its English parent, was still the country's 'Established' Church, but its influence was waning. By 1850, it could claim the adherence of no more than 20 per cent of the population and, in Gladstone's words, 'bore all the marks of the decrepitude of age and of approaching inevitable dissolution'. We can see this reflected in Father Daly's remarkable personal progress. He rose to take over the city's commanding heights. It is even more remarkable to see that until at least the late 1840s these heights had been occupied by 'the enemy', namely the Church of Ireland, whose Rev. John D'Arcy was manager of the Gasworks, secretary to the Harbour Commissioners and the Town Commissioners Office, treasurer of the Reproductive Loan Office (which offered small loans to 'the industrious poor') and local inspector of the imposing town jail.

D'Arcy's demise might be seen as the culmination of a battle launched back in 1824, when the thirty-six-year-old Father Daly first attracted public attention. His target was Archbishop Trench, or to give him his full name and title so redolent of the Protestant Ascendancy, His Grace the Right Honourable Power le Poer Trench. The Church of Ireland's Galway bowsprit, he was a man of gaitered dignity, accustomed to deference by virtue of his rank and perhaps even more importantly in that stratified society, his family ties to the Earls of Clancarty.[26] But on 19 October, when he was chairing a public meeting of the Galway branch of the 'London Hibernian Society for Establishing Schools and Circulating the Holy Scriptures', the proceedings were disrupted by a noisy crowd of Catholics, led by Father Daly, protesting at attempts to disseminate an alien Protestant doctrine. Daly made the first of the many tub-thumping speeches of his public life. His supporters declared him 'chairman' of the meeting and the Archbishop scuttled away protected by a phalanx of militia with drawn swords.

The Father was to remain centre stage in the city's public life for the next forty years, a dynamic combination of do-gooding energy, demagoguery and a brisk business mind, a mix which was bound to bring him into conflict with the Roman Catholic hierarchy even more than the Church of Ireland. Though as far as we know no one actually wanted Daly dead, it is not too fanciful to imagine his frustrated – and no doubt increasingly jealous – superiors echoing King Henry II's call, 'Will no one rid me of this troublesome priest?', which sparked the murder of Archbishop Thomas à Becket. His detractors failed to lay a finger on him with an allegation of lustful impropriety after he had escorted a young Dominican nun to a convent in Paris, and neither Sloth nor Envy were charges that could be laid at the door of a man of such energy and self-confidence. Yet several of the other Deadly Sins were strongly in evidence in Peter Daly's complex character. Avarice certainly; he built up a large property portfolio, including Villa Albano, a 'handsome mansion' set in thirty-two acres of grounds outside the city, owned at least two other fine houses and a Monopoly-like accumulation of city tenements and small farms.

He soon earned the reputation of a landlord who would not hesitate to evict tenants, even if they were up to date with their rent, if he had plans to develop the property more profitably; he spent one Church Holy Day in court attending to the eviction of twenty-nine hapless families. He died a rich man. Wrath too; his scrupulous biographer, Father James Mitchell, tells us that Daly would fly off the handle at both public and private meetings. 'Hold your tongue, sir,' he yelled at one of his fellow members of Galway's Town Commission, 'you are most insolent always. You lie . . . you are a disgrace to society.' Little wonder then that the stream of hostile comments about him to the Vatican refer to his 'unduly rough disposition', and paint him as 'contumacious' with 'presumptuous capabilities' and an 'indomitably insubordinate spirit'. 'The untameable Hyena', one of his bishops wrote of him in an un-Christian fit of fury. He was so widely known as what might fairly be called a 'Holy Terror' that when in 1856 a Dr Fallon was nominated as Bishop of Galway, he turned the honour down 'through sheer fear of Father Daly', as one of Daly's colleagues wrote

1. 'The doors of the most respectable banking houses were besieged and throngs heaving and tumbling about Lombard Street made that narrow thoroughfare impassable.' 'Black Friday', 10 May 1866.

2. Doré Print of Ludgate Hill with a view of Saint Paul's Cathedral.

3. Lombard Street.

4. 'Samuel Gurney the Great.'

5. Elizabeth Fry, the famous Quaker reformer and sister of Samuel Gurney.

6. The Gurney bank in Norwich, 1780. Cornerstone of the family's remarkable wealth.

8. Henry Edmund
Gurney.

7. Grove House School.

10. Greek novelist and entrepreneur,
Stefanos Xenos.

9. John Henry Gurney.

11. (*opposite*)
The dapper and devious
'Baron' Albert Grant.

12. Father Peter Daly whose
idea for a new transatlantic
shipping line led to one of
Overends' nastiest
financial disasters.

13. An architect's vision for
the Galway deep harbour.

14. Transatlantic ships in
Nova Scotia.

15. The Isle of Dogs, site of the last of Overends' major calamities.

16. Charles John Mare's Shipyard.

17. Brunel, Russell and Lord Derby at the launch of the *Great Eastern*.

18. The failed launch of the *Northumberland*.

19. An Overend share certificate, in the end not worth the paper it was printed on.

20. Overend and tombstone: the cover of the final company file.

21. The trial of the Overend directors, with Henry Edmund Gurney wielding his famous brass ear trumpet.

22. The almost extinct Gurney's Pitta.

23. Samuel Gurney's memorial, Stratford, East London.

to the Irish College in Rome. However, one of the good Father's well-honed skills was nurturing useful contacts and his access to the highest, dustiest power corridors in the Vatican, which included several meetings with Pope Leo XII. Criticisms of him in that direction tended not to have much effect. Even the sin of Gluttony might, at a stretch, be entered in the record, if a local apocryphal story is true. It claims that Daly was hosting Bishop MacEvilly of Galway to a rich dinner at Villa Albano when a lad came to the door asking him to come to his home to administer the last rites to his dying father. Father Daly retorted that he wanted to finish his dinner before it got cold, and enjoy his wine, and would come along later. The embarrassed Bishop went in his place.

These and other anecdotes about Daly are only one side of a remarkable coin. The other shows a man who became a local hero, a man of immense energy who built churches and a home for the local clergy, and persuaded the Sisters of Mercy to open a convent in Galway to help deal with the sufferings of the famine.[27]

However, his comments on Ireland's tragedy seem to reflect genuine pastoral concern; either that or breathtaking hypocrisy. He told a committee of enquiry, with a perceptible lilt in his language, that

> the houses in my parish are going to decay for want of trade and commerce in the town . . . The people subsist generally on potatoes . . . there is a change for the worse in the clothing, feeding and habitations of the people and it is worse such things are becoming every year . . . in many houses there may be twenty families having between two and seven persons . . . the beds are generally straw or chaff and the bedclothes tattered dirty blankets or quilts and many houses or rooms of them having too much ventilation for want of being able to glaze the windows or otherwise close the opening . . .

According to the *Galway Vindicator*, the town's main newspaper, on Christmas Day in 1846, Father Daly 'provided each of one hundred families with three pounds of beef and a large loaf'. But, by the following February, in the year known locally as 'black '47', the *Vindicator* was reporting that, 'No language can depict the ghastly suffering of the poor destitutes of this city. On every side nothing but cries of destitution and starvation are heard. The poor are literally dropping on the public highways . . .'

Galway's sufferings and poverty drove Peter Daly to apply his energies to reviving the city's fortunes. If frayed relations with colleagues and bruising controversies were the price, it was worth paying. Probably for him at least it was also rather fun; but those like Overends, Xenos' sometime friend George Lascaridi and a slew of Irish investors, all of whom paid a colossal financial price for their involvement in the Father's chimera, would have had a different view. Daly joined the Galway Town Commissioners towards the end of 1847 and soon became their chairman. His public life was taking over from parish duties. In May 1849, he was in London giving evidence on the famine and the workings of the Poor Law to a House of Commons committee; in June, he was appointed to the Board of the Galway Gas Company; in July, he joined the Harbour Commission; and in August, we see him in Dublin presenting 'an address' from his home town to the visiting Queen Victoria. A year later the shape of his dream became clearer, when he pushed through a proposal to be submitted to Whitehall to make Galway a 'transatlantic shipping terminus' by designating it as an official 'packet station' for the mail between the British Isles and North America. The pieces all fitted neatly. As chairman of the Commissioners he held many of the reins of civic power. He was also a director of the Midland & Great Western Railway Company and persuaded them to run their line from Dublin right into the heart of the city; a comfortable alternative to the Royal Mail Coach which rattled out of Eyre Square to Dublin at 2.20 p.m. daily (Sundays presumably excepted) via Ballinasige, Athlone, Moate, Killbegan, Tyrells Pass, Kinegad, Clonard, Innfield and Maynooth.

In a country which had folk memories of the twenty-one galleons of the Spanish Armada washed up along the Irish coast, and a French attempt, providentially thwarted by Ireland's secret weapon, the weather, to land 14,500 men at Bantry Bay in 1796, railway stations were usually sited some way away from the coast, close to the local garrison's barracks, to make them less susceptible to quick capture by a hostile landing party. In contrast, thanks to Father Daly's influence, the Midland Line ran to the heart of the city, right to the edge of Eyre Square. But as in London, what self-respecting station was without its integral hotel? Daly convinced the Railway to build what was then the biggest hotel in Ireland, now 'The Great Southern'. No expense was spared. The swing doors through which railway passengers could walk, under a glazed canopy, straight from the platform into the hotel lobby, though now blocked off, are still to be seen. The hotel's proportions have been marred by the addition of a modern top floor, but its simple, classic lines are evident and in marked contrast to the grandiose exuberance of the London station hotels. To this day locals claim, not without a touch of pride, that Father Daly was the secret owner of the tenements which stood on the hotel site and that he evicted the tenants, sold the land to the Railway for a handy profit, and the next Sunday beseeched his parishioners from the pulpit to give generously to the collection plate to help those so sadly dispossessed.

Tying together the railway, the hotel, the harbour and a shipping line into one integrated operation made sense, on paper. After all, Galway's magnificent natural harbour, its mouth sheltered by the Aran Islands, was 300 miles nearer to North America than Liverpool. A local shipping line linked to Britain and Europe via the railway to Dublin could capture a large piece of the growing two-way transatlantic traffic and, in Xenos' words 'annihilate the space that lies between the Old and New Worlds'. All the more if its running costs were underpinned by a British government subsidy to carry mail to and from North America.

Had Peter Daly been less sure of himself, and as superstitious as his fellow countrymen, he might have seen Fate's lighthouse flashing an early warning of things to come. A trial run across the ocean by a small paddle steamer in 1850 turned into a nightmare of gales, fog and icebergs and ended with the vessel wrecked on the rocks of Nova Scotia. But Daly pushed on, lobbying the Lord Lieutenant in Dublin and even the Prime Minister Lord Derby in London, in an unsuccessful attempt to get British funding for new docks and harbour installations, the absence of which was one of the scheme's major flaws.[28]

There were probably few important visitors Daly did not find a way to meet. He certainly met old Samuel Gurney when he and Elizabeth Fry, Quakers with a conscience, came to see what might be done to help the famine victims; Elizabeth Fry later sent Daly £40 for one of his food kitchens.

Sometime in the late 1850s, Daly had a more significant meeting with the Manchester entrepreneur John Orrell Lever. Lever was then a thrusting thirty year old, who had made money during the Crimean War from chartering supply vessels and troopships to the Government, and who was now running the West of Ireland Steam Navigation Company.

The two men pushed the transatlantic project forward. (Praising Father Daly's efforts, the *Vindicator* also gave credit to 'the mighty Lever which he has put upon [Galway] to raise her to future greatness'). It was characteristic of the times that getting the mail subsidy which was so essential for the Line's income subsidy involved coarse politics, even coarser bribery and double-dealing. No government could ignore the 106 House of Commons votes of Irish Members. But political balances shifted with the winds and Lever wanted to make sure of success by offering a firm of 'parliamentary agents' £100 if they could persuade Whitehall to underwrite the Line's first voyage, and up to £10,000 if the Line received the mail subsidy. When this came through – £78,000 a year for a fortnightly service – and the 'agents' sued for their money, Lever refused to pay, brazenly alleging fraud since the 'agents' did not have the influence they had claimed. He was ordered to pay £1,000. Lord Derby as Prime Minister and Disraeli as his Chancellor, feigned ignorance of the whole affair, while parliamentary committees growled ineffectually. The Line was born amid much fanfare and high hopes, which were soon to be sadly dashed as the Line began what Father Mitchell describes succinctly as 'a calamitous six year career'.

Rear Admiral the Earl of Shrewsbury, the Hereditary High

Steward of Ireland, was chairman and a firm then known as Philip Cazenove & Co. was its lead stockbroker. Promoted as 'a national and commercial enterprise of the first rank', the share offer raised £500,000. Many of the original shareholders were Irish and the list, published by the Line's diligent maritime historian Tim Collins, provides a surprising counterpoint to the stereotype of a country ground down and impoverished by famine. As the poor dropped dead in the ditches, the country's merchants, professional men and shopkeepers, even the gentry of Galway and the depositors who lost £500,000 with John Sadleir's fraudulent 'Tipperary Bank' (another Irish folly of the era), had cash to spare. Likewise, the Line's original shareholders' list included a broad cross-section of the community from Guinness's to grocers.[29]

How did Overends become involved in such an extravagant dream? As we saw, to save Lascaridi and their own reputation, they had to bail him out from his involvement with Xenos and the other blizzard of Bills he had signed, probably again without his family firm's knowledge but in their name, to fund the Galway Line. As the Line began to swirl into a nightmare, again The Corner House had a choice: pull out, or put in more money. Again, they made the wrong one.

An even more interesting question is how Lascaridi became embroiled in the first place.

13

That Sinking Feeling

For the answer, we need to return to the small seedy world of the City's back alleys and moneylenders' offices. According to Xenos, it was Lever, with the financial blade-runner's gift for spotting a naïve target, who gulled Lascaridi into becoming involved, dangling the prospect that backing such a prominent venture would bring him a knighthood. Visions of kneeling in velvet breeches before Queen Victoria so that she could tap him on the shoulder with a small sword were more than enough to induce him to accept liability on £200,000 of Bills to finance the first purchase of ships. In a parallel 'con' worthy of a David Mamet screenplay, Lever induced an elderly cotton mill owner from Hyde, Thomas Howard, to add his own name to the Bills; if trouble came, there was no question of any liability for Lever. His two 'partners' would have to pay up.

The Bills were 'melted', turned into cash, for the Line by Henry Barker and Albert Grant. Given the latter's fertile mind and his ability to connect up the dots, it may well have been Grant himself who nudged Lascaridi in Lever's direction.

Daly had done his part and turned vision into reality. He had even invested £1,200 of his own money in it; a tidy sum for a parish priest. But as he told the townsfolk, referring to himself in the third person like many demagogues before and since, 'Don't wonder at that, for to tell the truth, Father Daly has a little money. There is birdlime on his hands and the money sticks to them'; sadly, not in this case.

Even before the Line started to operate, Lever was bilking the shareholders and Lascaridi by buying ships at one price and, after adding a handsome margin, selling them on to the Line at Lascaridi's risk. The origin of many of these vessels offers yet another glimpse into an incestuous world. The most egregious example was the *Indian Empire*, bought for £8,500 and mortgaged to Lascaridi for £25,000, the profit pocketed by Lever, who also skimmed off some of the proceeds of the initial share offer to his Great Ocean Telegraph Company to fund an unsuccessful attempt to lay a transatlantic cable from Galway to Halifax, Nova Scotia.

However, the Line's problems went far deeper than self-dealing and the unstable pyramid of Bill finance, which had become a defining feature of Corner House ventures. To paraphrase Cole Porter, it was the wrong time, the wrong place and, though its ships were charming, they were the wrong ships.

Although emigration flows from Ireland were still high, and trade and the first stirrings of a two-way transatlantic tourist and business traveller trade were being felt, the blockade of the South, which was a key part of the North's strategy in the American Civil War, was playing havoc with both passenger and freight levels, and it would not be long before the first underwater cable would make mail subsidies a questionable benefit. It was also the wrong time to challenge Merseyside, the business centre of powerful vested interests, among them Cunard, who had more capital, more staying power, better management skills and more direct access to the Whitehall corridors of power. Liverpool also had the edge because emigrants to North America were not just Irish; for the tired and huddled masses from Germany, Eastern Europe and Scandinavia, Liverpool was a far more convenient destination.

Galway was the wrong place. Its harbour was indeed magnificent, but the closest it came to building the docks, which might have made it more efficient as a destination, was an architect's fanciful Canaletto-like sketch. Passengers and cargo had to be ferried in open launches, waves breaking over their heads and their luggage, to and from the steamers anchored off Mutton Island; the emigrant poor, hunched in their shawls and travelling 'steerage', could hardly object. Those who had paid sixteen guineas for first-class treatment were more vocal in their discontent.

The biggest weakness, however, was that the Galway Line had the wrong ships for crossing the Atlantic Ocean, which is as unpredictable, as terrifying and as unforgiving as the financial markets. The Line's vessels were puny and unreliable. In that age of transition from sail to steam, many of them were powered by a creaking compromise. There were lumbering engines which swallowed coal at an alarming rate as they cranked the two side paddlewheels at a ponderous twelve revolutions a minute, backed up by a spread of sail Nelson would have recognised; the specifications for one noted that it was 'a barkantine rig with topsails on the fore- and mainmasts and long poles permitting topgallants if necessary'. It was an 'either/or' choice; the sails could not be spread when the engines were running because of the risk of hot embers from the funnels setting them ablaze. Early propellers had long, thin blades, rather like those on a pre-jet aeroplane engine, all too easily smashed or bent by driftwood or reefs. Mid-Victorian engineers were still discovering the hard way that fitting propeller shafts into wooden hulls was a problem; the constant flexing of the ship's frame meant that the shafts were constantly pulled out of alignment.

Ships were changing, but the systems to bring them safely across the seas had not yet caught up. There was no radio, radar, or weather forecasts. The Line's logs are studded with references to 'hurricanes', 'gales', 'icebergs', 'fog', 'laying to for a week to allow the winds to abate', burst pistons and boilers, not to mention terror-stricken passengers. In the early winter of 1858, the homeward bound *Indian Empire* was caught in a south-easterly gale, stretching its voyage from the normal five or so to nearly thirty-five days. When its coal ran out near the Irish coast, the boilers were fed with its cargo of cotton and timber as well as the ship's backup set of spars, bulwarks and any other gear that could be unscrewed and burned. The *Empire* was then blown over 100 miles westwards again before the gale finally spent itself and the ship made landfall in County Mayo on Friday, 26 November, when hope was fading in Galway of her safe arrival. It had been a great piece of seamanship by the skipper, but whether the 400 passengers bothered to praise his skill when they complained loudly to the press about the horrors of their experience in the Line's hands is doubtful.

Just a few months later, the Line's *Pacific* ran into squalls, which 'washed away the cutwater, bulwarks, boats, fittings and everything else on the deck from the figurehead aft to the paddle boxes'. This diverted neither the Line – now the Atlantic Royal Mail Steam Packet Company – nor Lever who, with Daly's enthusiastic support at the hustings, was elected MP for Galway City on a rather basic platform of making sure its people were well fed, well clothed and well educated. 'If ye will h'elevate me I will h'elevate ye,' he is reported as promising, though the phonetics are more Irish than Mancunian.

His fine words did not calm the restless waves. In May 1859, *The Argo*, outward bound from Boston, ran at full speed onto the rocks of Trepassey Bay, off Newfoundland. Its 220 passengers and 150 crew were saved, but the ship was a total loss, though the Line or Lever – it is not clear who received the benefit – had the consolation of an insurance payment from Lloyds.

According to Xenos, shortly after this Edward Edwards, Henry Barker and Ward Chapman – *prima facie* a rather un-nautical trio – in effect took control of the Line and pushed Lever out; possibly on account of his backstairs flirtation with a Canadian competitor to start a rival line out of Londonderry, a flirtation which was never consummated. Here again was a turning point. At this distance we do not know what their real options were. On the face of it, Overends had other choices. They could have cut their losses and shut the Line down; they might have put in professional management and a modicum of capital to steer it back to profitability; or they might have tried to sell it to one of the larger competitors. Instead, they resolved to 'go for broke', in both senses. In September 1859, they commissioned five new ships and bought a sixth, at a cost of some £600,000, financed by another new share issue and by Bills taken up initially by a new Barker and Grant enterprise, the Imperial Mercantile Credit Association. The Imperial bought the Line's new Bills, but shrewdly insisted that The Corner House should guarantee them, saddling Overends with a large contingent liability which would become pressingly real if the Line failed to pay. In turn Overends held mortgages over the ships. Xenos, who tells us he talked the whole imbroglio through later with Lever himself, claims that the ships were badly designed, chewed through far too much coal and were worth at best half of what they cost. He claims that Edwards had persuaded the Board to do this, 'though he had never been a seaman, a merchant or a naval architect'. There is no reason to doubt it and the role played by Imperial adds to the flavour of Edwards in the middle of an orgy, wheeling and dealing with money changing hands in various directions. Xenos puts it nicely: 'small commissions, brokerages, douceurs, charges for bonus, interest, etc. which tend to draw off the vitality of the concern.'

Xenos' comment about Edwards' lack of technical knowledge is true, in fact, of everyone involved with the Line's destiny, an object lesson in what happens when over-confident men get into complex businesses about which they know nothing. Lever was at heart a speculator. Daly may have believed in miracles, but was a man of the mind, not a mechanic. Lascaridi and the cotton spinner Howard were as lambs to the slaughter, and The Corner House partners' combined shipping experience was probably limited to travelling across the Channel as rug-wrapped first class passengers or watching their infant children play with model yachts on the Round Pond in Kensington Gardens.

But the issue was more than technical. The perils of the sea made the mail subsidy a mixed blessing. It was already highly politicised, closely scrutinised by parliamentary committees and much coveted, and therefore robustly lobbied for, by Liverpool, US and Canadian lines. Allegations flew that the Galway Line had paid at least one lobbyist £10,000 to secure the mail contract. Given the Line's fragile earnings, it could make the difference between loss and profit on every voyage. The Post Office contract meant that the Line's vessels could add the prestigious 'RMS' or 'Royal Mail Ship' tag to their names, but against that, the terms and conditions were so tight that even a relatively minor delay, let alone meteorological misfortunes on the scale to which the Galway Line was prey, could bring penalties and even suspension of the contract.

By the time the Line's Annual General Meeting was held in March 1860, losses, expenses and claims of mismanagement were attracting shareholder wrath, all the more vehement since the meeting was in London rather than Galway. By July, the pressure came to a head when word got out that the company was secretly negotiating to sell the subsidy rights to the Canadian Allan Line. Though the talks came to nothing, there was a storm of local indignation, the verbal equivalent of a nasty Atlantic squall; Lever was a 'charlatan' and Galway had been 'taken in and done for' were among the milder comments. Even the *New York Times* weighed in, playing to its Irish emigrant readership with the thought that Lever was a 'pecuniary traitor', whose name would go down in history 'laden with the fearful execrations such as have hitherto been monopolised for Cromwell'.

In September, the Board was reshuffled and Lever stepped down as chairman, but remained a director. In September, the gods struck again, keeping up a rhythm that Xenos with his Classical background would have well understood. One of the Line's new vessels, its Jarrow-built pride and joy, the lavishly fitted, paddle-powered, 3,000-ton *Connaught*, began to take in water 150 miles off Boston, on the return leg of its first and last voyage, and soon caught fire. It would take the loss of the *Titanic* some half a century later to bring home to the world that passenger ships were being exposed to the treachery and bullying of the ocean with far too few lifeboats. The *Connaught* had just eight for her 467 passengers and crew of 124, and would have been in the record books as a major maritime catastrophe had the American brig *Minnie Schiffer* not splashed out of the night and taken everyone on board to safety minutes before the *Connaught* went down.

In May 1861, after more fierce lobbying by Canadian shipowners, the Galway Line lost the mail subsidy, though not without a valiant if ill-judged last-ditch sortie by Father Daly to London to put pressure on the British Prime Minister, Lord Palmerston, to reverse the decision. Daly's name must have commanded respect since Palmerston agreed to see him at his Piccadilly home on a Saturday morning, but the Father was up against a far shrewder political operator, and a man who knew how to read the Irish. Palmerston had inherited a large estate in Sligo, in the north-east, and his title was Irish, one of the 'potato peers'. He also knew about the Atlantic run: when the Great Famine struck in the mid-1840s, he had paid for several thousand of his tenants to sail away from starvation to a new life in Canada.

Daly knew that Palmerston's minority Government, dependent for survival on the votes of Irish Liberal MPs, was facing a critical budget debate, and his offer had a crude simplicity: the votes would be delivered if the subsidy were restored. There was one slight problem: he was bluffing. He had not even spoken to the Irish MPs, a touchy group at the best of times, let alone secured their support for such barefaced blackmail. Palmerston must have known or sensed this, and refused to budge. In the end, he got his Irish votes anyway. Though an enraged House of Lords tried to have Daly summoned before Parliament to justify himself, nothing came of it, and the Father went home to one of the triumphal welcomes his supporters often laid on on such occasions and told a cheering crowd that he had done his best. A *Punch* cartoon a few days later shows Palmerston thumbing his nose at the sackful of Irish 'votes' proffered by Daly, caricatured as the British stereotype of a balding black-robed Catholic priest. 'Oho! Father Daly! Now I think I understand you', the caption ran.[30]

Though the ever resourceful Lever chartered out several of the Galway Line ships to run the American blockade of the South (whether or not in partnership with poor Zachariah Pearson is unclear), its mainstream business fell away until 1863. In February of this year another London foray by Father Daly wrung a promise from Lord Palmerston that the Line might re-qualify for the subsidy if it could demonstrate that it had reliable ships which could maintain a regular schedule.

The Board was restructured yet again, joined by 'Samuel Gurney', otherwise unidentified but presumably the MP who was old Sam's son and an inactive partner in The Corner House, and a 'John Chapman', who may well have been related to David and Ward and who later became chairman. In August 1863, with the usual local rejoicing, the company was back in business. The celebrations were not only expensive and roundly platitudinous, but proved sadly premature. Fog, ice and storms again upset the schedules, a ship ran aground, and the US Consul opined that the new sailing schedule offered little benefit to the United Sates or indeed to Galway. In a last-ditch attempt at financial *legerdemain*, Edwards advised Overends to inject several of the Galway vessels into a new public company, East India and London Shipping. This, of course, also collapsed, adding to the pile of worthless paper stacked in Overends' vault. In a final insult, the expensive furniture and fittings of the Galway Line head office were auctioned off in the now victorious Liverpool. In June 1864, the company was wound up.

Lever's gullible partner Howard, then close to eighty, found himself in the Bankruptcy Court, after 'the Gurneys got all that I had, and the great portion of the cotton mill. They frightened me out of it and got it from me clandestinely.'

Lever himself, undaunted by the Line's failure, the loss of his Commons seat and bankruptcy, tried to establish a local flax mill and stood again unsuccessfully for Parliament in 1865. In 1880, however, he was back again to find that memories had faded; he was re-elected and remained a Member until he resigned his seat in 1886 after a spat with his Party.

Some memories lasted longer. James Joyce was not born until 1882, long after the Galway Line had sunk beneath the waves, yet he too caught swirling fragments of its history in *Ulysses*. Bloom and Daedalus are in a Dublin cabmen's shelter, in the improbable company of a lighthouse keeper and a drunken, lice-scratching sailor. The keeper remembers the time the Line's *Empire* ran aground 'on the only rock in Galway Bay' and the local rumour that British shipping interests had bribed the captain to wreck it deliberately. 'Ask the captain how much palm oil the British Government gave him for that day's work, Captain John Lever of the Lever Line.' This prompts the sailor to chant:

> The biscuits were as hard as brass
> And the beef as salt as Lot's wife's arse
> O Johnny Lever, Johnny Lever, O,

a ditty whose deeper significance, if any, can happily be left to Joyce scholars to puzzle over.

A more relevant puzzle is the link between this Irish shipwreck and our next chapter, yet another maritime mishap, this time on dry land.

14

Going to the Dogs

'It's a long, long way to Tipperary', British soldiers sang as they trudged to their deaths in the First World War. From Galway to London's Isle of Dogs, setting for our study of the last of Overends' major calamities is a fair stretch too. But there is a direct link. Yet again we are back to ships and shipbuilders such as John Scott Russell, and Charles Mare, with their bold but bankruptcy-inducing bids – not least the *Great Eastern* – to conquer the new technology of iron. Yet again we see on the stage many of our now familiar troupe of strolling players: The Corner House partners, Edward Edwards and the agile Albert Grant; even John Orell Lever has a walk-on role. Again it is a story of staggering stupidity, whose beginning is hard to find, and whose twists and turns need to be simplified in the telling. The Millwall Shipyard, nearly 30 acres on the Isle's western banks, was Overends' graveyard, where many of the vessels that pitched and tossed across our pages, spraying losses in their wake, were built. Curiously it also has ties that seem to predate Overends years of trouble, with old Samuel Gurney 'The Great' and the family's Norwich Bank. These links, fragmented and elusive as they are, allow us to speculate that the root cause of many of The Corner House's problems may have been the Yard itself. Though a space that had to be rented out to cover its cost, tenants consistently overreached in their borrowings from Overend, forcing the latter into a web of financial and commercial stratagems to get the vessels sold and keep them gainfully employed.

The Isle of Dogs was an appropriately unpleasant and appropriately named setting for our Victorian melodrama. A marshy peninsula around which the Thames loops from Poplar back up to Blackwall, lapping dankly at Deptford and Greenwich on its way, it is said to have got its name as the site of Charles II's Royal Kennels when the Court was in residence across the river at Greenwich Palace. The cold winds nagging and tugging off the river, and the foetid humours of the swamps, must have kept the poor hounds lean and mean. By the early nineteenth century, London's ever growing shipping trade had outgrown the wharves and warehouses which had sprawled for centuries along the Thames' banks and the first major dock, the West India, was cut, cofferdammed and brick-buttressed in the mud across the top end of the Isle. A new era began. Other vast docks followed.

Even now older Londoners can still dredge from the fringes of their memory images of the bows of merchant ships and slow-swinging cranes looming like film-set props over the high brick walls curving along the narrow West Ferry Road; dockers in cloth caps, white mufflers and sturdy boots, clattering and coughing their way down the cobbled side streets, hand-rolled cigarettes drooping from the corners of their mouths. So key were the Docks that until the 1950s, strike action by handfuls of militant workers could often paralyse British trade. But the world changed and the Docks died. In a feat of energy and imagination worthy of Victorian times, for which a small group of American bankers can take much credit (a fact which would have reinforced old 'Monadnock's flinty feelings about British effeteness), they were eventually replaced by the glittering towers of Canary Wharf and its outrider blocks of high-priced flats complete 'with stunning river views' and Phillipe Starck sanitary fittings.

Fringing the civil engineering triumphs of the docks were less attractive buildings; the industrial plants exiled there because the miasma of smoke and smells which were the unregulated, unfiltered by-product of their money making, were too much even for nineteenth-century London. The air was gritty and the river streaked and glazed with waste from the machines which boiled crushed and ground away, day and night, to spew out tar, white lead, candles, disinfectants, boot polish, toxic chemicals, dyes, paints, quicklime, and antimony. Even that humble Victorian, staple, household and office glue oozed out of stinking vats in which the bones and hides of cattle and horses were steamed into what a contemporary Encyclopaedia rather nicely called a 'tremulous jelly'.

Of direct relevance to our story, the Isle of Dogs was also where London's shipbuilders had clustered for centuries, across the river from the Navy's huge yards at Deptford and a little further downstream at Woolwich. Though Clydeside and the North-East were both emerging as major centres, much of British shipbuilding was still concentrated in the London yards. Like the country as a whole, shipbuilding was going through a massive technological change; the transition from wooden hulls to iron, another of those great leaps forward of Victorian times.

The rich paraphernalia of Nelson's world of 'Hearts of Oak', the white oak and pine planking, cedar masts, saws, adzes, hammers and nails, 'coakes', garboard strakes and futtocks, had begun to give way to the new world of iron around 1830. Thirty years later, when iron shipbuilding in London reached its peak, the Isle's industrial fog blanket was overshadowed by the steam and smoke of the yards. A stream of horse-drawn carts clanked over the cobbles piled high with scrap iron horseshoes, mangles, cooking pots, lengths of worn-out railway track, bits and pieces of agricultural machinery, even rusting hull plates from earlier generations of iron barges and ships now beached and dead. These were just part of the raw material the production lines needed to feed their growing appetite, and were supplemented by plates and ingots barged down the Thames from ironworks across the country. The Yard furnaces disgorged a lava-like hissing red outflow which, as it cooled, was moulded, rolled, cut, bent and stamped by towering machines, winched up piece by piece into a wooden frame, and hammered and riveted in place, the whole yard a clanging flame-spouting inferno. But this was not just some giant version of the village blacksmiths shop. The industry was driven and underpinned by the intellectual curiosity and practical research so characteristic of the age. Iron's role and risks in the construction of railways and bridges had even been the subject of a 435 page report by a Royal Commission in 1845. Enquiring minds then turned to ships, to optimal hull shapes and wave patterns, the tensile strengths of different grades of iron and how they could be improved, the optimal configuration for ship beams, even the relationship between the number of rivets and the stress lines on an iron plate; each minute detail of a ships construction was rigorously analysed. The manufacturing process itself was 'engineered' to produce one of the earliest versions of the integrated industrial production line. From it emerged many brilliant technological triumphs: iron warships, river cruisers, cargo boats, tugs, passenger liners and luxury yachts for the Viceroy of Egypt and the Pope, the latter clearly not a hair-shirted ascetic. He may even have had a sly sense of humour; the yacht was named *The Immaculate Conception*. The immense folly of Isambard Kingdom Brunel's *Great Eastern* stands as a reminder, highly relevant to our story, that brilliant engineers are not necessarily brilliant men of business.

Traces of this high-water mark of the Victorian machine age still remain. The blocks of flats on the eastern side of the Isle are called the Semuda Estate, after the brothers whose yard was one of the better run in an industry that was high on hope and engineering brilliance but woefully short on financial and management skills. Another yard, once a farm, was where Trinity Wharf is now, at the Isle's north-east corner, where the River Lea oozes into the Thames. Some of the original steam-driven machine tools still stand, rusting peacefully next to the Edward Hopper incongruity of 'FatBoy's Diner', authentically American red plastic and chrome, perched on the water's edge with the Millennium Dome bulging behind it across the Thames like a giant yellowish goitre; a reminder that bankers are not the only ones who make bad mistakes. The curious explorer can find what remains of Overends' watery grave on the western side of the Isle, about a mile down West Ferry Road from Canary Wharf. A slip road on the right between two blocks of flats leads to a sweeping embankment with a view across the slate grey water to Deptford and the distant glory of Greenwich. On a grassy patch between the walkway and the communal gardens of the flats, a skeleton of heavy wooden beams lies half buried in the ground, like the bones of some prehistoric animal. That and a pile of heavy chain links looped over an iron bollard are all that is left of the slipway used for the disastrous launch of the disaster-prone *Great Eastern*. The river frontage of what was once the Millwall Yard, then a 27-acre site most of which lay on the land side of West Ferry Road, is now a lattice of small streets with names which once cut through the waves on the bows of Royal Navy ships: Cyclops, Harbinger, Hesperus, Thermopylae. Even the Yard's long vanished 'Mast House' has a street named after it.

It was a site for dreams and innovation. But it was an industry where the risk of failure was high. 'English finance', reliance on short-term Bills being rolled over every 90 days, was the norm. Competition was fierce, and with accounting and proper cost control, in their infancy, applying the uncertain new technologies to contracts often taken on at fixed prices meant that the line between profit and loss was hard to calibrate and all too easy to cross.

Even so, superstitious observers might have wondered whether some especially malevolent jinx had squirreled itself away in the mud of the Millwall Yard. The Yard's first victim, and the only one with no apparent tie to Overends, had been the Manchester engineer and ironmaster William Fairbairn, who bought it for £50,000 in the mid 1830s to turn his carefully researched theories of how iron ships should be built, into commercial reality and Government contracts. By 1848 though he had built 100 iron hulled vessels, mainly for the Royal Navy, financial pressures forced him to retreat back to his still profitable Manchester base, selling the Yard for a mere £12,000 and nursing accumulated losses of some £100,000. In a memoir published in 1865 he laid the blame on 'opposition and competition from . . . the great builders and shipwrights of the capital' who had forced him into an 'unequal contest', though part of the problem may have lain in Fairbairn's inability, like those who came after him, to resist taking on projects such as bridges which brought prestige but no profit.

The next tenant, John Scott Russell, was another 'one of a kind' character in the Daly and Xenos mould, a brilliant physicist and a less than brilliant man of business. The later attribute made him a natural candidate to be drawn into the orbit of Edward Edwards and The Corner House. His career was also marred by episodes that suggested an occasional inability to distinguish other peoples' money from his own. Born in Scotland in 1808, he made his lasting mark in the academic world with his studies of how waves worked, from which he extrapolated unique ideas for the design of ships' hulls. By his late thirties, he seemed set to blend into that amoeba-like creature, 'The British Establishment'. Though together with two partners he had already begun a small scale shipbuilding business at Millwall in 1849, public recognition and exposure to 'the great and the good' were emerging in parallel when he was nominated as Secretary to the Prince Consort's Committee organising the Great Exhibition of 1851. He decided to step down early to devote himself to shipbuilding full time (some unkind voices said the Committee was not unhappy to see him depart). His early years at the Yard seem to have been reasonably successful, but the Millwall jinx lay waiting patiently. Its first and potentially fatal sally was a fire in 1853 which devastated the Yard and its equipment. Russell managed to recover, only to founder a few years later on the wreckage, almost literally, of the world's most ambitious shipbuilding project.

The saga of the *Great Eastern* has been told and retold; Russell's connection, although seemingly only small scale, with The Corner House is a new aspect. The vision of Isambard Kingdom Brunel, who had already been working with Russell on designs for ships to be used on the long haul across the Pacific, the *Great Eastern* epitomised the ambition and vision of the age. Conceived as an all-conquering behemoth to replace the sailing clippers on the long run round the Cape of Good Hope to Australia and the Far East, it would combine size – 20,000 tons and room for 4,000 passengers – with the best of the new and the old: a glorious Rowland Emmett-like mix of six mighty steam engines, sails on six masts, five funnels, twin 56-foot diameter paddle wheels and a screw propeller, all cased in an iron hull 700 feet long and 100 feet wide. It was a commercial catastrophe from start to finish.

Though Russsell was the builder and thus the man ultimately in charge who carried the financial risk of construction, Eastern Steam Navigation, the company created to back the project, had appointed Brunel as Chief Engineer. Brunel's terms of reference allowed him to check and recheck every detail, make design changes, and generally 'second guess' the Scotsman and delay progress. His vigilance and interference increased when he began to suspect that Russell was diverting some of the *Great Eastern* materials and maybe even funds to meet obligations on other contracts the Yard was trying to complete in parallel. As with almost every other such project of its time 'cash', the solid foundation of permanent invested capital, and disciplined budgeting, were sorely lacking. It was 'English finance' yet again. Russell had grossly underestimated the cost of the contract and had made his cash-flow problems worse by agreeing that instead of money he would take Eastern Steam shares in part payment. It is hard to pay wages and clamouring suppliers with share certificates, however elegantly engraved, and though at that stage Russell's bankers were Martin's, it is not unlikely that the first brush with Overends came, probably via Mercantile Discount, when these illiquid shares needed to be melted into liquid cash. The roller-coaster of crises in the Yard ended in ignominy when after all the pomp and ceremony of the launch, an event of such popular interest that Eastern Steam sold tickets to the viewing stands, the gigantic hull stuck fast on the slipway; a calamity blamed by Russell on Brunel's passion for experimentation, in this case insisting on using iron runners rather than the traditional grease-slathered timber. The Yard jinx had reappeared. But it was not yet done. On the ship's maiden voyage to New York, it had sailed only as far as Hastings when a boiler exploded, ripping the heart out of the expensive interior and killing five men. This was just the first in a series of calamities.

Seeing his dream become a nightmare was literally the death of Brunel. Russell went out of business and then started up again, with the benefit of Navy contracts. In January 1860, wracked as always by money problems and chewing his fingernails waiting for payment of an arbitration award in his favour against the *Great Eastern*'s owners, we see the first hard evidence of his ties to Overends, those generous lenders of last resort to shipbuilders and operators in distress. On the security of progress payments owed by the Admiralty, Russell borrowed an initial £15,000, not a great sum but every penny helped. Edwards reappears as supervisor of 'the financial arrangements connected with my factory', as Russell accepted in a letter to Edwards dated 1 January, which also obliged Russell to pay 'any commission due to you'. We are so often reminded that the world of The Corner House was curiously small. When it became clear that as a business venture the *Great Eastern* was a great white elephant, John Lever, ever alert for a quick profit, put in a cheekily low offer to buy it for the Galway Line, the middleman being none other than Edward Edwards. The offer was turned down. But as we shall see the *Great Eastern*, shorn of glamour and glory, turns up again in the final stage of our story and leads us back to our opening page.

Russell went bankrupt in 1861 and, though discharged in 1862, he was finally forced to give up shipbuilding and turn from the drama of the yard to the humdrum drawing board as a naval designer. His new profession did not curb his entrepreneurial instincts. He became entangled as the middle man in an American Civil War arms deal, which characteristically ended with both supplier and customer screaming that Russell had pocketed their money.

In London shipping's boom years, yards rarely stood empty for long. The Millwall Yard's next tenant was Charles John Mare, another Overends' bad debt waiting to happen. That will be no surprise; nor by now will be the jack-in-the-box appearances of Edwards.

It is easy to dismiss Mare as a charismatic playboy and gambler, which he was, and a poor businessman, which he may have been. But he knew how to build ships, or rather he had the vision of how to do it and the gift for attracting brilliant engineers and naval architects as partners. Sharing with Fairbairn that burning Victorian drive to apply the force of new technology, Mare was one of the pioneers of the iron hull; his was the first yard to integrate iron founding into the shipbuilding process, creating what was by any standard an important industrial complex. Though there is no suggestion that he was of Quaker stock, in his gift for mastering and harnessing new techniques, Mare was much in the mould of the Society's early industrialists. He also emulated them in his 'enlightened self-interest' for his workers, though in his personal life he was far closer to the flashy David Ward Chapman, not least as 'a familiar figure at Brighton during the season' and a 'warm supporter of horse racing' with a stable at Newmarket and estates in Cheshire and Staffordshire. Like Chapman, Mare was a lavish entertainer with what today might be called a 'trophy' wife, the rich, beautiful high-Society daughter of the timber merchant Peter Rolt, MP for Greenwich. One rather breathless press report of the time claimed that Mrs Mare had once been a lady-in-waiting to Queen Victoria; the Royal Archives at Windsor do not bear this out. Like Albert Grant, and many other self-promoting men of business, Mare himself ran – unsuccessfully – for Parliament, a self-indulgent foray which cost him £16,000; multiplied by fifty this is a staggering sum and it is hard to imagine quite where it all went.

Like Edwards, Mare had been called to the Bar, but when his father died in 1837, he sold the family estate and went into iron shipbuilding with Thomas Ditchburn, a talented naval engineer, who was 'Mr Inside' to Mare's ebullient 'Mr Outside'. They started out at the Dickensian-sounding Dudman's Dock in Deptford making small paddle steamers, entering a closed trade that resented the upstarts; their first yard was torched by jealous wooden hull builders. Undeterred, Mare and Ditchburn moved up to larger passenger and warships, and the partnership ran successfully until 1844, when Mare's burgeoning ambitions outstripped Ditchburn's. Mare took over the Orchard and Bow Creek shipyard, now Trinity Wharf, as the site of C. J. Mare and Co., expensively rebuilt and equipped. By 1853, in the words of Professor Tony Arnold, the painstaking historian of the London iron shipbuilders, 'never before had the firm's output been so high or its prospects so encouraging', something men might well have said of Overends around the same time.

In another of the coincidences that riddle our story, several of the vessels which slid into the Thames in those busy years to cheers and the blast of sirens, had been commissioned by the General Screw Steamship Company, which ran them on the first mail service between London and Cape Town, later extending its reach to India. Scott Russell built the *Pacific* and the *Adelaide*, and Mare the ill-fated *Argo*, the *Jason*, the *Brazil* and the *Golden Fleece*. In 1857,

General Screw went out of business and its ships were taken over by another company, which soon, in Xenos' phrase, 'also came to grief'. At this point, Edward Edwards, the second failed company's Official Assignee, sidles on to the scene. Advertising the fleet for sale, he did not have to look far for a buyer, none other than John Orrell Lever, who was being financed by Overends. Lever first used the ships on an abortive venture to operate a service to Brazil and then sold them to the Galway Line, at rather higher prices than he had paid.

Meanwhile at Millwall the contracts rolled in and at the peak Mare had a workforce of over 3,000 men. Back-of-the-envelope costing, poor accounting and an ill-judged foray into ironworks' contracts for the Westminster, Menai Straits and Saltash bridges and the roof of Fenchurch Street station, all of which were taken on for prestige rather than profit, meant that money rolled out even faster.

In September 1855, Mare went bankrupt in a welter of debts totalling some £400,000, about £20 million today. His affairs were put in the hands of the Official Assignee – at this point in the story there are no prizes for guessing his name.

In the aftermath of the bankruptcy, Mare was spared much pressure and many awkward questions by Edwards' deft touch in arranging a 'private settlement' with a committee of creditors, chaired by Mare's father-in-law Peter Rolt; conflicts of interest were not confined to the much maligned Edwards. The settlement, for a few shillings in the pound, was not without its critics. Short-changed creditors claimed bitterly that Rolt had bought up a large amount of Mare's debts himself, giving him the votes needed to force the other creditors into settlement.[31]

In 1859, with the brazen resilience characteristic of so many Victorian entrepreneurs, Mare re-emerged as a shipbuilder on the Isle of Dogs, but now on its western shores, taking over Russell's space at the Millwall Yard. In Russell's day, the Yard had been mortgaged to Martin's Bank, but when Mare took over, Overends took on effective ownership of the Yard by taking over the debt. True to form they bought a totally illiquid asset of dubious value by putting into circulation another paper edifice of ninety day Bills, kick starting another misjudged deal which would cost them at least £450,000 and maybe half as much again (between £20 and £30 million today).

Mare was now running the biggest iron shipbuilding works in Britain. By Victorian standards he treated his 5,000 men well, with a half day on Saturday, though the workday in the week was from 6 a.m. to 6 p.m., punctuated by an 8.30 a.m. breakfast break and a lunch hour. The Yard had rowing and cricket clubs; even a library and a winter programme of lectures, which was well attended. Though it might be a stretch to apply the term to modern Millwall Football Club fans, Thomas Wright, who wrote a study of the Isle in this period, commented that the shipyard workers were 'admirers of muscular Christianity', preoccupied in the summer months with 'boat racing, foot racing and other athletic sports, and flocked eagerly to boxing matches'. Wright was struck by the preponderance of Scottish workers who had moved down from the Clyde; the area had 'a very comfortable little kirk' and pubs such as 'The Burns' and 'The Highland Mary' reminded the men of home. 'It must be confessed that on the island the public houses are a much greater success than the kirk,' he sighed.

Mare built for the British, the Italians and the Russians, including a huge iron shield for the Tsar's Kronstadt fortress. He expanded back across the Thames into a yard at Deptford and employed experienced and energetic managers. But he was to learn yet again that high business volumes did not necessarily mean high profits, or for that matter any profits at all. As with the other elements of the story, the figures are hard to disentangle, but the Millwall Yard was twice reorganised. The second time in 1864 was when Mare departed and The Corner House, feeling the pressure of juggling with short-term finance to try to keep another large business afloat, decided, or more likely were persuaded, that a public offering of shares was the way out. In their small, introverted world, to whom should they, or could they, turn to but the dapper Albert Grant, whom they had first met when he had melted so much paper through the Mercantile Discount Company.

15

The Baron

We have lost sight of Grant. It is time to bring him back into our narrative and catch up with his remarkable trajectory as it intersects again with the macabre world of Overends. Mercantile had gone out of business in 1860, loaded well past danger level on the Plimsoll line with 'finance' paper, now good only for papering the walls of its Abchurch Lane offices. Just a few weeks before its collapse it had reported a year of 'prosperity' and declared a generous dividend. Shocked shareholders were left nursing losses while Grant banked a carefully pre-arranged contractual pay off of several thousand pounds.

Following a prudent spell out of the City limelight and insulated from the complaints of his shareholders, there emerged from the ashes of Gottheimer, the Phoenix of Albert Grant; company promoter, the man behind the new and supposedly all-powerful finance houses the Imperial Mercantile Credit Association and the Credit Foncier and Mobilier of England. His promotion of the company that built the Galleria in Milan was rewarded by the King of Italy with the accolade of Commander of the Order of St Maurice and Lazare, and the title of 'Baron'. Grant's enemies claimed he had slipped the financially pressed monarch a fat fee for the favour, circulating a jeering couplet around the Stock Exchange:

> Kings can titles give, but honour can't,
> So a title without honour's but a barren Grant.[32]

Though many in the City rightly suspected him, not many shunned him, much as later greedy bankers and brokers who should have known better would flock to do profitable business with Robert

Maxwell as he looted his companies' pension funds. Fees and commissions cover a multitude of sins, all the more if the sins are only rumours. Grant acquired an additional veneer of popularity through share tips and well-paid sinecure directorships he could offer to those whose names or titles looked good on the corporate letterhead. He was a fount of lavish hospitality. None of that shielded him from being sneered at for his pushiness, his pretensions, his flashiness and, more validly, for his reputation for fleecing the unsophisticated middle-class investor with his 'bubble' companies, whose shares were pushed by bribed journalists and prices manipulated by backstage operations. All of which was true. However, he was not the only player in this lucrative game and his investors were as greedy as they were gullible. Above all of course, this being England, he was despised for his success as well as his Jewish roots, usually behind his back. As he once eloquently put it himself, his reputation was always 'at the mercy of backbiters and slanderers in holes and corners who lick your boots by sunlight and assail your honour by candlelight'.

Many rogues are shrewd, but Grant had a formidable intellect. Hardly surprisingly given the trail of commercial wreckage he left in his wake, he was constantly embroiled in litigation, and a speech he made before the Lord Chief Justice shows a supple mind, a mastery of the law, wit and a gift for eloquent, if prolix, advocacy; the printed copy runs to 258 pages.

A 'Selected List' of Grant-promoted companies circulated by a group of his shareholder victims is a catalogue of multinational mendacity. As well as Emma Silver and the ventures with which we are concerned, he dangled before investors the glittering prospects for the Imperial Bank of China, India and Japan, the China Steamship and Labuan Coal Company, the General Irrigation and Water Supply of France, the Central Uruguay Railway Company of Monte Video, the Odessa Waterworks Company and the Imperial Land Company of Marseilles, among many others. He also had time for the domestic market, peddling shares in the more homely Somerset and Dorset Railway, the Louth and Lincoln Railway, and even the Nantyglo and Blaina Ironworks in Ebbw Vale, whose long and tangled history of labour exploitation and unrest was characteristically not mentioned in the share offering circular. Not all the companies on the list had met their final end by the time it was circulated, but even so the table showed that the £25 million raised had already shrivelled in market value to £5.6 million. Grant's technique was not that complicated, nor given the infancy of company law was it fraudulent, at least technically, however shrilly the shorn investors screamed. To call it a 'confidence trick' is to do less than justice to a well-honed operation, which depended as much on the greed of those investors as it did on Grant's ability as a conjurer; the audience know the magician is deceiving them, but they want so badly to believe their eyes rather than their common sense. The Victorian barrister Montague Williams, who penned a thinly disguised portrait of Grant in his autobiography, stressed the illusion of wealth and power. Grant's City offices, which at one point were in Lombard Street just a few doors from The Corner House and a far cry from the rabbit warren of Abchurch Lane, were designed to impress, 'built in the most costly style'. At the top of the broad marble staircase hovered a deferential pageboy, taking visitors' cards, and passing them to Grant on a sliver salver as he shuttled, smooth and serene, in and out of the several Board meetings simultaneously taking place in the half-dozen panelled conference rooms. Grant's clothes were in the same 'most costly manner' as his office, tailored by Henry Poole of Savile Row; Williams recalls his 'well cut velvet jacket, and a double breasted white waistcoat, across which hung a gold and turquoise watch chain . . . I don't think I ever saw a man more calculated to inspire persons with confidence.' Fortunately for today's international bankers, the firm of Henry Poole has outlasted Grant and still has in its dusty leather-backed ledgers the entries showing, in neat copperplate, his expensive penchant for alpaca, cashmere and doeskin.

The second essential ingredient was a flow of investors to whom this display of corporate 'flash' was the hallmark of success and the virtual guarantee of profits. Among them, Williams recalled, were 'noblemen, officers in the Army, clergymen, fashionably attired ladies, and mothers and wives of the middle class'. Though Grant always denied it, his enemies claimed his clerks combed obituary columns, Army and Navy retirement lists and Church notices in *The Times* to build what nowadays would be called a 'database' of wealthy widows, pensioned officers and rich bachelor clerics to be targeted with offers they could not refuse by his army of Stock Exchange half-commission touts.

The third leg to this Bermuda Triangle, into which so much money disappeared, was an unregulated Stock Market, which did not require much in a prospectus beyond fine words and a few distinguished names on the Board. The names, also procured by agents working on commission, were often given a large fee or a parcel of shares for agreeing to join; they were not usually called on to do more than 'come to sign their names, take a glass of sherry and a biscuit and pocket their two or three guineas' for each meeting. The more illustrious the names, the better. In 1864, Lord Derby noted in his diary that 'Lord Claude Hamilton is full of a steam navigation company of which he is Chairman. The difficulty now is to find a peer or titled person not engaged in this kind of business. Lord Elcho last week refused £1,000 a year to be Chairman of the Millwall Iron Company. I have had half a dozen similar offers . . .'

The shares were then vigorously promoted by a venal press and their prices ramped by surreptitious dealings, fuelled with money slipped to the seamier Stock Exchange jobbers by Grant from the company's own funds until the day of reckoning came. When it did and the frantic public rushed to sell, buyers were thin on the ground. Grant and his associates had long since pocketed their profits and moved on to the next deal and the next set of victims, like morning-coated muggers.

To judge from the fawning profile of Grant it published on his fortieth birthday, the editor of the magazine *Spy* was among those on his payroll; the *New York Times* declared flatly that the article was 'one of his most recent investments'. 'Banker. An art critic, a man of taste, an *homme de salon*, a millionaire in money and a statesman by household suffrage,' it swooned. The latter phrase was a convoluted way of underscoring Grant's election as MP for Kidderminster, helped by local bribery on a scale profligate even by the standards of the time.

Spy suggested that Grant was being eyed as a coming man by both the Government and the Liberal opposition. 'But his enormous occupations will probably prevent him from acceding for some time to any proposals that may be made to him and he remains therefore a future rather than a present Chancellor of the Exchequer.' 'For some time' is a nice touch, which suggests that the words were Grant's own dictation, even though, as David McKie has pointed out, the view from the political heights was more nuanced. Lord Derby observed that Grant had 'done too many dirty acts to be whitewashed, and too many that are useful to be neglected'.

Grant was a pragmatic philanthropist. His gifts were large but chosen to promote Grant even more than the public good. As Osbert Sitwell, product of a later generation, elegantly put it, he 'was almost the first Englishman to realise the possible personal benefits to be derived from the practice of public benevolence combined with a high patriotism', a realisation without which the twenty-first-century Honours Lists would be painfully short of names. A Landseer for the National Portrait Gallery was small beer compared to his dramatically self-aggrandising gesture in 1873. Having bought the 'neglected area of Leicester Fields occupied by dead cats and other refuse surmounted by a broken statue of George I', he converted it into handsome gardens complete with statues of the artists Joshua Reynolds and William Hogarth, the surgeon John Hunter and Sir Isaac Newton, all of whom had lived in or around the area in its palmier days.[33]

He then donated the site to London. Not everyone cheered. The *New York Times* told its readers about Londoners' 'soreness . . . they do not like to accept favours from Mr Grant'. The Prince of Wales declined to attend the opening, a prudent move since men were hired to walk around at the ceremony with sandwich boards displaying messages that attacked Grant in doggerel, whose metre had distant reverberations of the elephantine style of William Topaz MacGonagall, Victorian Dundee's deservedly underrated 'poet and tragedian':

. . . But will the world forget these flowers of Grants
Are but the products of his City 'plants'?
And who for shady walks will gave him praise
For wealth thus spent, when gained in shadier ways?
In short, what can he hope to gain from this affair
Save to connect his name with one thing Square!

Lord Derby's diary said much the same thing in less contrived prose: 'In any man this would be called an act of public spirit; in a disreputable speculator who has more than once narrowly escaped prosecution for fraud it is an ingenious device for putting himself right with the world. And in that point of view it will be a very good investment.'

As the problems of the Millwall Yard mounted, and The Corner House's other difficulties made it ever harder for them to raise money to keep the pyramid from collapse, the beleaguered partners turned to Grant, the financial magician, to pull a rabbit out of the hat, or in language Lord Derby would have understood, to raise fresh capital by convincing Stock Market investors that the Yard was not a spavined nag but a thoroughbred, destined to win many major races.

16

Millwall's Last Hurrah

Riding high, Grant now ran two share-promoting houses; The Imperial Mercantile Credit Association[34], of which Xenos' nemesis from Smyrna, Henry Barker, was the manager, and the Credit Foncier and Mobilier of England. They had largely overlapping Boards, which, not unlike our own cast, included two leading members of the London Greek banking community, a Manchester merchant, an eventually bankrupt Irish railway contractor who was the prime mover of the National Gallery of Ireland, a director of the London Chatham and Dover Railway and Lord Otho Fitzgerald, a minor courtier dismissed by an anonymous contemporary as 'a mercenary little fortune hunter'. In April 1864 these two firms, the Castor and Pollux of speculative share offerings, jointly touted to a still credulous public, the shares of the Isle of Dogs yard now grandly renamed the Millwall Iron Works, Shipbuilding and Graving Dock Co. Ltd. The latter's directors (minus the circumspect Lord Elcho), with David Ward Chapman as deputy chairman, told investors, in a formula which would later be used to similar spurious effect, that 'the profitable results of the undertaking may be considered as assured'. The offer which, reflecting the 'anything goes' markets of the time, shared its Stock Exchange debut with the Royal Sea House Hotel, Worthing, and another Grant promotion – with loud Melmotte echoes – the Imperial Bank of China, was Grant at his classic prime: assets injected into the new company at an inflated value, press 'puffing' and price ramping by Grant's tame brokers.

The offering was a success and, with the company floated, some permanent capital locked in and the delusional safeguard of uncalled share capital as a fallback, everything seemed set fair for the future. For the next two years orders rolled in and ships rolled down the slipway. But the jinx had not gone away. Adapting an ancient Greek saying, the twentieth-century writer, Cyril Connolly, quipped that 'Whom the gods wish to destroy they first call promising'. Overend & Gurney had been the epitome of promise for many years, and if the prospectus was to be believed, so was the Millwall Yard. The gods did not even bother to invent a new punishment, but simply decreed a replay of the *Great Eastern* débâcle.

It came on 17 March 1866, just a short while before Overends' own death rattle.

London was cold, and the Isle of Dogs even colder, with a skin-scraping wind slicing off the Thames into a yard packed with chilled dignitaries, headed by the portly Prince of Wales. They were there to launch HMS *Northumberland*, a 7,000-ton warship, one of the heaviest vessels to be baptised in the Thames since the unhappy *Great Eastern*. Red-coated bandsmen fifed, drummed and puffed their shiny brass trombones. A beribboned bottle of champagne crunched across the ship's towering bows as the 'brilliant and numerous assembly' watched – and watched and watched. The ship slid a few feet down the slipway and then stopped, stuck fast. Divers were sent down into the freezing water to try to see if they could free the keel. Tugs fussed and tooted trying to haul the hull into the water. In the end, the bandsmen packed up their instruments and marched away to their tea, the crimson-faced chairman did his best to mollify the Prince and the 'brilliant assembly' dispersed, muttering. Over the weekend cables were strung across the river and sixty men strained at two huge capstan on Deptford dock, trying to tug the *Northumberland* free by brute force. It took four weeks, four specially built wooden flotation tanks known as 'Camels', hydraulic rams, extra costs of some £12,000 and the blessing of an exceptionally high tide before the slipway gave up its grip and the 500 feet of 5-inch armour-plated cast-iron hull, with an internal sheath of 5 inches of teak, finally floated free.

The cost of the abortive launch hit the Millwall company hard and it fell back on the next line of defence, making a call on its horrified shareholders for another instalment of the unpaid capital. Those unfortunates included Robert Birkbeck and others linked to

Overends. Already up to their necks in a swirling tide of problems and demands, the call must have come as the last terrible turn of the screw. The waves of worry were washing all the way to Norwich. When in the time ahead the creditors were picking over Overends' bones, it came to light that The Corner House had only recovered a derisory £7 10s from the collapse of Millwall, and that no more was expected. Surprisingly, this was because Overends' security turned out to be second in line; the Norwich bank had the first mortgage and the luckless Corner House creditors and shareholders had only what was splendidly called 'the equity of redemption', or in lay terms, whatever might be left after the Norwich debt was paid off. On the face of it this is more than a touch incestuous, and it is odd that none of the vigilant and vigilante creditors pressed for details. It was fortunate too, since the details of the deal are not clear, that it included the release of Robert Birkbeck from liability for the unpaid calls on his Millwall shares, cancellation of Millwall Bills held by the old firm, and payments to both Martin's Bank and the liquidators of the short-lived public company. This shuffling was perhaps no more than a last-minute effort by the Norwich partners to plug the hole in the dike. But it did not save the day. The yard closed, the fires in the furnaces died back to grey ash. Where there had been the hiss of steam, the wail of workshop sirens, the clang of hammers, men swearing and shouting, there was now silence, broken only by the mewling of gulls on the Thames and the murmur of the liquidators' clerks as they chalked sales prices on the rusty stock of iron.

Before we leave the fatal Isle and watch bemused as the drama plays out, one question nags: what were Overends doing there in the first place?

17

East Enders

The connection between Quaker bankers, with their roots in East Anglia, and the Isle of Dogs is not immediately obvious. The links are speculative, thin gruel rather than a feast of archival facts, but they do seem to be grounds for guessing that Gurneys arrived there by a process of long-term familiarity rather than the scheming of Edward Edwards.

Victorian East London conjures up another stereotype of slums, docks and factories, poverty, disease, drink and Jack the Ripper. In the first half of the nineteenth century, this was true of its pestilential inner core, but beyond Stratford the country began. Trollope hunted there and, as we saw, Walthamstow, long since overtaken by Kensington and Fulham as the senior banker's habitat of choice, was home to Barclays, Gurneys and Bevans. Henry Ford Barclay, later to become a director of the 'new' Overends and a partner in the Norwich bank, lived at 'Monkhams', a mile or two further out in Woodford. A short carriage ride to the south in Whipps Cross, the 'Barclay Estate' is still an area touted as 'desirable' by local agents. In an 1851 survey quoted by Elizabeth Isichei, Essex and Hertfordshire stand out in the South of England as counties with a particularly high proportion of Quakers relative to the general population. Closer still to East London was Samuel Gurney's estate, brought to the marriage by his wife. Since the 1830s, he had lived in what is now West Ham, and on most business days travelled down the Bow Road through East London on his way to and from the City. Over the years he had become a major donor to East London causes; a drinking fountain was put up at Stratford to recognise his generosity. Gurney endowed the Brickfields School, later West Ham and Stratford British School, and both he and the shipbuilder

Charles Mare, were much involved with fundraising for the Poplar Hospital for Accidents. While still at the Orchard Creek Yard, Mare had been shocked when he realised that because there was no closer hospital, one of his men, badly hurt in an accident, had to be jolted on a cart along the cobbled streets all the way to the London Hospital in Whitechapel Road. He died before he could be treated. This prompted Mare to put his energies behind the construction of the Poplar Hospital to specialise in industrial injuries. As the Hospital opened in 1858, and the fundraising must have preceded it by some time, we can see that Mare and the Gurneys knew each other long before the Millwall adventures began.

Samuel Gurney had also been a major benefactor of the London Hospital, another major East End institution. Henry Edmund Gurney and John Henry Gurney were among the City worthies who served as governors over the years, again suggesting a level of acquaintance and a commitment to the area. Interestingly, so too did Charles Mare.

The Gutta Percha Company, where Henry Ford Barclay made his fortune, had its first factory in Stratford, before moving across the river to Greenwich. As his chemical business grew, Luke Howard, definer of clouds, moved his factory from Plaistow to Stratford and then to Ilford.

What does this all add up to? It suggests that to this generation of London Quakers, the East End and the Isle of Dogs were not uncharted, hostile waters, no *terra incognita* peopled by Cockney dockers, Irish labourers, Scots shipwrights and Jewish immigrants, but an area whose people they knew and, more relevantly, whose business potential, with shipbuilding as its core, they could readily appreciate. Once involved for good or ill in shipbuilding, it was not a long voyage into financing the entrepreneurial ship buyers. When those buyers fell on hard times, the temptation, as our story shows, to try to 'work things out' by asset shuffling and the certainty of more debt, rather than admit mistakes and bad debts, created the fatal vortex.

Grant too had more to do with the area than was at first apparent. The Corner House had resorted to his dexterous promotional services to take the Yard public. We now know that just two days before the Millwall Yard collapsed, Grant's Credit Foncier and its Doppelganger Imperial Mercantile, had jointly sponsored the offering of shares in a new company which owned – or, more accurately, claimed it had the right to acquire – 198 acres of freehold land right next door to the Millwall Yard. They told investors that they planned to build a huge dry dock for ship repairs with the balance of the land developed for housing; a forerunner of the various twentieth-century Docklands' schemes. 'It is believed that so sound a scheme . . . is seldom brought before the public,' Grant's prospectus writers purred. Insulated from 'all character of speculation so often the leading feature in all public companies . . . it should doubtless be appreciated by those who, while expecting good profits from their investments, yet look for good security.' As with so many of Grant's offerings, it was a mere chimera. More to the point, it is hard to see how Grant can have become involved with an ambitious project next door to the Yard without having some dialogue with The Corner House, as the latter's main backers.

Grant's appetite for grand titles gives another elusive hint that he had been active in East London. In 1868, he was offered the honorary post of a deputy lord lieutenant, not, as one might expect, in one of the counties in the West Midlands where he had his parliamentary constituency, or in Sussex where he had a home, but in Tower Hamlets, at the top of the Isle of Dogs. No doubt, Grant being Grant, favours of 'hot' stocks and low prices, or offers of something even more tangible, lay behind it. Nevertheless it does hint at some broader interest in the locality, even if it only helped him spot that such an arcane title existed. He lived up to the title, paying his tailors, Henry Poole, over £3,000 in today's values for a silk-lined uniform replete with gold braid epaulettes and a sword belt.

The last, but in its odd coincidence not the least, interesting link is the recondite relationship between the Gurney family and the Thames shipbuilders, via the concrete bulk of West Ham United Football Club's Upton Park stadium. As we have seen, Charles Mare was a good employer; canteens, libraries and organised sport were features of his original Thames Ironworks, which his father-in-law Peter Rolt took over, and later of the Millwall Yard. The Thames Ironworks football team became West Ham United, still nicknamed 'The Hammers' from the Victorian shipwrights' heavy metal-working tools.[35] The original Upton Park estate was Samuel Gurney's home. With Ham House, a Jacobean manor, at its centre, it ran north to what is now the complex of streets – Clova, Sprowston and, in a nice reminder of those Norfolk roots, Norwich and Earlham – bounded by the railway line into Forest Gate Station.

The southern edge is marked by what is now the Jewish cemetery in East Ham. After Samuel's death, the estate was broken up and sold off, and soon covered with houses, cemeteries, schools and shops, an entire new community in the driving Victorian spirit of renewal.[36]

As the estate was broken up, what is now the stadium site, once part of Samuel's extensive gardens, passed into the hands of the local Roman Catholic diocese, which sold it to the 'The Teetotallers' in 1897.[37] West Ham's tribal chant, 'I'm Forever Blowing Bubbles', now swells over a featureless suburban landscape, where the loudest noise was once the squeal of excited Gurney grandchildren and the shrieks of old Samuel's prized peacocks. Where gardeners once hoed and pruned and old Samuel admired his magnificent flowers, shaven headed shell suited fans now shamble into the ground between lines of police vans and yelping Alsatians, like the inmates of an East European penal settlement being released into the exercise yard. This curious, almost circular, passage from Gurney hands back to an offshoot of a Mare-related enterprise may just be coincidence; if so, it is at the limits of the word.

18

Storm Cones

We now know, from outside, much of what the partners of Overends were grappling with, the chronicles of disaster which, amazingly, were successfully kept from the world at large through the years of struggle and, even more incredibly, through the public share offering.

But what was going on inside The Corner House? To adapt a phrase from the Nixon era of American politics, 'What did they know and when did they know it?' And why when they finally faced reality, did they adopt a solution so fraught with further risk?

The first daring dips into the piranha-pool of the 'finance business' came in 1859. There were no reports to be filled in for regulators, no shareholders expecting quarterly results, no securities analysts asking awkward questions. Reflecting the Victorian way of signalling bad weather, *The Times'* weather reports all too frequently advised that 'storm cones were hoisted' in a series of coastal spots, a phrase not out of place in a saga so involved with shipping. The cones went up in Birchin Lane in 1861 and the hoister was John Henry Gurney.

Forty-two years old, rich, cultured and sensible, he had up till then been an inactive Corner House partner, though he was involved in the Norwich bank and even more involved in ornithology. He soon became a central figure in trying to steer The Corner House out of trouble and finally reaching for the flawed solution.

Whether his London partners owned up to the difficulties, whether he spotted them for himself by a careful reading of the private ledgers, or whether he was alerted by a loyal senior clerk – not improbable in a tight-knit family firm – we do not know. But they must have come as a nasty shock, even to a man who knew that banking always involved some losses. As Bagehot wrote later, 'everyone must feel sympathy with him personally, great as is the evil that his firm has brought upon the world . . . he was resident in Norfolk engaged upon the quiet local business of the bank there and had no share in the rash local management which has ruined the family and disgraced its name.' Even so he was personally liable for London's debts – and, as the richest partner, the one on whom most of the burden of a failure would fall if the others could not meet their obligations – and he might be faulted for being too trusting too long.

His surviving letters show him to be a shrewd and decent individual, and with hindsight it is clear that he should have simply shut the whole 'finance' business down. However, these decisions are never as clear-cut. The reality of the time was that his London partners were convinced, based on their own psychological need to be bolstered by Edwards' ingenious advice, that ways could and would be found to work their way through the nastiness buried in the books. They also seem to have convinced their polite Norwich inquisitor, who was, after all, not an active partner and did not know all the details. The Quaker urge for consensus, whether in the affairs of the Society or in their own businesses, may also have played on him; who was he to rock the boat? There may be echoes here of his father's sage advice to fellow Quakers, reprinted by a later generation of Friends in 1854: 'Never act from motives of fear contrary to thy judgment. When thou art anxious on any subject do not magnify evil in the anticipation and learn to expect good rather than evil.'

Edwards, who had by now been fire-fighting for two years, tells us that when John Gurney saw what was going on, he was 'frightened at the involvement of the House' admitting to him privately that the 'House was in a mess', but 'nothing which it could not perfectly pull through'. According to Edwards, Gurney 'begged me to continue my supervision' of the junk portfolio and above all, to keep the bad deals 'out of the bankruptcy court by every means in our power' so as to give the core business a chance to survive.

John Gurney may have been more passionate about bitterns than banking, but he knew his trade and if Edwards was really the 'villain of the piece', as he was later painted by the high-powered legal team whose job it was to defend the Overends' directors, Gurney would surely have sensed it early on. Instead, he clearly accepted Edwards as a man who had his hands around the problems and was adroit in offering solutions.

Edwards was no doubt a greedy double dealer who rubbed shoulders with an unpleasant crowd, notably Grant and Barker. But such was the world, or the underworld, of the Official Assignee. Nor is there any doubt that he must take considerable responsibility for advice which led to the problems escalating beyond any hope of resolution. But the responsibility for the decisions was, in the final analysis, that of the firm's partners, not their advisor, and they were men of business, not naïve country parsons. Moreover, if his mission, which was never contradicted, was to keep the crippled companies alive at all costs, his advice would inevitably have involved strategies with a higher degree of risk. It is hard to argue that his appetite for fees and commissions, and his disregard for conflicts of interest, did not taint the objectivity of his advice. But his account of how he got to The Corner House, and his role in their affairs, was never disputed on the record by the main protagonists, nor for that matter his assertion that they were all well aware that he took fees wherever he could get them on the deals he handled. We shall tell more of Edwards' side of the story later.

Though there were a few knowing rumours after John Gurney's arrival that 'Overends are not to go on like this any more. The Norfolk people have come to town and shut the till,' this did not happen. But for the partners themselves, the till was indeed closed. John Gurney may have hesitated to write off the bad business, but he had no compunction about forcing the working partners to count the cost, insisting that none of the firm's profit from its core discount business – then running at an average of £220,000 a year, or £10 million today – was to be shared out. It had to stay in the business to balance the losses oozing out of the basement drains. For the richer partners this may have been irksome; for Ward Chapman with his extravagant lifestyle, it must have been a serious blow and may help to understand the terrible lapse of judgement he later committed, with Edwards' connivance, and which so shocked his partners and the public when it came to light.

The four years that followed 1861 were the years of living dangerously. Having followed the twists and turns of Xenos, Peter Daly and Charles Mare, and the later history of Millwall, we know that there were also other problems. What we do not know is what it felt like to grapple with these things day by day. The continuing profitable flow of trade-related Bills business provided some cushion, some reassurance, but equally it ratcheted up the pressures. If the ever-sensitive money markets had an inkling of the existence, let alone the size, of the leprous junk portfolio, their blind faith in Overends would have been fatally corroded. Deposits would trickle or, even worse, flood out, and the mainstream business would wither and die. So to the world Overends had to show a brave face, even a proud face, and the anxieties kept for private moments among the partners and their conclaves with the dexterous Edwards.

It came out in later evidence that for those troubled years the profits were not even 'ascertained'; in other words, there was no attempt even to draw up annual accounts. Any auditor going through the books would see all too soon that the all-powerful Corner House was more like a charnel house. It would be interesting to know what the firm's loyal managers and staff suspected or knew about what was going on. Even though the 'exceptional' deals may have been booked to a partners' private ledger, or some similar accounting device, to try to keep the knowledge to a small circle, the underlying Bills were flowing in and out daily. As the pressures mounted, The Corner House was reaching out to other banks and to Grant's Imperial Mercantile to remortgage some of those jinxed ships and railway bonds they held as security. They also persuaded Imperial and others to accept Bills, backed by a Corner House guarantee of payment, so that worthless paper could be renewed and camouflaged with the endorsement of a new name. They even pledged to another bank, title documents to a cargo of wheat that Xenos had given them as security. The staff must have suspected that odd things were happening, but family loyalty and worry about losing their jobs reduced the risk of gossip.

The partners were in fact acting out a script painfully familiar to anyone who has been involved in a failing business. Mistakes, small at first, have been made, but no one wants to admit them. Those in charge are convinced in the face of all reason that the problems will solve themselves. They don't. They escalate. The Botox of 'creative accounting' is injected into the sagging figures (in Overends' case, the frequent use of 'front men' or sham structures as borrowers so that names such as Xenos or David Leopold Lewis did not show up in their ledgers). Half answers are preferred to whole truths and bad deals are kept on a cash-draining life support system instead of being allowed to die, in the forlorn hope of recovery. Seemingly experienced and resourceful advisors murmur as they take their fees that there is a cure for this disease. To mix a vegetative metaphor, weak straws are clutched at while the nettles are not grasped. The actors find that they can square their consciences by convincing themselves they are not telling outright lies. They do not have to. 'A cocktail of truth, falsity and evasion is a more powerful instrument of deception than undiluted falsehood', in the words of a senior London judge in a modern fraud case. Those at the centre are gripped by a sort of bipolar disorder. At the low points they wrap themselves up in a comfort blanket of self-delusion, muttering the mantra that the mess they are in is not their fault and that they are being got at; the problems must therefore be kept secret. Then the mood swing brings conviction that 'it will all work out fine if we can buy just a little more time'. There is never enough time. As in the case of Overends, some often unrelated outside event, malign serendipity, tugs the comfort blanket rudely away. As a Wall Street sage remarked after the Crash of 1987, 'It's only when the tide goes out that you find out who was swimming naked.'

The evidence given by a manager at the Crown Agents is a reminder of the comparison we made at the outset to demonstrate that nothing really changes. When it became clear in the early 1970s that their huge loans to the dapper, dexterous and devout property speculator William Stern were in jeopardy, the mood of terror in its Millbank offices must have been much as it was at Overends:

> We were living in a waking nightmare . . . we had so much with him by then, wrongly though it be, that he came in the category as we saw it of people whose collapse would trigger off our own collapse through a crisis of market confidence . . . During those difficult times we thought we were walking a tightrope of confidence in the market which we must not fall off; in other words we could only survive if we had a continuing ability to borrow . . .

Towards the end of 1864 Robert Birkbeck rounded on Edwards in a fury, yelling at him – uncharacteristically for a man of his quiet upbringing – to get out of The Corner House and never come back. In Edwards' words, he charged that 'my connection with the firm had been most injurious and that I had been the cause of all their losses'. None of those involved ever specified what had actually prompted the explosion. If we extrapolate from Xenos' account, it was most likely when it dawned on Birkbeck what a catastrophe it had been for the Galway Line, on Edwards' advice, to order those five new unsuitable and unprofitable ships at a staggering cost.

Though Henry Gurney did his best to calm Edwards down, saying soothingly that he did not share Birkbeck's harsh view, the partners nevertheless decided that, in modern Divorce Court parlance, the relationship had broken down irretrievably and Edwards had to go. He went, though with the balance of his contract paid up and armed with a generous testimonial to the 'assiduity which you displayed in attending to such matters as we placed under your care and also that we feel well satisfied whatever advice you gave us representing them was dictated by a regard for our interests and a desire on your part to promote them'. Though the pay-off was handled by David Ward Chapman, the flurry of letters that surrounded it makes it clear that Henry Gurney and Birkbeck were fully in the picture and no doubt agreed with Chapman's rationale, set out some years later in a letter his father forwarded to *The Times*.

The grim secrets had to be kept in the cellar; if not the business would die:

> Now the position we were in was simply this. Here was a man who . . . had become possessed of sufficient knowledge to have forced us to put up our shutters within 24 hours of his revelations, if he had chosen to make them. Now I ask you what would you have done under such circumstances. Would you not have smoothed him down in the best way you could and made the best terms in your power?

The words can be read as carrying a subtle implication that Edwards had applied pressure, blackmail even, but Chapman himself is not a reliable witness and if Edwards were the 'guilty man' of history, the threat of exposure is hardly the route he would have chosen. Moreover, the phrase 'become possessed of sufficient knowledge' can be read as suggesting yet again that Edwards was, as he claimed, an advisor who came to understand, and saw rather than caused, the problems he was asked to deal with, even though his dealings may have made the problems worse.

19

A False Dawn

John Gurney had been agitated and agitating since 1861, but it was not until 1865 that the cold light of reality finally pierced the dusty windows of The Corner House. They were close to bankruptcy. Though the mainstream business was still generating healthy profits, these were more than eaten up by the heavy day-to-day interest burden of financing the junk portfolio, leading to an annual net cash drain of some £500,000. This was unsustainable. None of Edwards' nostrums had worked. As we have just noted, it was also a burden that required some *legerdemain*. Even in a greedy market where high interest rates and commissions deodorised the smell of risk, it was becoming harder and harder to renew every ninety days or so the Bills which kept Millwall, Greek & Oriental, the various Galway emanations and their other bad dreams in business; thus the ship remortgaging and the use of guarantees and 'front men'. A London-based Italian merchant, a client of the private bankers Curries, had the good sense to check with them about a suggestion from Overends that he might like to earn a generous fee for simply putting his name on Bills drawn by one of their nominees. He took Curries' advice to steer clear. Curries became even more suspicious when Henry Edmund Gurney asked their senior partner a short time later if The Corner House could 'borrow money of us at a special rate against securities which seemed to me of doubtful value. I remember his indignation when I threw some doubt upon them, and his remark, "Do you presume to question the credit of Overend Gurney & Co.?" '

But the emperor had no clothes. When on the worst nights even the phlegmatic John Gurney must have jolted wide awake, sweating, he would have had to admit to himself the doleful truth that because the portfolio was worthless, and should have been written off, the firm actually had no capital. In a moral, if not yet at that time a legal sense, it was trading fraudulently. Here was another crossroads, and here again the partners took the wrong turning. They finally began to talk about the choices to a handful of trusted friends, notably the quartet of City worthies who were, as we shall see, about to join the Board and become unwitting companions in misfortune. We can only wonder if these frantic men ever talked to their wives about what was making them taciturn, abrupt, distracted, depressed and sleepless; one of those Victorian engravings of a ruined man, slumped and wilting in an armchair, staring blankly into the fire, all hope lost. If Trollope is any guide, as he should be, the wives were told little or nothing. If they asked questions they would have been told, gently or curtly depending on the man, that it was none of their business and nothing to worry about.

One idea after another was canvassed: new capital from friends, new partners and even a last-ditch effort, which must have been excruciatingly galling, to sell the firm to their conservative competitors, the National Discount Company, an offer the latter refused, no doubt having a good sense from the marketplace of how serious the problems were.

In the words of W. T. C. King, 'there seemed but one alternative to liquidation, the formation of a company' which would take over the Overends' partnership and would then sell shares to the public to replace the lost capital. With the mainstream business thus reinforced, the junk portfolio could fade discreetly into the back pages of the ledger, with the former partners meeting any shortfall out of their own assets. Limited companies had become a vehicle for investment and speculation after a change in the law in 1862, but were still regarded with some suspicion, rightly, as they were seized on by Grant and his fellow financiers as a handy tool for sucking up suckers' money; he cannot have been far away as this answer was canvassed. We do not know what was in their minds, but to modern eyes there may well have been other, better solutions. Almost anything would have been preferable to exposing a business which they well knew, though their shareholders would not, was on the knife-edge of bankruptcy, to the cruel manipulations of the Stock Exchange. To be at the mercy of speculators and each new wave of rumour, and even the minimal public scrutiny of the times, seems almost the ultimate in foolhardiness and disdain for investors. These were, of course, both Grant hallmarks. They knew him and his skills from the East India and Millwall share offers. They were using Imperial Mercantile as a 'front' for some of their Bills by adding its name, and Grant was far too shrewd not to have guessed why. Maybe he promised to provide some discreet background help in finding investors and pushing the share price to a confidence-boosting premium.

King takes the charitable view that 'this project was not as it at first may seem to be, an open fraud on the public. It was an honest attempt to segregate the valuable discount business from the rotten financing commitments and to provide for the gradual liquidation of the latter.' Whether even by mid-Victorian norms it was really 'honest', we shall see. When the truth came out, most commentators and the various judges who dug into the facts did not wholly agree. Nor, fatally, did it achieve the aim of separating the good from the rotten. Bagehot later suggested that, 'if the great loss had slept a quiet sleep in a hidden ledger – no-one would have been alarmed and the business of Overends might have existed until now', although he probably did not appreciate just how fast the notional profits were being overtaken by real losses. The way the deal was set up demonstrated the naïveté and lack of financial 'savvy' which got them into trouble in the first place. If going public was what Germans call *die Flucht nach vorn,* 'fleeing danger by advancing towards it', or less emotively 'taking the bull by the horns', the way it was done made a bad ending almost inevitable – for the wealth and reputation of the Overends' partners, for the public and maybe for the London financial system as a whole. What makes it all the more surprising is that the partners of the old firm – men by now on the edge of a nervous breakdown, men drowning in delusion, whose always suspect judgement must have totally deserted them – persuaded other City figures, men of reputation and experience, men with cool heads who knew the markets and who knew the real facts, to join them on the Board of the new company and that the deal made sense.

Thomas Gibb was a respected City banker, Harry Gordon was chairman of the Oriental Bank and William Rennie was senior partner of Cavan, Lubbock & Co., merchants and bankers. The fourth, Henry Ford Barclay, then forty years old, was a direct descendant of one of the Society's early thinkers, David Barclay 'The Apologist', and had married Samuel Gurney's younger daughter, Richenda, when he was twenty-one. He was a man in the classic Quaker mould. He too had been educated at Grove House. Though no doubt backed by adequate capital to start with, went on to make what his obituary called 'an ample fortune' with the Gutta Percha Company, whose resinous product was in huge demand for insulating the network of underwater cables spreading like weeds across the world's ocean beds. The only thing he had in common with Edwards was gout. In another human touch, it was nice to find out that in his spare time Barclay, whose Grove Park education had encouraged a latent mechanical aptitude, was an enthusiastic builder of clocks and mechanical engines.

What did the new men know? A letter, which surfaced during the various post-mortems, was carefully drafted. It was written by John Gurney to the new Board on behalf of the 'old' firm, no doubt as part of what lawyers today would call 'due diligence', or in lay terms, as evidence that on the one hand the old partners had disclosed there were problems, and on the other, that the new directors had asked the sort of questions prudent men of business might be expected to ask. However, it too was a gloss. It gave considerable detail about the firm's substantial profits from its core business, but though it admits to 'various transactions by way of investment, loan or discount which were entirely extraneous to the legitimate concerns of our business but upon which we unadvisedly entered', the staggering total of £4 million, or £200 million today, is not given. But as it was central to the problem and the solution, it must equally have figured large in the long discussions that led up to the share sale; discussions, some of them in John Gurney's St James's Square home, which were rooted on the one hand in trust, and on the other, in fear. The trusting new directors took what they were told at face value, concluding that they didn't need to bring in an accountant to audit the books. The fearful 'old' partners knew that if an outsider had even a brief glimpse of the ledgers, it would mean instant ruin when word of the horrors inevitably got out. To use a simile from more than half a century later, the old partners were like a First World War patrol, trapped in desperation in a waterlogged shell hole in no-man's land. The new directors loomed out of the mud as a gallant rescue party, half-aware that they might be risking their lives, but supremely confident they could all make it back through the barrage and German sniper fire to the safety of the British trenches and a cup of cocoa. Maybe they were using a sketch map drawn by Grant – one that did not show the minefields?

20

Buyer, Beware!

On 12 July 1865, even City men might have turned first to the story that the previous day the Gentlemen had beaten the Players by eight wickets after a two-day game at Lords. The result would have seemed entirely appropriate. The Gentlemen were just that; the Players were working-class professionals who played cricket for money – on a par, in the minds of many of those who read the story, with gamekeepers or tradesmen. The only cloud was the uninspiring batting of the Gentlemen's new star W. G. Grace, a lanky seventeen-year-old who had yet to bulk out into his iconic image as a white-flannelled giant with an Old Testament beard; his elder brother Edward had a far better game as a bowler. The class division (the professional of the Bolton Club in Lancashire lived up to the stereotype, probably provocatively, by wearing wooden clogs when he bowled) was another slice of Victorian double standards; as an amateur and 'Gentleman', Grace earned far more through appearance fees in his career than any of those who supposedly played for wages.

A second story was of more business interest and gossip value: Overend, Gurney & Co. was turning itself into one of the then new-fangled 'Limited Liability' companies and offering shares to outside investors; 'going public', in twenty-first-century City Page language.

As they brushed the toast crumbs out of their whiskers after breakfast, and later as they met their partners in City banking parlours, some of those with their fingers on the pulse of the markets wondered why, though not very loudly. As *The Times* reminded its readers, 'the name of Gurney is honourably known among men of business all over the world'. Rumours about the firm had come and gone across the City like wisps of fog for some years, but apart from the leather and spelter losses there were no hard facts, and the terminally metastasizing 'junk' cancer was a closely held secret. Moreover, as successive financial crises roiled the markets in the 1830s, 1847 and again ten years later, there had hardly been a banking name to which some rumour of poor judgement, a nasty loss, or impending calamity had not been attached. Crossing swords with the Gurneys and their network of banking and industrial families and friends was not advisable, and there were commissions to be had and handy dealing profits to be made from the share offering. So '*caveat emptor*' – 'let the buyer beware' – remained the City's lodestar, all the more since investors had, as always, learned nothing from earlier boom and bust cycles and were ready, in the financiers' slang, to 'fill their boots' with anything that looked like offering the chance of a quick profit. It was a time, as a Whitehall assessment of the period put it in rotund Victorian phrasing, when 'long continued prosperity in commercial affairs and the general wealth consequent on it have produced their ordinary results in encouraging speculation especially of a monetary or financial nature and fostering hopes of acquiring wealth by more speedy means than are presented by the ordinary methods of commercial industry'. In today's terms, the country was caught up in a speculative frenzy on a par with the dot.com bubble, a mood reflected by the *Bankers' Magazine*, when it gushed uncritically that in its reincarnation as a new public company Overends represented 'the greatest triumph of limited liability'.

Behind his editorial desk at *The Economist*, Bagehot was less euphoric and closer to the truth, commenting that the public might now learn more about Overends' navigation outside the mainstream Bill discounting business at which it was adept, into the altogether trickier currents of longer-term financing entanglements. As he put it, it was a 'matter of public notoriety' (the word then meant little more than it was 'quite well known') that for some time Overends had been doing business which, while 'not at all in general of an illegitimate or unprofitable character, was still of a sort different from those conducted by bill brokers 'pure and simple''. For Bagehot, the most compelling argument in favour of the transformation was that the new public company would be obliged to produce audited accounts. He was right in the sense that the public did learn more, but not until it was too late; while the company lived, no accounts ever saw the light of day. The share offering prospectus, published the day after the first brief report, sought to make up for a singular lack of hard facts – the substance of it ran to no more than 400 honeyed words – with a roster of the new directors, men 'with whom everyone would delight to do business', in Bagehot's view. An extra lustre of respectability was added by naming the Bank of England and another pillar of Quaker finance, which then had the rather clumsy if reassuringly rural name of Barclays, Bevan, Tritton, Twells & Co., as Overends' own bankers. The Barclays, Bevans and Gurneys had been linked by marriage, business and belief since the mid-1700s. To underscore that this was a 'community' effort, the stockbrokers handling the sale were Overends' accomplices in the failed banknote imbroglio, the Quaker house of Sheppards, Pelly & Allcard. It was not thought in the least odd to see the Bank's name coupled in apparent commercial harmony with the three firms which, just a few years earlier, had acted as a 'concert party' in that clumsily handled affair.

A sharp-eyed reader might have wondered about a bland reference to the former partners' guarantee that they would bear any loss on the assets to be transferred over to the new limited company. Its vagueness was to be at the heart of the accusations of fraud and deception levelled later at those involved, since they all knew only too well that a crippling proportion of those assets were indeed of a highly 'illegitimate or unprofitable character' and were in truth a ledger full of the worthless junk whose sorry history we have followed.

The meretricious 'financial engineering' behind the share scheme, which emerged later after Overends' collapse, must be attributable to some slick hand other than the family's, possibly an off-stage Albert Grant. It was simple, deceptively so. The Overends' partners would sell the entire business and 'goodwill' of their firm to the new limited company in exchange for shares. The new company would have the Overend & Gurney name and also the strength of a capital of £5 million in 100,000 £50 shares. But here lay one of many flaws: investors would pay up only £15 per share, or £1,500,000. The remaining £3,500,000, it was implied, would be called up only if and when the profitable growth of the business required it over the years ahead. Partly paid shares were a frequently used capital-raising technique of the time, as for instance when the Millwall Yard was floated, and indeed later; they were last used on a large scale in the Thatcher-era 'privatizations' of British public utilities. None of those who bought Overends' shares (including customers of the Norwich bank) dreamed that the unpaid element was soon to become a horror story of its own.

Henry Gurney and Robert Birkbeck would stay on to run the new company (for a generous salary and a slice of the profits), but all the other partners, David Ward Chapman among them, would retire – 'retire' in one sense but not in another. They would leave their money in the new company and would share responsibility with Henry and John Gurney and Robert Birkbeck for the £4 million of junk bills. The crucial 'but' that underlies all of what happened next was that the new directors decided to keep the existence, let alone the size, of this problem a secret. The statement in the prospectus that 'the assets and liabilities to be transferred will be guaranteed by the vendors' is a commonplace piece of legal boilerplate. Even the most eagle-eyed and cynical investor could never have guessed its real significance. It was not just that these were real guarantees of very real problems, but the survival of the new company was wholly dependent on the guarantees being worth at least as much as the likely losses. If there were a gap, the loss would fall back on the new company. This was in many ways the most egregious error of all. Optimistic calculations made by the new Board showed that when various pluses and minuses were taken into account, the net liability under the guarantees might not be more than £1.3 million, a sum which the guarantors' estates and wealth were more than sufficient to cover. The one-page statement of assets on which they relied was written out by John Gurney and does not seem to have been backed by any supporting schedule, let alone any auditors' or estate valuers' certificate. It is hard to follow, especially its separate references to 'Gurneys Norwich' and the 'Norwich Bank'. Though it does bear out the claim that in theory there was enough there to cover the liabilities, with a surplus at the end of the day of some £670,000, in practice it was crucially dependent on two flimsy assumptions. First, that when it was finally liquidated, the junk portfolio would produce at least £1,250,000, and second, that the partners' asset sales could be sold at good prices and without attracting attention. Even so, the conservative John Gurney struck out of the final draft of the prospectus the claim (a gloss of the kind so often added to unflattering portraits by a delicate Grant paintbrush) that the liabilities would be 'most amply and satisfactorily guaranteed'. He also struck out another claim that 'the company will thus have the advantage of entering at once into a large and profitable business'. It was not enough to ward off the later accusation that the document as a whole was utterly misleading. To compound the concealment, although the guarantee deed was available in the company solicitor's office to be inspected by potential investors (few if any bothered to do so), a second deed, which made clear that this was not just boilerplate but a guarantee that had a time frame and specific circumstances in which it might be called on, was kept under wraps.

The family worries about the real risk of the guarantees are evident from the letters that went to and fro between John Gurney and his uncle Daniel, old Sam's brother. Though another quiet man, Daniel knew a risk when he saw one. He told his nephew, 'I certainly feel a great objection to our joint and several guarantee for the deficiency of the new company.' It created a liability, which would rank equally with the marriage settlements he had made on his children and with his obligations as a partner in the Norwich bank. He hoped that the new Board would at least allow the marriage settlement to come first if his assets were attacked. 'I am sorry to trammel the negotiations in any way but I doubt whether this proposal . . . is quite honourable to the families into which my children have married.' John Gurney, who was probably the richest in the family at the time, offered to shoulder some of his uncle's liability. Daniel thought his 'willingness to make a sacrifice in my favour when it comes to the appropriation of losses . . . a great kindness', but remained 'very uneasy about this and especially the marriage settlements . . . in the case of a real catastrophe all my family and myself would be in total destitution or almost', and his sons-in-law would be 'almost if not quite ruined'. In the end, Daniel, clearly already resigned to the fact that having to face up to losses was a matter of when rather than if, had to concede realistically that 'the case is urgent . . . I leave the matter in your hands'. Jane Austen would have understood the dilemma perfectly. Despite his nephew's support, Daniel's story was to end much as he had feared.

Though they reflected, through rose-tinted spectacles, about what each guarantor was worth, and concluded that there was enough there to meet the guarantees, the new Board had spent too much time looking inwards and playing with words, blind to the dynamics of the real world. It was all very well to say that an estate was worth say £100,000. But while losses could and did become real overnight, country estates could not be sold that way. Moreover, these were substantial, well-known properties, of the kind which today would be given prominence in the first few pages of *Country Life* advertisements. Owned by men equally well known, the mere fact that one or more was on the market would send distress signals to a vigilant City. As we shall see, this is indeed part of what happened.

The carefully fudged guarantees in the prospectus only surfaced years later. At the time, all the public really had to rely on were assurances from the directors, who, to underscore their confidence, would also be substantial shareholders and would 'give their zealous attention to the cultivation of a first-class business only [a phrase later adapted by a more successful banker, J. P. Morgan] . . . it being their conviction that they will thus most effectually promote the prosperity of the company and the permanent interests of the shareholders.' The terms of the offer 'cannot fail to ensure a highly remunerative return to the shareholders', the directors purred, echoing the hollow promise engraved by Grant's silver pen in the prospectus for Millwall. Sadly they did fail, totally. The word 'conviction' would come to hang over the directors' heads, resonating nastily with a totally different meaning. The investors would soon pay a high price to learn that fine words and fine names, the powerful pheromones of elite Quaker wealth and business connections which the Gurney association generated, were no substitute for audited accounts.

For the present, despite Bagehot's nuanced scepticism and the *sotto voce* gossip, investors reacted, as *The Economist* later put it, with 'a sort of wonder that a benevolent deity should have decreed that even the humblest might share in the great riches and power of so mighty an institution'. Their appetites whetted and their critical faculties dulled by the speculative climate, investors subscribed enthusiastically to the new company, buying 100,000 £50 shares, of which they only needed to pay £15 down, with the prospectus headlining the soothing assurance that there was no intention to call up the balance. The shares jumped to a gratifying premium and by October had doubled in price. 'I told you so,' the investors preened themselves.

Like the Eton boys observed by Thomas Gray in our opening quotation, they were blissfully unaware of what lurked around the corner of The Corner House. How could they be otherwise, since the share prospectus, at best a gloss on the truth, and by any common-sense standard false and misleading, told them nothing about what one commentator rightly later called the 'wild advances'.

The sighs of relief were deafening, but those most dangerously deafened were those most centrally involved. After years of silent worry and pain, they believed, for a brief and glorious interlude, that they were out of the wood. But it was only a short stroll across a small sunlit clearing; they were soon wandering in an even darker forest, stalked by even worse nightmares. Disraeli, whose liberal father had sent him to Quaker schools where unidentified Gurneys were among his fellow pupils, and who in his twenties was himself an unsuccessful Stock Market gambler, once remarked that 'it is very difficult for people at the summit of life to believe in the possibility of ruin'. As 1865 melted fast into the fateful 1866, the former Corner House partners and the distinguished new directors finally saw the possibility becoming a reality. The skeletons in the closet were once again rattling their chains.

21

'Fictitious Capital'

The 'finance business' was an accident waiting to happen. It was a bubble, and when it burst the businesses it was keeping afloat would founder like a Galway Line ship in an Atlantic gale. Looking back later *The Times* charted the course of the shipwreck:

> The finance people who have urged their clients, the contractors, to enter into the most serious works insist that before these unhappy people can be allowed another farthing they must give up every available asset they can lay their hands on and even on these conditions pay double terms for whatever may be granted them.
>
> In the next stage they are told they cannot have the slightest support. The victims then stop payment, the works on which they have been engaged are rendered comparatively worthless and the finance people whose securities consist in a great measure in a lien on these works become wild with helpless terror and endeavour to put out fresh paper by offering the most tremendous bribes meanwhile comforting their shareholders by the issue of special reports to induce them quietly to pay calls [on their unpaid shares]. But these companies now find that the treatment they have accorded to their own clients the contractors is to be inflicted on themselves. All the leading banks which have thus far made high profits by discounting and thus encouraged the circulation of their paper forthwith intimate that it will no longer be touched . . . the reins thus tightened with a violent jerk snap altogether . . .

Among those that snapped was the Financial Discount Company, which sold shares to the public in 1864, its chairman none other than George Lascaridi, either unfazed by his Galway losses or seeking to recoup them. Like the old Mercantile, it combined fast and loose lending with dividends paid out of non-existent profits and by 1866 its shares were worthless.

Even as events closed in, Overends tried to battle on, but the pressure of events was simply too great. It is hard to say against this backdrop of general market uncertainty that there was any single 'tipping point'. Some claim that it may have been in January 1866, when a firm of railway contractors failed owing some £1.5 million, and was soon seen to have been in the middle of a web of backstairs finance companies and 'finance' Bills. The Jacobean twist hinted at earlier was now played out as the contractor's name was Watson, Overend & Co. It had no business or other connection with The Corner House and, as far as anyone knew, no family link with the original Corner House partner, but in febrile times people react to the headline and are less concerned to know all the facts. The coincidence of name was enough to start tongues wagging and deposits draining away. At the same time, rumours began to surface that The Corner House partners were selling off their estates to meet the guarantees they had given for liabilities, whose significance had been so smoothly glossed over in the prospectus. Bigger depositors drew their own conclusions. The Ides of March brought the collapse of Millwall. In early April, a firm of merchants trading with Spain, Pinto Perez & Co., collapsed. They were known to be heavily in debt to Overends, and it soon emerged that they too had been trading fraudulently. The Corner House now began to feel the real pain of being a public company, as 'bears', the Stock Exchange dealers who thrived on potential bad news, sold the shares 'short', betting that by the time they had to deliver, the price would have fallen even further and they would make a handsome profit out of others' misfortune. Some market men were convinced that the 'bears' were a 'well-organised gang' and there is certainly anecdotal evidence of similar concerted operations being mounted against other weak financial companies. But whatever prompted the heavy selling, unnerved depositors seeing the shares in free fall began to pull their money out of The Corner House even more urgently.

Banks failed, companies failed, the stock and bond markets swooned. By March an unidentified newspaper cited by King was led to comment that 'company winding up seems likely to become one of our national institutions'. Grant's Imperial Mercantile was on the ropes, calling up unpaid share capital only to find few investors responding, perhaps because many of them had never existed in the first place. Outside events added to the nervousness. On the Continent there was the unsettling belligerence of Prussia, poised to establish dominance over North German states in the Seven Weeks' War with Austria, which ended with its victory in the Battle of Sadowa, and there were fears – proved correct a year later – that a Fenian uprising in Canada could be replayed in England. Hard on the heels of the Millwall failure came the collapse of the Contract Corporation, a profligate issuer of Bills, which was linked to Watson, Overend.

On 3 May, the Bank of England raised its lending rate from 6 to 7 per cent, and on 5 May came a further hike to 8 per cent. Each turn of the screw made City men more apprehensive that a new and nasty storm was about to break over their heads and slice into whatever profits The Corner House imagined it was making under its own 'Alice in Wonderland' accounting. For old partners trying to find buyers for their assets at any price, it was made increasingly more difficult by the day.

To those beleaguered in Birchin Lane, it must have seemed that Shakespeare had been right:

> When sorrows come they come not as single spies,
> But in battalions.

John Gurney, doughtily fighting a losing battle in Birchin Lane, was also well aware that the contagion might affect the family 'crown jewel', the Norwich bank, all the more if it became know that Norwich had helped out with funding for The Corner House. In March, we see him writing to Samuel Gurney Buxton in Norwich to tell him that Stock Exchange dealers were using rumours of 'a bank in Norwich' being in trouble to knock down the Overends' share price. He advised that any money Norwich had borrowed from the Bank of England should be repaid, presumably as a gesture of strength, and the Norwich books balanced 'by Saturday'. The Yarmouth branch should be told to offer any gold it held back to Norwich, rather than fuel rumours by selling it in London. He added that the once remote, now looming, guarantee liability should be discussed with others in Norwich 'gently and judiciously'. The delicacy of the balancing act is suggested by the fact that several months before the failure, John Gurney was reminded from Norwich that 'the family' was paying him £2,000 a year to 'keep up appearances' and that to dismiss all his servants and cut all his expenses might send the wrong message to a suspicious world. 'It may prove to the advantage of the Limited Company that you should not appear to be utterly cleaned out all at once.'

The family were also increasingly worried about what London's problems might mean for the Norwich bank, if, or ever more likely when, they saw the light of day. Several of those in the London firm were partners in Norwich. If London crashed, the waves of worry might carry away the East Anglian business. Even if that did not happen, if the London partners' Norwich holdings were seized by The Corner House creditors and sold, the delicate stability of the family bank would be undermined. Writing to Daniel Gurney in the immediate aftermath of the Pinto Perez failure, John Gurney commented that it 'is not creditable to the old firm or the new and I feel is a reason for concluding the Norwich Bank deeds as rapidly as possible'.

When Overends went public, the selling partners' share of the Norwich bank's goodwill, valued at £300,000, had been cited as one of the personal assets which the incoming directors had relied on as part of the underpinning of their guarantees. Now it was to fade quietly away, like the Cheshire Cat, leaving only a mirthless grin behind. The deal John Gurney was so anxious to conclude was designed to ensure, as he wrote to Daniel, that none of those involved in Overends any longer had an 'ascertainable interest' in

Norwich. *The History of Barclays Bank*, published in 1926, addresses the point rather coyly, perhaps because it was still sensitive. It shifts the time frame of the shuffle of holdings to 'shortly after the death of Hudson Gurney [in 1864]' and tells us only that 'a rearrangement of the two businesses [Overends and the Norwich bank] was carried out.'

Writing in 1966 on the centenary of 'Black Friday', Sir Anthony Tuke, one of the three chairmen his family provided to Barclays over the years, gave a fuller account. As the problems began to mount early in 1866, the Gurneys involved in Overends realised that their heavy guarantee liabilities had 'serious repercussions' for the profitable Norwich bank. With what Tuke called 'characteristic realism and courage', a new Norwich partnership was created, excluding the men who had signed that ill-fated guarantee. Four new partners were brought into Norwich. Though new as partners they were hardly strangers: two Buxtons, another Birkbeck, and none other than Henry Ford Barclay, one of the directors of the new company. As he had never been involved in the 'old firm' of Overends, he bore none of its former partners' liability under their guarantees, a liability as contagious as the cholera bacillus. The new members are said to have injected new capital of £635,000, £150,000 of which Barclay put up himself. They were only just in time. The 'new' bank started its legal life on 23 April 1866; nothing else changed. When 'Black Friday' arrived just a couple of weeks later, it was able to tell the world that 'Gurney & Co. of Norwich are in no way affected by the affairs of Overend, Gurney & Co.'. Like so many comments by the various interested parties throughout the history of the sad affair, it was true on its face, but glossed over a key fact or two. The Norwich bank had extended a substantial standby credit to The Corner House to try to keep it afloat, which is presumably how the Millwall deeds came to rest in the vaults of Norwich rather than in the hands of The Corner House creditors. Local support was underpinned at a meeting in Norwich, convened at an hour's notice on the Saturday by its mayor and the chancellor of the Norwich diocese, which affirmed 'its unbounded confidence in the house of Gurneys and Birkbecks and unabated reliance on its perfect financial security'.

Fortunately for all concerned, neither the 'new deal' in Norwich nor the latter's financial support were looked at in any detail in the various legal post-mortems. Wherever the shift in shareholding came up in the hundreds of pages of legal transcript, it seems to have been neatly deflected, and each exchange between lawyers and witnesses produces a slightly different version. One suggests that the new Norwich partners simply put in the entire £635,000 of new capital; another that they paid their outgoing colleagues only the £300,000 originally given as the value of the latter's interests; while according to a third, the money they owed for their shares was payable only out of future profits from Norwich to begin after 1870. Whatever the facts, Tuke rightly told *Times'* readers that the episode had been 'a narrow shave'. Following him almost forty years later, with the added detachment provided by distance, Margaret Ackrill and Leslie Hannah in their vivid update of Barclays' history, see it as 'another remarkable example of the cousinhood's capacity to limit financial contagion by acting as a lender of last resort.'

Though John Gurney was a realist, Henry Gurney and Robert Birkbeck went on pretending that the bank was not in trouble. When William Peek, a City man who had a large shareholding in the public company and who kept his ear close to the ground, wrote at the end of January to ask why there had been no Annual Report and no General Meeting of shareholders, Birkbeck wrote back smoothly that the reasons were technical, to do with the dates laid down in the new company's bylaws:

> . . . no-one can have been more annoyed at the rumours relative to the company than we have been. I can only assure you the company has not lost anything and that the business is going on as satisfactorily as we could desire . . .

On 14 April, almost a month after Millwall began to unravel, Peek asked more questions. Birkbeck wrote to him again, his message quite remarkable for a man with the Sword of Damocles hanging on a single, fast-fraying hair just a few inches over his head:

... I can assure you that there is not the slightest ground for the report you mention or that any of the directors or any of us have been selling a single share since I wrote to you on 1st February. Except as noticed in the *Times* today by frauds of Pinto Perez & Co the company has not made a single bad debt. I still believe that when July come[s] you will be perfectly satisfied with the accounts ...
Believe me, in haste,
Yours truly ...

It is hardly surprising that, in the light of such blatant misrepresentation, Peek eventually mounted a legal action of his own, which failed on legal technicalities rather than the merits of his claim.

Three days later, Henry Gurney himself fobbed off another anxious investor:

I beg to inform you that we have no intention of making a call [on the unpaid shares]. None of the shares belonging to the late firm has been sold since October. Any loss made by the Millwall Company belongs to the old firm; till Pinto Perez let us in we had not made a single bad debt. I am sorry to say that they have by fraud let us in to a considerable extent but how much it will be we cannot at present tell, but I have no fear of our being prevented from paying a fair dividend ...

This answer was on its most charitable interpretation not just economical, but downright miserly with the truth. That a dividend could even be contemplated was perhaps the pinnacle of self-delusion; deposits were haemorrhaging and there was not a penny piece of real profit out of which it could properly be paid.

The Millwall Yard may have been one of the 'excepted accounts' for which the old partners and not the new firm were responsible, but Henry Gurney knew all too well that it was a bad debt of over £500,000, or in modern terms some £25 million, which would take a lot of personal asset sales to cover; all the more as we shall see since The Corner House held no real security. We can only guess at the stresses in the partners' room in those last months and days and their beleaguered, hopeless defiance as one piece of bad news followed another in a malign chorus.

The directors were in fact in meeting after meeting, agonising about making a call on the unpaid shares, only to decide that the money would not reach them in time to save the day, and that in any event it might only add fuel to the flames.

Back in Birchin Lane, behind the crumbling façade of 'business as usual', the men in The Corner House were fighting a losing battle. Other banks, worried about how much money they had left in the vaults, had to take care of their own suddenly fragile future and would not, or could not, help. On 9 May, along with the Bank rate increase, came the final straw; a court ruled on a technicality that Overends had no power to enforce what seemed a bona-fide debt owed on Bills by the Mid Wales Railway. Though the amount involved was small, if this debt was not collectible, what did that say for the millions of pounds of railway obligations floating around the marketplace?

In the final moments, Birkbeck finally admitted to Peek that the game was up. Told of a 'disagreeable rumour . . . that they were about put up their shutters', Birkbeck stopped pretending. He told the anxious Peek that the Bank of England had unexpectedly refused to lend them money though they had offered them 'ample and first class' security. 'It was done to gratify an old grudge on the Bank's part and would bring on a catastrophe which would result in an enquiry in Parliament. If the Bank had not turned them down, the company would have declared a dividend of 7 per cent!', he claimed, reiterating the foolish statement made a few days earlier by Henry Gurney. He added lugubriously that he 'would feel better if you abused me', which, given the answers he had been fobbed off with up to that point, Peek would have been perfectly entitled to do, though being a gentleman he probably restrained himself.

For Birkbeck to blame the Bank is sadly characteristic of any businessman facing the wall, Xenos no exception; it is their bank manager's fault. One more week, one more loan, and the corner would have been turned. In fact, the Bank's behaviour was professional and set the pattern for its approach to other crises; Barings' problems with Argentina in the 1890s, the reprise at the hands of rogue trader Nick Leeson some 100 years later, the 'secondary banking crisis' and the BCCI scandal. First get the facts. Then see whether the risk they represent is 'localised' to one bank or group; if so, the arguments for riding to the rescue are thin. If the risk is 'systemic', the soundness of the wider financial market threatened, more radical action may be needed.

The Bank was far less well informed than it might have been even thirty years later. David Kynaston's research shows that while strong hints of 'rather reckless business' had reached Threadneedle Street, the Bank, like the rest of the financial community, had been comforted, maybe deliberately misled, that 'profits are commensurate' with the losses they were incurring. Moreover, 'capital is ample to meet any contingencies'. So when Overends suddenly called for help, Governor Lancelot Holland must have been taken aback. He sent two senior City bankers and Kirkman Hodgson, his immediate predecessor, round to The Corner House to look at its books. We can fairly wonder whether the biblical lament, 'How are the mighty fallen, and the weapons of war perished', rang half-remembered in their ears. We do not know what they saw, or what they were told, but their obviously shocked and negative conclusion led the Bank to refuse that last-gasp advance and allow the firm to die. These decisions are rarely clear-cut and in the end they are a matter of judgement based on experience and 'gut feeling', courage too, rather than numbers set out on spread sheets. They are decisions which the press, politicians, lawyers, liquidators and historians will pick over and second-guess. It is thus all the more frustrating for researchers that neither the report of the 'Three Wise Men'[38] nor any account of the key meeting about Overends' fate, are to be found in the Bank's Minute Books; probably because the problem was handled directly by the Governor and a small inner core of colleagues, then presented to the full Court as a fait accompli.

We know that relations between the Bank and its biggest competitor were complex and competitive, but while achingly remembered on both sides, that 'old grudge' – the banknote affair –

had ended in victory for the Bank and an Overends' climb-down. It seems improbable to say that the vindictiveness festered and became the decisive factor in whether or not to rescue Overends. It is far more likely that even at that early stage in its evolution as the British central bank, what weighed most heavily in Holland's mind was the stability of London's financial system. Would the City, banking and trade all be put at peril if Overends were allowed to fail? It was decided that they would not, provided that they had government backing to pump more cash into the financial markets to calm things down. Others might fail, but on balance the risk of a far-reaching 'domino effect' was containable. And if Overends were bailed out, how could the Bank refuse to help other firms who were sinking fast in the flood of 'finance' paper? It is not fanciful to see, behind the Banks overridingly professional assessment, the conditioning of years of the liberal Tory philosophy, enunciated by Sir Robert Peel in the 1830s and quoted by Boyd Hilton, that the natural order of things involved 'a system of social retribution' with its 'just reward of merit and just penalty of folly and vice.' Hilton has pointed out that in 1826 the liberal Tories had refused to help out certain firms in distress. For the Tories, in Hilton's words, 'businessmen like working people must stand on their own feet and not expect outdoor relief when they got into difficulties.'

The curtain came down. But it signalled only the end of Act One in a drama that would keep the public enthralled, and those centrally involved twisting in the wind, for years to come.

22

Shipwreck

The letter pinned on The Corner House doors at 3.30 p.m. on 10 May 1866, and sent out to the banking world – the death certificate of Overends, and a sad coda to Samuel Gurney's achievements and ambitions – was the epitome of banking courtesy:

> Sir,
> We regret to announce that a severe run on our deposits and resources has compelled us to suspend payment, the course being considered under advice the best calculated to protect the interests of all parties. Mr. Turquand of the firm of Messrs. Coleman, Turquand Young & Co and Mr. Harding of Messrs. Harding, Pullein, Whinney & Gibson who are now occupied will prepare a statement of the affairs of the company to be laid before the shareholders at a meeting which will be fixed for as early a date as possible.
> I remain your faithful servant
> William Bois, Secretary

The message for those on the inside was terser. J. Plummer, a Norwich clerk of the Electric and International Telegraph Company, wrote out in fine copperplate a telegram from John Gurney to Fowell Buxton in Norwich, now in the Gurney files: 'Overend Gurney & Co. payment cannot be made. This is now public. Let me see you tomorrow.'

That the Turquand firm had briefly, years before, counted the vilified Edward Edwards amongst its partners went unremarked; the City was a small world.

Not that many years ago, ghouls and abolitionists would keep vigil through the night outside British jails waiting for a nervous warder to put up on the high, metal-studded gates the official notice announcing that a convicted murderer had been hung at dawn. The Overends' death notice attracted a crowd too. It started to gather on the Thursday afternoon and by noon on Friday the 'tumult became a rout . . .The doors of the most respectable banking houses were besieged and throngs heaving and tumbling about Lombard Street made that narrow thoroughfare impassable,' *The Times* reported. Several bankers strode angrily around to the Mansion House to protest to the Lord Mayor that traffic and business were at a standstill. The Mayor arrived a little later with a platoon of police headed by Inspector Foulger, but it took time to disperse the crowd. The *Bankers' Magazine*, conveniently forgetting that only a little over a year before it had heralded the sale of Overends' shares as a 'triumph', recorded that the news had come like 'the shock of an earthquake. It is impossible to describe the terror and anxiety that took possession of men's minds for the remainder of that and the whole of the succeeding day. No man felt safe. A run immediately commenced upon all the banks, the magnitude of which can hardly be conceived.' The Bank of England's Discount Office on the ground floor, to the right of the main doors, was jammed with bankers, brokers and traders trying to borrow money.

As the news buzzed along the telegraph lines, country bankers found their halls besieged by anxious depositors trying to withdraw money and begged their London agents to send them gold and cash. Through the heavy gates of the Bank's Bullion Yard on Lothbury, carriages with armed guards clattered to the main stations and out onto the main post roads, creaking under the weight of boxes of sovereigns.

It was not just the many millions of other people's cash that Overends held on its books that were at stake. The firm's pivotal role in keeping money flowing to trade and industry raised the spectre of the banking system and industry grinding to a halt.

The Minute Books of the Bank's Court, or Board of Directors, and of its key Committee of Treasury, bound in leather and written in fine copperplate, are overwhelmingly 'housekeeping' records:

replacement of lost bank notes, salaries, promotions, pensions, donations, investments in high-quality debt such as the new Thames Embankment, the day-to-day minutiae of a large bank. The 'blip' in the otherwise dull recitative comes on 'Black Friday' when the Court met twice, at 11 a.m. and again at 3 p.m., with Holland in the Chair. The calm, formal record does not reflect the chaos outside in the City. The banks and discount houses froze their business in its tracks, while traders and merchants could not discount their Bills and pay their creditors. It was even impossible to borrow against 'gilt-edged' government securities, 'Consols' and Exchequer Bills. According to his Chalk Farm admirer Karl Marx, Samuel Gurney was convinced that, 'When a panic exists a man does not ask himself what he can get for his banknotes or whether he shall lose one or two per cent by selling his Exchequer bills or three per cent. If he is under the influence of alarm he does not care for the profit or loss but makes himself safe and allows the rest of the world to do as they please.' But making oneself safe was now impossible. The Stock Exchange dealers shut up shop and already panic-stricken investors became frantic. They could not borrow against their shares, nor could they sell them. So acute was the fear that Lionel de Rothschild and his son decided that financial *force majeure* outweighed religious duty and came into the City to pass an anxious Saturday in their New Court offices. A draft scrap in the Bank of England files suggests that, hardly surprisingly, their firm was among Overends' creditors – as indeed was the Bank – but was relatively unaffected either directly or more broadly by what Charlotte, Baroness Lionel de Rothschild, described in a letter the following day as 'yesterday's appalling panic', followed by 'immense excitement in the House of Commons . . . even at Lady Downshire's ball, every body spoke of the immense city failures'.

For half a century most of England's country banks had turned first to The Corner House as the home for their surplus short-term cash. Now until the liquidators had crawled over The Corner House books, bankers from Newhaven to Newcastle, from Bognor to Bodmin, had no idea whether they would see a penny of it back.

The men seated round the Bank's long, rectangular Court table had their own worries; all were bankers or merchants and even the most solid was not immune from the contagion. Even though as directors their firms could look to the Bank for support in time of trouble, who knew today what that support might be worth? They sat soberly as Holland told them that as the result of 'the failure', the Bank had come under very great pressure for assistance and he thought it right to summon the Court and propose 'an advance in the rate of discount'. More important was to prime the pump. The Bank's ability to put money in circulation was limited by the Bank Charter Act. The cash crises of 1847 and 1857 had been quenched by the governments of the day agreeing to suspend the Act temporarily so that money could be injected into the system. It had worked each time, mainly by its psychological rather than its practical effect, and would, they all hoped, work again. The Court therefore approved a letter to Lord John Russell, the Prime Minister and First Lord of the Treasury, and Gladstone, Chancellor of the Exchequer, which reported in measured rather than panicked terms that it had responded to 'Black Friday' by lending £4 million, 'an unprecedented sum to lend in one day', and had not refused any 'legitimate request'. The next day, Saturday, was a working day for banks and business. But even if the run continued the Bank believed that it could handle it, with the important proviso, 'unless the money advanced is entirely withdrawn from circulation', i.e. if the banks and others who borrowed it simply kept it in the vaults and refused to lend it out.

Nonetheless, while suspension of the Act, or rather an under-taking that a breach would be retrospectively sanctioned, was not on balance essential, it was a prudent step to calm the markets. They were pushing at an open door. Gladstone had been softened up by a deputation of City men in a state of 'extraordinary distress and apprehension', as he wrote when replying to the Bank. They were 'persons of the greatest insight and influence, who had urged with unanimity and earnestness' that the State must intervene. And intervene it would, with permission to breach the Act 'to compose the public mind and avert the calamities which might threaten British trade and industry'. However, there was a price: the bank rate had to go to 10 per cent and he reserved the right to demand it be pushed even higher. Thinking of everything, the canny Chancellor added the rider that after 'a fair charge' to the still privately owned Bank 'for its risk, influence and trouble', the profits from this higher rate were to be handed over to the Treasury. While conceding that the Government's action had been essential, *The Times* was not sympathetic to those 'distressed' bankers. The Bank had been prudent in maintaining an adequate reserve, the commercial and private bankers had failed to do so. When the panic came, the thrifty Bank was 'mulcted for the unthrifty . . . the foolish virgins made so much clamour they compelled the wise virgins to share their carefully collected oil,' it added, confident that its readers knew their Bible.

It was not just the City that needed reassurance. The world's money flowed through London. The Foreign Secretary, Lord Clarendon, sent an immediate cable to British embassies and legations, laying out the line ambassadors were to take in their host countries. Published in *The Times* ten days later, it is probably the best contemporary summary we have of how Whitehall saw cause, effect and response; 'Long continued prosperity in commercial affairs and the general wealth consequent on it have produced their ordinary results in encouraging speculation especially of a monetary or financial nature and fostering hopes of acquiring wealth by more speedy means than are presented by the ordinary methods of commercial industry.' In today's terms, it had been yet another bubble. That it would always end badly had been 'anxiously apprehended', all the more because of growing concerns over political developments on the Continent. But the collapse of The Corner House had burst the bubble 'with a severity and suddenness in regard to its immediate consequences which could not have been anticipated'. It was a banking crisis that had been focused in London but which could have spread fast throughout the country; Overends held 'many millions sterling which in other times would have formed and, perhaps, ought to have formed the reserves of the various private and joint stock banks of the country'. The phrase 'perhaps ought to have formed' was a not-so-veiled dig at the greed of the banks in chasing higher returns by depositing with Overends, than they might have got in the safer hands of the Bank of England. The Bank was ready to help, and the Government had agreed that it could breach the Act 'if the exigencies of the times' required it. Any solid and well-managed business 'will be enabled to withstand the shock'. The Government had no reason to suppose that the crisis reflected any general lack of soundness in the country's trade. It was confident that the measures taken would see the crisis abate; indeed, the 'panic' had already begun to recede. In a fine Victorian flourish he added 'all that is required is that all classes should cooperate with the Government in endeavouring to allay needless alarm and in acting with prudence and forbearance while so much agitation prevails.'

In the chandeliered chancelleries and banks of Europe, suspicion of 'perfidious Albion' was ingrained, so it came as no surprise when cynical readers concluded that if London was putting out such soothing words, the problem must indeed be serious. For some time 'every English signature [on a Bill or a Letter of Credit] was suspected abroad.'[39]

Other than the click of the lock as the doors are shut, banks make no noise when they close. If they did the reverberations after 'Black Friday' would have been like a Second World War bombing raid on the heart of the City. Down went the Bank of London, the Consolidated Bank, the British Bank of California, the Contract Corporation and Grant's Imperial Mercantile, none of which would be much missed or lamented. The crisis also swept into liquidation the Agra and Masterman's Bank, taking with it the savings of hundreds of retired Indian Army officers and civil servants, another target of the Stock Exchange 'bears' who replayed, with far less justification but even more sophistication, the tactics they had used on Overends: selling shares they did not own to push down the price and buying them back at a profit when nervous depositors took fright and pulled out their money, driving the price down even further.

'Black Friday' also sucked down many businesses that had become dangerously addicted to the temptations of the 'new style' of Bill finance. Perhaps its most prominent casualty was the international contractor, Peto & Betts, whose driving force, Sir Samuel Morton Peto, had masterminded the building of the symbol which in itself and in its setting, epitomised British power and mastery of the seas; Nelson's Column in Trafalgar Square. He had also been responsible for the Reform Club, where the Anglophile Xenos was a member. Peto and another major contractor, Thomas Brassey, had poured skill, engineers and navvies into laying Canada's Grand Trunk Railroad and the vital Crimean War rail link between Sevastopol and Balaclava. About to go bankrupt and resign from the House of Commons, The Corner House failure pulled down the pyramid of Bills through which he and promoters of the London Chatham and Dover Railway were financing its construction. Brassey survived and flourished, leaving his sons an estate of £6.5 million, a figure which did not include his landholdings and which was noted by Lord Derby, who kept a keen eye on his own and other people's fortunes, as 'the largest amount for which probate has been granted under any one will'.

The crash also halted forever another smaller, if no less ambitious project, to build a 'pneumatic railway' under the Thames. Based on a successful experiment at the Crystal Palace, the trains were to be sucked by vacuum power at 25 mph through a tunnel from Great Scotland Yard to Waterloo Station. The navvies had just started digging the underwater stretch when the money vanished.

One important building project did continue, the grandiose Albert Memorial in Hyde Park, just across the road from the homes of David Ward Chapman and Samuel Gurney Jr. As *The Times* reported on 14 May, as a diversion from the financial gloom, most of the granite and marble was already on site and 30 feet of brickwork had been erected. Londoners would soon see a centre of flowers and fashion in place of 'the howling wilderness, scarcely frequented save by such of the Knightsbridge garrison as loved solitude,' it added, in what may have been a sly dig at red-coated guardsmen's reported readiness, for a few coins, to accommodate London gentlemen afflicted by what was known at the time as 'Scarlet Fever'.

On a more human scale, the crash forced the publisher Sam Beeton, whose wife Isabella had died in childbirth the previous year, to sell the copyright of her classic *Beeton's Book of Household Management* and the rest of his publishing assets. Even Karl Marx, busily rethinking the world from a distinctly unrevolutionary address – No. 1, Modena Villas, Maitland Park – in Chalk Farm, North London, and rather behind with his rent, told Engels that he had come under renewed pressure from his landlord: 'because of the Overend affair the fellow is reduced to living off his house rents and . . . won't take Bills of Exchange'. In studied contrast to the excitement of the *New York Times*, a Hong Kong correspondent cabled home to *The Times* in London, with the understatement expected of British expatriates, that the news of the collapse 'had a most depressing effect on business'.

There was perhaps one ray of light, recently recounted by the always-acute *Spectator* commentator, Christopher Fildes. The day after the collapse, the Fellows of an unnamed Cambridge college [clerics to a man], which had also deposited a large amount of cash at Overends, gathered in a fustian funk waiting for their bursar, a layman, to tell them that the college was ruined. Not so. 'I am pleased to report, Master,' he declared, 'that the College's funds are secure . . . when I was in London last week I happened to call on Messrs Overend and Gurney and looked in on the manager. I found him reading the Bible. So I at once withdrew our balances.'

The crash was no respecter of persons. Its ripples destabilised investors and bankers, and prominent businessmen. But through the collapse of Millwall, and compounded by the vagaries of nature, it also dealt a cruel blow to the East End poor, those least able to defend themselves. After Millwall closed down, other London yards shut their gates and laid off their men. It may be, as some have argued, that this domino effect was a direct consequence of Overends' failure. But The Corner House was not involved with the other yards and on balance it seems more likely that even if Overends had not gone under, the London industry was headed for trouble. Millwall would have been among the first to fail; like all Overends' enterprises, it was so precariously financed that even brilliant management would probably not have saved it. Ship-building was cyclical, and the London yards themselves were poised on the edge of a downward swoop of its business roller coaster. At first their proprietors thought it was no more than what they had come to know as a 'slap of dull trade', but this was to be the final slap, a phase from which the Thames yards never really recovered. Economists still debate the causes: high London labour costs compared to Clydesdale or the North-East, which already benefited from easier and thus cheaper access to coal for their furnaces; the transition from iron to steel hulls and armour plate, which would have required major new capital investment; and the fact that the yards and the Thames itself were becoming too cramped to build and launch ever bigger vessels.

But the unemployed had no time for economic analysis. The cold spring of 1866, with hail, gales and frost as late as May, was followed by a wet summer and a poor harvest, which meant higher grain and bread prices; this was not a major problem in St James's Square, but it struck hard at those without work on the Isle of Dogs. By autumn cholera bacteria were multiplying invisibly but lethally in the East End's contaminated water, communal dung and refuse heaps and street gutters greasy with household slops. The winter too was harsh and The Port of London ice-bound. Twenty thousand dockers, bargees and lightermen joined the shipyard workers in the despair of joblessness.

As Professor Arnold writes, dockers and shipwrights marched together in the cobbled streets of Limehouse and Poplar chanting, 'We're all froze out, we've got no work, we've got no work to do.' The 1866 report of the Poplar Hospital's management committee recorded that, 'Since its first establishment there has never been a year so pregnant with disaster both public and private and the pecuniary distress which has fallen so heavily upon the country more especially upon the eastern portion of the metropolis has necessarily affected in great degree the interests and prospects of the Poplar Hospital.'

After a touch of arrhythmia here and there, the smoky heart of industry slowly began to beat again, if more slowly. Job statistics quoted by Hoppen make interesting, if sad, reading. In 1867, the year after the collapse, the unemployment rate in Britain as a whole jumped from 2.6 per cent to 6.3 per cent; in 1868, it climbed further to 6.7 per cent, before easing off to 5.9 per cent in 1869 and a more normal 3.7 per cent in 1870. It is hard to claim on these figures alone that this was a result of the 'Black Friday' panic and the ensuing shrinkage in business and investment credit; it seems equally plausible that the figures reflect the bursting of an economic bubble, which blew Overends away with it. Nonetheless, hard times arrived and the gross follies of Overends did not help.

According to the *Glasgow Herald*, it had been a singularly English phenomenon. 'Scotch [*sic*] banks were never sounder, more prosperous nor their resources more ample,' it declared patriotically to a background skirl of pipes. *The Scotsman* pointed out that banks north of the border kept substantial reserves of gold and government securities and were not dependent on the Bank of England for help in times of crisis.

Summing up some months later, Governor Holland patted the Bank and the London community on their collective backs: 'I think I am entitled to say that not only this house but the entire banking body acquitted themselves most honourably . . . Every gentleman who came here with adequate security was liberally dealt with and if accommodation could not be afforded to the full extent which was demanded no one who offered proper security failed to obtain relief from this house.'

Back-patting was cold comfort. As the shock and pain set in, the hunt was on for answers and for scapegoats. It was all the more intense because the Overends' partners – conservative, professional, supposedly the essence of Quaker straight dealing – turned out to have built up, and kept hidden, the pile of worm-eaten debts on a scale that beggared belief; that it also came close to beggaring them was little consolation. As Bagehot later volleyed at the old partners, 'They ruined a firm almost inconceivably good by business so inexplicably bad that it could hardly be much worse if they had of set purpose tried to make it bad.'

23

Truth and Consequences

For the old firm's partners and new directors a new episode in the long horror story was only just beginning. The first blows would be felt by the public shareholders, a saga which would take years to bring to a finale. A dispassionate inquest into the facts by the Official Liquidators revealed, to a thunderstruck world, the existence of those 'illegitimate advances' that, in the new company's short life, had grown like some money cancer from £4 million to over £5 million, as interest clocked up and the problems metastasized. The mortuary analogy struck John Gurney, who wrote, stoically, to Norwich as the enquiry unfolded that 'the post mortem examination of so unsavoury a carcass is by no means agreeable.'

For the shareholders there was nothing but bad news. The gap between what the company owed and what its liquidators could hope to collect from its core business, i.e. its portfolio of 'conventional' Bills and other securities, plus what might be realised from the personal properties of the former Overends' partners, was too big. It became quickly and nastily clear that even after the partners' private assets – their estates, town houses, pictures, insurance policies – had been liquidated and the proceeds put 'into the pot', the banks and other depositors who had put their money with Overends would only have a chance of being paid out if the shareholders paid up the uncalled balance of £35 on each share they had so blithely bought. It was not quite the unlimited, 'down to the last collar stud' liability that so many unfortunates who were duped into underwriting Lloyds of London's insurance obligations in the 1980s believed would never crystallise in a million years, but it was serious enough. A middle-class investor who had relied on the bland prospectus and subscribed for 100 shares, fortified by the directors' statement that 'it is not intended to call up more than £15 per share', now found that 'intentions' were not 'promises'. Not only had they lost their £1,500 stake, but they now had to put up another £3,500; in today's terms, £75,000 had been flushed away and they now had to find another £175,000, or risk having their homes and assets seized by the liquidators' seedy bailiffs.

Though the Victorian author Charles Manby Smith was writing, and somewhat overwriting, about a company collapse some ten years before Overends (lessons were clearly not learned), he catches the flavour of what the bland phrase 'a call on unpaid shares' might mean in reality:

> Independent country gentlemen, West Country manufacturers and merchants of substantial capital were summarily pounced on by the fangs of the law and all simultaneously stripped of everything they possessed in the world. Professional men, the fathers of families genteelly bred and educated, were summarily bereft of every farthing . . . Others accustomed perhaps for half a century to the appliances of ease and luxury and who were the owners of hospitable mansions . . . hide their heads in cottages and huts and eleemosynary chambers where they wither in silence and neglect under the cold breath of alien charity . . . it has wrought wretchedness and ruin for those whom it promised unexampled prosperity.

Overend & Gurney had some 2,000 shareholders, as far as can be seen almost all individuals or families. There were none of the 'institutions' one might have expected to see even fifty years later, let alone today. Largely this is because they did not exist; there were no pension funds and no mutual funds. It also, in part, reflects that among the directors of the handful of insurance companies that did exist, and the trustees of college endowments and the like, not only was there no 'cult of the equity' but shares in general were (rightly as it happens) viewed as little more than gaming chips, totally inappropriate for serious investors.

What is also striking about the list of shareholders is the essentially middle-class flavour of the addresses: '10 Park Crescent, Stockwell', '71 Peascod Street, Windsor' and '5 Wormwood Street, London EC' do not suggest plutocrats at play. Though there are also many country addresses from Truro to Tunbridge Wells, these give the impression of nice houses with a few acres, rather than castles and rolling estates. A feature which might suggest, to a cynic, the operation of Grant's well-honed marketing machine; that each of the list's thirty pages contains what at first sight is a significant proportion of maiden ladies, widows and clergy. But whoever they were, the overall sense is of people to whom a call on the unpaid liability would come as a shock and a hardship. Their dreams of profits soon turned into a real life nightmare, brought to front doors across the country first by stiff legal letters and then by seedy bailiffs demanding payment.

The shareholders argued that they had been defrauded by a false prospectus and should not have to pay. As the usual post-crisis fog of facts, anger-fuelled allegations and rumour swirled through London, it became daily clearer to the directors of the stillborn company that years of legal wrangling lay ahead and that it was quite likely that the road on which they had so confidently embarked was going to lead them into the dock of a criminal court.

Some shareholders paid as the calls came in, some tried to hide, and many, as the Lloyds' victims would do a century later, rushed to form a defence committee to fight the claims of the creditors, retaining George Lewis, fashionable London's favourite solicitor – the Victorian Arnold Goodman. The creditors and the Official Liquidator also organised themselves as well, the latter retaining no less a figure than the Attorney General Sir Roundell Palmer (in those carefree days law officers of the Crown were allowed to take private work). The two groups launched into protracted legal trench warfare. The legal arguments are complex and subtle, but for the shareholders it was simple: the prospectus had been a blatant fraud and they were under no obligation to pay. In the final analysis, based on the law as it then stood, the Judge, Sir Richard Malins, and later the House of Lords disagreed, but not before both had castigated the directors in terms which would have made even the

most self-confident or self-righteous of them quiver in their polished
boots. Taking aim at the new Board members in particular, Judge
Malins expressed his 'astonishment that four men could be found
who having had such facts communicated to them, could have
thought it not only prudent but justifiable to proceed with the
company [and] induce others to advance their money to an insolvent
and ruined concern. Could they on any principle of morality and
justice be right in concealing so appalling a fact?' 'His Honour', *The
Times*' law reporter declared, 'was decidedly of the opinion that they
could not,' even though somewhat contradictorily he felt that
they 'could not have intended to do wrong' but had acted in good
faith and had been deluded by 'too sanguine a view of the prospects
of the concern and too great a reliance upon the guarantee of the
[former] partners'. But if the shareholders' hopes rose as the Judge
spoke, expecting that this would mean a verdict in their favour and
releasing them from liability, they were chagrined when he declared
that this was not the issue. Creditors had advanced money and done
business with the new company, relying on what they had been told
about its capital. The unpaid calls were an integral component of
that capital, a contractual underpinning on which those who
deposited money with the new company were entitled to rely and
the Liquidator had a valid claim against the shareholders on the
creditors' behalf.

In August 1866, when the judgement was appealed to the House
of Lords, Lord Cranworth, the Lord Chancellor, flanked by Lords
Westbury and Colonsay, expressed a view that the sponsors of the
company would not have liked at all, and which again might briefly
have boosted shareholders' hopes of relief: 'I wish I could have
believed that the prospectus was honestly and fairly framed. But I
cannot. I must believe that the truth was intentionally concealed and
hopes held out which those who framed the prospectus must have
known would deceive those who trusted to it.' But after another
complex analysis of the law, he and his colleagues agreed that Malins
had been right. The call obligation was a binding contract and the
shareholders had to pay up. A report some months after the judgement showed that out of the 2,219 shareholders, 43 had declared

bankruptcy, 151 had 'demonstrated their inability to pay in full' with 40 'whose present residence is unknown'. The anguish was countrywide.

The Overends' partners saw all too clearly where allegations of this kind might lead and quietly retained two of the country's leading lawyers to defend them if any charges were brought (a fact which only emerged in a House of Commons debate two years later). This was prudent. It was again testimony to the permeability of barriers between public and private office for which Edward Edwards was berated. Sir Roundell Palmer, who was still representing the Official Liquidator, was asked to hold 'a watching brief' for the Gurneys (though it was never specified, we can assume his brief was in fact on behalf of all the likely targets), along with Sir John Karslake, then Solicitor General, who a year later would take Palmer's place as Attorney General.

Looking at the Norwich correspondence files there can be little doubt that getting top legal help was an initiative of John Gurney. He had moved to London and was tidying up the remains of The Corner House, disposing of his own assets, sorting out family issues and still finding time to chase the Norwich bank, in which he supposedly held no 'ascertainable interest', on the minutiae of business.

In June, when the echoes of the firm's explosion were still ringing loudly in wounded ears, he was writing to the Norwich bank about an 'unfavourable' article in *The Economist*; it would be 'desirable if you could prevent it from being copied into the Norwich newspapers'. Without any hint of sentiment or nostalgia for what might have been, he recommended that Norwich's substantial Bill business should now be channelled to Overends' closest competitors, Alexander's, happily also a Quaker firm.

Just after the collapse he was clearly strapped for cash and rather touchingly asked his Norwich partners to find a good home for his mare 'The American' and to carry on his annual contribution, via 'Mr. Mall of The Black Bull', to buy bread for the city's elderly poor. But money must have come from somewhere since by August he was insuring his life to provide annuities for his wife and son, and cannily asking a Norwich partner to hold the policy as trustee 'to keep this matter clear of my affairs'. In September, he agreed with the Overends' liquidators that any further properties that had to be sold could be bought by family trusts without going on the open market, provided the liquidators thought the price acceptable; a nice way to keep good property in the family circle. 'Advise all interested parties,' he tells his country cousin, which may well explain why the family's Catton Hall estate passed from John's hands to those of his cousin Samuel Gurney Buxton. Around the same time he wrote regretting that his son, Hay Gurney, had been seen around Norfolk 'driving a four in hand', behaviour which John Gurney thought 'an extravagant indiscretion'.

In The Corner House itself, soon to be sold to its neighbour Glyn Mills for £29,000, he worked with the 'front man' Koch on a settlement of debts relating to 'the Belfast railway', and on liquidating exotic ephemera such as interests in the Swedish Land Drainage Company and land in Pensacola, Florida. Yet it was matters close to home which really interested him. The Norwich partners needed to take 'a stiff hand' with the manager of their Fakenham branch to make sure that he did not lend 'more than is absolutely necessary' to the local farmers. 'If you do not look out very sharp he will not only lock up money but also make many bad debts.' Another warning shot came around the same time when he heard that the bank's Yarmouth branch had been seeking to raise money on Bills in London, fuelling rumours that it was short of cash. The Norwich partners should 'double bar the door' to stop this happening.

November saw the St James's Square home, which he had inherited just two years earlier, sold for £35,000 (demonstrating, as with the sale of The Corner House itself, the weakness of the Fifty Factor when applied to real estate; the price today would be in the region of £15–20 million).[40] Hudson Gurney, who had held court there for so many years, would have turned in his grave to the delight of the clerks in Lombard Street, though the house did at least pass to another banker, one of the Hoares, rather than some parvenu tradesman. The contents fetched 3,500 guineas at auction. Among the pictures, sculptures and candelabra, perhaps the most bittersweet reminder of the past was *The Thames at Millwall*, a watercolour by the prolific Pre-Raphaelite marine artist Edward Cooke RA. Touted by the auctioneers Robinson & Hetley as 'an elaborate and brilliant example of the great master', its hammer price of 215 guineas stood in pathetic contrast to the £7 10*s* The Corner House and its creditors retrieved from the entire shipyard affair.

Samuel Gurney Jr had also been a buyer of Cooke's work, paying £450 in 1860 for his *HMS Terror in the Ice of Frozen Strait*, catalogued by the Royal Academy, unconsciously echoing what life was like inside The Corner House, as 'the whole scene . . . as far as the eye could stretch was confusion worse confounded'. Earl Grosvenor bought it for 400 guineas and it was last recorded, rather appropriately, as a bequest to the Scott Polar Research Institute in Cambridge.

John Gurney's calm deliberation under what must have been extreme pressure suggests that, if only he had been able to impose his will more firmly when he first became aware of the London bank's problems, failure might – but only might – have been averted.

But there was far worse ahead. The losses, the press comments, the pointing fingers, the sibilant whispers of gossip and the family strains were nothing compared to the vengeance of Dr Adam Thom.

24

A Doctor Calls

Dr Thom – the title was an honorary legal distinction – was a 'son of the manse', born into a Scots clerical family in 1802, who had taken a law degree at the University of Aberdeen. He emigrated to North America at the age of thirty-seven to make a fresh start after his first wife died. What a start it was. He was the first judge appointed in the immense landmass that was then the fiefdom of the Hudson's Bay Company and now makes up a large part of modern Canada. His official titles – 'Recorder of Rupert's Land and Legal Advisor to the Governor of Assiniboia' – only hint at what life was like for a man set in judgement over a territory populated by 'wild and peculiar people': native Indians, the Metis or 'French half breeds', and rugged settlers. Or what it must have felt like when he sentenced the Indian Cappinesseweet to hang in 1845 for killing a fellow Salteaux tribesman. At a trial in 1849 of a Meti accused of trading furs with the Indians, the show of armed force outside the court by the accused's supporters forced Dr Thom to step down from the bench for a year. English visitors who made it all the way to his home in Red River wrote of him as 'very active, energetic and possessed of considerable talent' and 'an exceedingly able man'.

He returned home to Scotland in 1854, probably to some sighs of relief from the Canadian administration. The territory had no national newspapers to which angry letters could be sent, but Thom had found outlets for his strong feelings on local matters by writing and publishing pamphlets on various contentious issues including a salvo of 'Anti-Gallic Letters' aimed at the then governor-general. With a fire-and-brimstone Old Testament mindset, he emerges as a sanctimonious and relentless pursuer, an Aberdonian granite fore-bear of Lord Reith, the towering, uncompromising Scots-born creator of the BBC, whom Winston Churchill once dubbed 'That Wuthering Height'. Thom also has a distinct hint of George Eliot's Dr Casaubon; he laboured for years over his first book, *The Chronology of Prophecy*. Dr Thom later moved to London, where, as he himself wrote, his arrival and the need to invest his capital unfortunately coincided with the issue of the Overends' prospectus. He bought sixty shares. When the collapse came and he was faced with the loss of his stake and a demand, in today's values, for some £100,000, he was determined to seek retribution. Much as Xenos was over-fond of classical allusions, Dr Thom was keen on biblical references; a floridly written pamphlet of his, seeking funds for his campaign against the directors, sets its tone with a line on the title page from the Book of Daniel. In his battle against the authors of the prospectus and their high-priced lawyers, he saw himself as David, ranged 'against a host of Goliaths' and Overends 'as an upas tree come to shadow the whole world with its blight'. The Corner House and the Norwich bank were 'centres of rottenness' and 'whited sepulchres'.

It was clear from the tone of the various judicial comments in the civil hearings that it was at least arguable, and to many like Dr Thom crystal clear, that the prospectus had been deceitful in the extreme. On the other side, the argument ran that while those responsible for it had been naïve and reckless, they had not acted with the criminal intent essential to a charge of fraud. Their defenders hammered home the point that they had lost a sizeable amount of their own money. If anyone was to blame, it was Edwards. Balancing the arguments, Bagehot felt that when the shareholders' case was dismissed, the directors were 'guilty with extenuating circumstances'; however, that had been a civil case. It is easy to understand why many felt that the case should now be tried in the harsher light of the criminal law.

This was not easy. In the 1860s Britain, unlike most continental countries, had no public prosecutor. Its rudimentary police force had no Fraud Squad and in any event, fraud was a concept whose definition was unclear. To the judges in the Chancery Court who listened to the shareholders' pleas, it meant something closer to betrayal of a trust and not necessarily a criminal offence, for which intent and motive had to be proved. As the *Pall Mall Gazette* commented, 'unless committed in one or other of the coarse and customary methods it is safe from legal punishment . . . A large proportion is committed under circumstances so peculiar that the law has never provided for them.' In the Overends' case, the Crown's two principal law officers had already been retained to act in any criminal defence, making it rather improbable that the Government would be in any rush to prosecute. Informed opinion would have sided with Bagehot, that there were extenuating circumstances and the directors had suffered enough already. One of them, Thomas Gibb, had died in the meantime, broken by the worry of the civil action.

In the absence of official action, Dr Thom was implacable and launched his own crusade to bring criminal charges privately, an aspect of the subsequent trial that has not, until now, been high-lighted. It was a trial with all the panoply of the law and, especially in its preliminary stages, the law's rigours. But it was not an investigation or a trial as we know those processes today. Nowadays, the Serious Fraud Office would lumber into action, sending police to seize books, records and computers, trawl through bank accounts and dustbins, tap a few telephones and put pressure on The Corner House managers and staff to trade leniency for themselves by incriminating the partners. Softened up by a flurry of anonymous leaks to the press, the targets would wake up early one morning as their front doors splintered, hammered in by warrant-waving detectives, so dapperly dressed that it would be an insult to describe them as in 'plain clothes'. By sheer coincidence, pressmen and TV cameras would be lurking behind the privet hedges to accentuate the process of softening up and shaming the accused, and the well-oiled wheels of modern British justice would start to turn.

Dr Thom had a much harder job. Even though he was advised by the ubiquitous George Lewis, it took an inordinate time to formulate his case. It was not until the end of 1868 that the tipstaffs appeared at the directors' offices with summonses to appear before the Lord Mayor as the City of London's Chief Magistrate, on 1 January 1869; ten years after the first spores of financial dry rot had taken root in The Corner House rafters. The Lord Mayor would decide whether there was a strong enough case for the matter to go first to a Grand Jury (a procedure long since abandoned by the British system, but alive and well in the United States) and then to a full criminal trial.

'Thou cannot hurt me,' Henry Gurney is said to have declared when handed his summons, but however confident he and his colleagues may have appeared, the charge they faced had a chilling ring. Drafted in the rotund English that lawyers love, it asserted that 'by various pretences and representations alleged to be false and fraudulent and by divers subtle devices and means', the directors had conspired together to defraud investors of £3 million. Almost ten years had passed since that first encounter with Xenos. However strongly they felt about their innocence, they must have been aware of the fate of J. F. Wilkinson, managing director of their short-lived competitor, the General Discount Company. Admittedly the charges against him were more serious. His lending to rogues had been egregious and he had used the company's money to speculate secretly in its shares to his profit. Nonetheless, for The Corner House directors, the knowledge that he was now in the Dartmoor rock quarries, chipping away the days of his sentence of five years' penal servitude, must have cast a chill shadow.

25

Facing the Lord Mayor

The directors' City world had its 'mean streets', but it also had its potent symbols of commercial power and civic majesty. The Royal Exchange, built in 1844 and modelled on the Pantheon in Rome, George Dance the Elder's Palladian style Mansion House and the impregnable Bank of England, faced each other across the ancient, bustling crossroads of Walbrook, Cornhill, Poultry and Threadneedle Street. The Mansion House was the Lord Mayor's 'home' during his term of office and the setting for many of the cigar-fumed social functions to which the directors, as senior City men, would have been invited in the course of a busy year. A few hundred yards away was Guildhall, its foundations laid in 1441 on the centre of old Roman London, and the only stone building, other than some of the churches, to have survived the Great Fire. It too was a seat of authority and ceremony, which was part of the directors' comfortable landscape. With the doors of the Bank slammed in their face, they were called to the Mansion House not as guests carrying gold-bordered invitations, but as six distinguished men – John Gurney, Henry Gurney, Robert Birkbeck, Henry Ford Barclay, Harry Gordon and William Rennie – accused of fraud and peremptorily summoned to appear in its Justice Room. There they would face their first judge, the Lord Mayor, James (later Sir James) Lawrence, flanked by his predecessor in office, Alderman Thomas Gabriel. Both men they would have known socially and professionally, were now set in judgement over them, a new relationship underscored by the bench's purple silk gowns trimmed with fur and the ceremonial gold collars around their necks.

The Times was convinced that the accused men had City opinion totally on their side. The tiny room, with its bustling beadles in red-collared uniforms with gold epaulettes, was certainly packed with a supporters' club of Buxtons, Gurneys, Hoares and Lubbocks, along with 'other persons of consideration'. Throughout the long process which was about to unfold, the daily bail for the directors (another demeaning aspect of the legal conveyor belt) was underwritten by many with the same surnames; a Rothschild and even Kirkman Hodgson, the former Bank of England director, now a partner in Barings and one of the trio of 'wise men' who had advised the Governor that Overends were beyond all hope.

George Lewis gave his client Dr Thom good value and entertained the Justice Room with several days of flailing attacks on what he saw as a 'monstrous fraud' – the deliberate concealment of the losses, the 'false, fraudulent and delusive' prospectus, the family letters showing that the Gurneys knew that the guarantees would be called, and a confused and incorrect account of how some of the directors, and even Barclays Bank, had known what was coming and withdrawn money before the collapse. He went through the bad debts and the accounting entries in painful detail, the pain relieved only when he hammed to the gallery with rather contrived quips; reciting the names of the Galway Lines ships, he joked that the *Golden Fleece* would have been a good name for the share offering itself.

After two days crammed in the tiny Room, the hearing was moved to the larger Guildhall Courtroom. In its dark-timbered gloom hovered the oppressive shadows of centuries. Though the directors faced no more than jail, others who had sat there before them, including Lady Jane Grey, the 'Nine Day Queen', and Archbishop Cranmer, had gone on to face the executioner's axe or the brushwood crackling around a wooden stake. The only concession to the directors' status was that they were allowed to sit on a bench in front of their counsel rather than in the dock. Even the larger room was jammed with spectators, and crowds milled around in the flag-stoned courtyard waiting for a seat. 'Judging from appearances', *The Times* remarked, 'the audience . . . has been of a much superior class than that usually found in courts of justice.' It seems certain that a large number of them were in fact a cross-section of the duped middle-class investors since the mood had swung perceptibly. Instead of the phalanx of solid City support in the Mansion House, the directors now had to squirm uncomfortably as the spectators made it clear that they had 'little or no sympathy with the defendants. At apparently telling points against them . . . the predominant feeling has been expressed in an unmistakable manner either in ill-suppressed murmurs of disapprobation or by ironical laughter,' *The Times* told its readers, and the defence lawyers objected to the Lord Mayor that their clients had 'enough public prejudice to bear without this chorus'. There was personal prejudice too. Day by day the flinty Dr Thom, their Nemesis, sat in court, his eyes fixed on the men he was convinced had robbed him and so many others.

However, the mood changed again when a week into the hearing George Lewis called Edward Edwards to the stand, a dramatic flourish worthy of Alfred Hitchcock in the film *Witness for the Prosecution*. It is clear from the transcripts that the defence and the Lord Mayor had been well briefed on the surprises Lewis was about to spring. The first and most damaging related to Edwards' dealings with David Ward Chapman. In January 1863, Chapman, on behalf of The Corner House, had signed a contract with Edwards entitling him to a fee of £5,000 a year in place of the loose deal-by-deal arrangement under which he had been operating. Was it really true, Lewis asked with feigned astonishment, that immediately this contract was signed Edwards had drawn the first £5,000 in notes from The Corner House cashiers and handed it straight to David Ward Chapman, right there in The Corner House partners' room? Edwards' stammered admission evoked visible shock from the directors on trial, loud murmurs of disapproval from the audience and scathing comments from the press the next day. Though Chapman's partners claimed to have been, and no doubt were, totally unaware of the compromised relationship the payment created, they must have known that Chapman lived above his means. Even his salary plus his share of Overends' substantial profits left him short, and in the late 1850s he began to overdraw his account with the firm. In any well-run partnership, this in itself should have raised enough red flags to supply the Stockton to Darlington Railway for several years, but already the firm was colour-blind to danger.

Edwards had an even harder job explaining away to his hostile listeners the little matter of the 80-foot steam yacht *Penelope*. In the summer of 1861, a London newspaper had reported its arrival in Paris, the ensign of the Royal Victoria Yacht Club in Ryde fluttering at its brass-trimmed stern. It was thought to be the first English yacht to have made the journey across the Channel and up the Seine 'and is therefore an object of great curiosity to the Parisians'. Little did the curious *flaneurs* know or care that the *Penelope* was yet another tiny part of the greater Overends' mosaic. Its 'owner' was Edwards. His guests – floating through a Paris which had yet to acquire its 'signature' Eiffel Tower, much as London would not see the Disney-like Tower Bridge until 1894 – were an ill-assorted pair. One was Lyster O'Beirne, a business partner of Edwards who scuttled around the fringes of London's financial underworld and who acted for a time as manager of the Millwall Yard. The other was the prolific author of Victorian historical 'potboilers' W. Harrison Ainsworth, whose story of the legendary criminal 'Jack Sheppard' outsold the first printing of *Oliver Twist*, much to Dickens' professional chagrin. The dandyish Ainsworth had earned a parallel reputation as a serial womaniser, so a trip to Paris no doubt held attractions beyond the art and artefacts of the Louvre, not least the nearby Théatre du Chatelet, whose managers had around that time hired '300 pretty girls . . . exhibiting them to the public in a condition so nearly approaching nudity as to shock even the sensitivities of the police', who ordered the 'adoption of less Paradisiacal fashion'.

The *Penelope* was one of two smaller craft Xenos had commissioned when he went on his first buying spree to create the Greek & Oriental fleet. Asked by Lewis how he had come by it, Edwards claimed that it had been a gift from Xenos, a gesture of friendship. This did not convince a cynical and contemptuous courtroom, who shared Lewis' view that Xenos must have been forced to hand over the *Penelope* to save his financial skin, but since Edwards was being pilloried without being the target of any formal charges, the allegation could not be pursued.

Whatever the strategy behind calling Edwards to the stand may have been, his evasiveness once there – 'I am exceedingly anxious to answer every question clearly but I have a very bad memory as to dates . . . I do not like to answer positively to anything at all. My memory is a perfect blank' – at least gave the crowded benches something else to laugh about. Without seeking to excuse him, it is clear that his confusion was compounded by the battering he got not just from the prosecuting and defence lawyers, but also from a hostile bench. The image is of a dazed mouse being batted around the Guildhall floor by sleek legal tomcats, who succeeded in portraying him as devious to a fault and a man comprehensively on the take. As *The Times* reported, 'He gave his evidence with an obvious reluctance and a hesitation which more than once drew down a reproof from the presiding magistrate and repeatedly provoked the audience to laughter.' His stuttered defence that he had been summoned from his office to the Lord Mayor's Court at a moment's notice, and that he had long since handed his files over to the creditors and had no way of checking the facts on deals, some of which had been done ten years earlier, cut no ice.

Lewis' motive for this theatrical *démarche* is puzzling. He was prosecuting the six directors. Edwards' shady dealings with Chapman and his taking commissions from all and sundry were deplorable, his role in the firm's problems was debatable and his advice questionable, but he had had no part in the prospectus, which was at the heart of the charge. If indeed he could be shown to have been the 'man who broke the bank', that was surely a line better taken by the defence, not the prosecutor seeking to send the six men to jail.

The most likely explanation is that these hand grenades had in fact been surreptitiously delivered to Lewis by the defence, perhaps for tactical reasons relating to the defendants desire to avoid giving or calling evidence themselves at this early stage. Exposing Edwards' underhand dealings with Chapman and painting him as a man of no moral fibre gave Lewis another chance to play to the packed gallery. More to the point, it gave the directors' lawyers the opportunity, without calling their clients to the witness box, to try to shift the blame by portraying the entire sorry mess the result of collusion between Edwards, whom they called 'an outsider who was betraying them', and 'a traitor in the camp', the absent David Ward Chapman (who had left Overends when the limited company was formed and was himself about to be declared bankrupt after the failure of another City project). The grenades exploded with spectacular effect, but the diversion, if that is what it was, served only to shock and entertain, and did not work as a tactic, even though in the eyes of history Edwards was forever damned as a conniving double dealer and extortionist, 'butchered', to adapt Byron, 'to make a City holiday'.

The speeches for the defence were rotund masterpieces of Victorian oratory, rightly stressing the reputation of all the directors and the heavy personal losses of the Gurneys. They were all honourable men, who had staked and lost their own money in a venture that had been brought down by outside forces. The core Overends' business was sound – and they were entitled to assume that the guarantees would meet any shortfall – while all the facts about the junk business had been most thoroughly gone into on their behalf by Mr. Gibb (who, then dead, was conveniently in no position to confirm or deny this).

'To see a man past middle life', Henry Gurney's counsel boomed with a sweep of the hand at his unhappy client, 'sitting in this court instead of as a venerated guest, charged with a criminal offence, must unless the heart be hardened indeed, produce feelings which I should be loath to attempt to describe . . .' To have acted 'unwisely and improperly' did not mean 'dishonestly and fraudulently . . . These gentlemen however imprudent have not been guilty of a crime.' There had been no intent to defraud and there was no case to answer. The directors should go free.

It was powerful, but was it powerful enough to convince the Lord Mayor and Sir Thomas Gabriel?

26

A Case to Answer

On Wednesday, 26 January 1869, the court was due to reconvene at
1 p.m. to hear the verdict. The entire morning the approaches to
Guildhall from Gresham Street, Wood Street and Basinghall Street
were 'besieged by an eager and excited crowd of well-dressed people'
despite the damp cold. When the doors were opened, they pushed,
shoved and elbowed to grab one of the public seats while City police
did their best to keep space free for the City dignitaries; among them
Newman Hunt, the new Governor of the Bank of England, who as
deputy governor, had been at the centre of the 'Black Friday' crisis
with Lancelot Holland. Now, almost three years later, the climax of
the drama might be in sight. First, though, there was an anti-climax.
In those pre-tape recorder days, the witness statements taken down
by the shorthand writers had to be read back and verified. Edwards
had to listen to an unemotional recital of his equivocations,
punctuated by 'derisive laughter' and ending, as he stepped out of
the witness box, with a volley of hisses as though it was an East End
music hall rather than a court of law.

The Lord Mayor called for silence. He was short and to the point:
the evidence was sufficient to send six men to trial. The courtroom
audience broke into 'loud cheers', which echoed back from the
courtyard when the news reached those outside.

'You are not obliged to say anything unless you desire to do so,
but whatever you say will be taken down in writing and may be given
in evidence against you at your trial.' With that warning, couched in
terms which are almost unchanged today, the Lord Mayor asked the
defendants if they wanted to speak. The accused men put their own
cases with dignity. After the cheers which had gleefully greeted the
verdict, William Rennie, who spoke at the greatest length, must have

been surprised at the reception of his own dignified apologia; 'for the misfortune which has fallen on so many shareholders . . . it is a calamity which has fallen with equal severity on myself and it arose from circumstances which no-one had foreseen'. This brought a burst of applause; had he been an actor rather than a man of money, he would have known how fickle audiences can be.

Edwards certainly learned that lesson. When he slipped out of the court, he found a hooting, jeering crowd hot on his heels. He dived into a hansom cab in Gresham Street, but those baying for his blood stopped it moving off and were about to drag him out when the police waded in to his rescue.

They could not rescue him from the embarrassed anger of the Lord Chancellor's Office, which, as administrator of the Bankruptcy Courts, demanded the following week that he appear before his chief, Bankruptcy Commissioner Holroyd, to explain himself.

This he did, with an equanimity and even conviction that had been so badly lacking when he came to the Guildhall. He was prepared, balanced and gave an interpretation of his financial dealings with Overends, which, while not without internal contradictions, makes some sense, especially against the background of the louche demi-monde which made up much of the Victorian City. As a British judge in a modern-day fraud trial remarked: 'It is a commonplace of judicial experience that a witness who makes a poor impression in the witness box may be found at the end of the day, when his evidence is considered in the light of all the other evidence bearing upon the issue, to have been both truthful and accurate. Conversely the evidence of a witness who at first seemed impressive and reliable may at the end of the day have to be rejected . . .'

Edwards' version of the facts may have been polished in the time between his two court appearances. He was after all a barrister, with a barrister's fluency. He had also skated long enough on thin ice to know how to spot the dangerous patches. Nevertheless, much of his side of the story has the ring of plausibility. First, he told Commissioner Holroyd, he had been conscious that as part of the drive to reform public service, Parliament was looking at the role and remuneration of the Official Assignees. He had told his superiors that he intended to look for outside work to augment his income. They had raised no objection providing any such work was done outside court hours. Second, though David Ward Chapman was an old friend, he had first met Henry Gurney and his partners on business matters when, as Official Assignee, he had been sorting out the debts of a trading firm – almost certainly the big leather market scandal, in which Overends lost several million pounds in today's values and which cost Grant's Mercantile Discount even more.

Henry Gurney had been impressed and had asked him to be available for negotiations of an 'occasional and exceptional nature' related to 'large transactions' outside their mainstream business. The first of these had been Greek & Oriental, but he had played no part in the introduction of the business. Yes, he had taken commissions from Overends' borrowers, the unlucky Zachariah Pearson among them, but he had been told by Gurney at the outset that while the firm would remunerate him for each matter in which he became involved, 'they did not care what I got from other persons for whom I had dealings with them'. The payments had been received with Gurney's 'full knowledge, approval and consent'. Indeed, several of them had been negotiated directly for him by other Overends' partners.

Third, it had been John Gurney himself, not Ward Chapman, who in 1862 had suggested moving from the ad hoc payment arrangements to the lucrative five-year contract, the revelation of which had so shocked the crowd in the Lord Mayor's Court. Gurney had even mentioned vaguely the notion that Edwards might become a partner at some point, and Henry Gurney told him, 'Friend Edwards, I don't know how we are to get on without thee.'

The thinnest ice approached when Edwards presented his version of his dealings with David Ward Chapman and just how he had come to 'own' the *Penelope*. Chapman had publicly conceded that the loan had been a gross lapse of judgement, but swore that the debt had never compromised his dealings for his firm. Defending himself, Edwards took the high ground. It had not been the first or indeed the last loan he had given his friend; he had advanced about £11,000 in all, prudently taking a life insurance policy as partial security. It was something any good friend who had money to spare would do for another who was temporarily embarrassed. They had known each other for twenty years, they were near neighbours in Brighton and their wives were good friends. 'He is the most splendid fellow I know and gives the most delicious dinners,' he once told Xenos, in a nicely Victorian phrase.

As to the *Penelope*, Edwards' version is that it had originally been intended as a gift from the shipyard to Xenos, a gesture of appreciation for the large contracts he had placed:

> Knowing that I was fond of yachting he offered to give it to me . . . simply because he had no use for it himself . . . I told Mr. Henry Edmund Gurney about it and shortly afterwards Mr. Samuel Gurney [Jr] came by invitation on a cruise in it, when the fact of the gift was mentioned and talked about to him. It was a matter of perfect notoriety [that Bagehot phrase again] at the time. None of the firm ever objected to my receiving it and if they did not – if they, knowing exactly the state of affairs between all the parties did not object – why should anyone else?

Another alleged gift, an Arab mare, had been given to him by Xenos, but deftly turning the tables, Edwards claimed that he had later handed it on to Robert Birkbeck when the latter had admired it in Edwards' stables.

When Xenos read the newspaper report of Edwards' evidence, he angrily wrote to *The Times* to give his side of the story. Edwards, who was then acting as The Corner House watchdog in Greek & Oriental, had become aware that the *Penelope* was due to be delivered and had virtually extorted it from him as the price for his continued support in his tricky relations with Overends. He handed it over, Xenos wrote, 'as a dove gives herself to the hawk'. The Arab mare had been a 'gift' in the same vein.

However we now weigh up the conflicting evidence, the system of the time came to the decision that Edwards had to go. He was dismissed and disappeared, maybe to Brighton, or, like David Ward

Chapman, to some 'little colony of English raffs' in a continental spa, like Thackeray's Becky Sharpe at the end of her bruising tramp up and then down life's slippery staircase.

27

In the Dock

Edwards' public humiliation would have been of little comfort to the directors, who were braced for their trial. However confident they were of their innocence, as magistrates who sat on rural benches themselves, and from Quaker experiences visiting prisons, they knew that juries were fickle. Britain's jails were full of men who had been equally confident and who still faced long, harsh years behind bars weaving or mat-making from 6.30 a.m. until 7 p.m., sleeping in cells 13½ feet deep, 7½ feet wide and 9 feet high.

First, in a formality that must have been especially degrading, they had to appear at the Old Bailey, with its doleful aura of forgers, felons and footpads, where a Grand Jury was empanelled to consider the Lord Mayor's verdict, which it duly endorsed. The defence lawyers had, however, managed to save the directors from the ignominy of being tried there.

If this were a novel, backstairs plotting and twists and turns would now build to the dénouement with a heady mix of rapier-like cross-examination, surprise witnesses, a blackmailed juror, missing documents found in a safe at the last minute and shocking reversals of fortune. Truth is stranger than fiction and though there were twists and turns, the end result was bathos rather than pathos.

Despite the noisy commentary from the claque in and around the Guildhall, Dr Thom had never had the backing of the majority of shareholders for his vendetta. Many were convinced that without his strident campaign there might have been some compromise with the creditors to reduce the amount shareholders had to pay. Instead, the latter were now insisting not just on their full pound of flesh but were demanding interest as well. Others simply thought the criminal case a lost cause. Some felt that the directors had suffered enough.

Even so, public opinion remained hard to read. The *New York Times* reported in July that 'scarcely an apologist for them [the directors] can be found in the whole range of the English press . . . in many quarters their conviction is regarded as a foregone conclusion'.

Dr Thom seems to have realised only late in the day that the last and crucial battle would need more money than he could spare. Solicitors, even those as illustrious as George Lewis, did not have the right to appear in the High Court, and the system rightly discouraged litigants from pursuing their case in person. Dr Thom needed to retain a barrister. Barristers needed to be paid and he was short of funds. An application to a judge to take £5,000 out of the Overends' assets was rejected, and Dr Thom resorted to pamphleteering and a letter to *The Times* to raise money for what he called his 'national battle'. This brought in one donation of £100, another of £5 and some postage stamps, an indication of the way the wind of public opinion was blowing. He then approached the Government for backing and was roundly rejected. Justifying the decision in the House of Commons, Gladstone asked rhetorically why the public purse should be tapped to help a group of speculative investors. In any case, it was too late. If Dr Thom had come to the Government at the outset, things might have taken a different course, Gladstone told the crowded benches, but Whitehall could not give financial support for a case it had no hand in mounting and which it could not possibly take over at this very late stage. Despite some froth blowing in the House of Commons, the Government stuck to its guns, no doubt aware that Members on both sides included many of the directors' powerful friends and relations.

'Celebrity' trials were in any event part of Victorian entertainment culture; a feature of life less in evidence today but which certainly continued well into the 1930s. Crowds would throng to the Royal Courts of Justice in the Strand (the apotheosis of Victorian Gothic architecture) to hear the forensic fireworks of an F. E. Smith or Patrick Hastings, and watch defendants and witnesses (the more socially prominent, the tastier) skewered and discomfited.

The *Illustrated London News* commissioned the American artist, Asher B. Durand, better known for his pastoral New England paintings, to sketch the directors' trial for its readers. Reduced to page size, the details are hard to make out. However, seen on a fuller scale Durand did a good job of conveying the sense of a crowded, stuffy courtroom, the press and the official shorthand writers huddled together scribbling down every word as the lawyers boomed, their clients squashed onto a narrow bench in front of them, spared again the indignity of having to sit in the dock. The deaf Henry Gurney is actually on his feet, his brass ear trumpet turned to catch the lawyers' comments like a Victorian satellite dish. As the afternoon light faded beyond the power of the 'day reflector', a metal panel hung behind the jury box to beam its rays around the room, the black-gowned ushers held their long wands high to tug on the ring pulls which popped on the overhead gas lamps.

The trial had been postponed several times. While this must have added to the strain on the directors, they could at least be confident that they had the best legal team money could buy; led by the Solicitor General, Sir John Coleridge, who would go on to become Lord Chief Justice, and Sir John Karslake, who only a few months earlier had vacated the post of Attorney General. Mr Sarjeant Ballantine and Mr Sarjeant Sleigh did not need their ancient legal titles to make them the Bar's most formidable (and highly paid) cross examiners; Hardinge Giffard QC would go on to become Lord Chancellor and, as Lord Halsbury, the erudite codifier of the Laws of England.

King's *History* states that the trial was held at the old High Court next to Westminster Hall to avoid the disturbances which had accompanied the City proceedings. While *The Times* Law Reports of the first day of the hearing is from Westminster Hall, all the subsequent reports are headed 'Guildhall', so the accused were at least back on familiar, if hardly friendly, ground.

For Dr Thom to launch himself against a line-up of this calibre was daunting, made even harder by the fact that not long before the trial George Lewis had ceased to represent him, no doubt deciding that a fashionable solicitor espousing a now unfashionable cause might find himself out of fashion quite quickly. The good Doctor's desperate last-minute choice of Counsel turned a daunting challenge into the legal equivalent of the Light Brigade charging into the mouths of the Russian guns. Dr Thom's new solicitor found a junior barrister, Dudley Yelverton, who in turn suggested Macrae Moir, a magazine editor and non-conformist minister who was also a member of the Bar. That Moir was a fellow Scot and Secretary to the Scottish Corporation in London must have given Dr Thom some comfort. The third of Dr Thom's 'Musketeers', who would lead the team, was the Irish Queen's Counsel Edward Vaughan Kenealy. Brought in at the last minute, he was an unfortunate choice. In the words of a contemporary, Kenealy was 'possessed of great pertinacity, of complete disregard for the feelings of others and of an absolute recklessness of statement', a man of whom 'it would be an affectation to pretend . . . his reputation was high among his fellow barristers.' He had a large chip on his shoulder about some alleged mistreatment by senior judges, was much involved in mysticism (his authorship of *The Book of God* and *Braghallan of the Deipnosophists* would have given him and Dr Thom something in common) and, to compound his failings in the eyes of his colleagues, a Radical. The Lord Chief Justice who was to preside over this unequal clash of talents, Scottish-born Sir Alexander Cockburn, had twice served as attorney general. When he moved to the bench, he found it hard, in one contemporary's view, to forget that he was no longer an advocate, and was inclined to make up his mind on the merits of a case too quickly and 'in consequence wrongly'. The same anonymous Encyclopedia contributor stresses that Cockburn was nonetheless 'beyond doubt always in intention, and generally in fact, scrupulously fair'. In the Overends' case, Kenealy tested Cockburn's patience to the limit, a test all the more severe since the two men were friends and Cockburn was godfather to Kenealy's son. He certainly tested the patience of the 'Special Jury'. The twelve commercial men, who, like the crew of HMS *Pinafore*, were 'sober men and true, and attentive to their duty', did not appreciate Kenealy's admission that he had not had much time to study the papers before launching into a barrage of confused facts and what Cockburn called 'reckless assertions' and 'serious impropriety'. Much of his presentation of a complex figure-laden case must have been almost incomprehensible, even to the financially sophisticated jury. Because of the way the charges had been framed, and after long wrangling about what the defendants could be cross-examined about on their statements at the civil trial, the six men did not give evidence. Each sat stoically day after day, heads aching as plummy voices boomed and blustered in the muggy courtroom air, listening to Kenealy bluster and rant about the share offer as 'a mock auction where the silver was not silver and the jewels were glass'. They also watched with pleasure as Oswald Howell, an accountant who had worked for the creditors' committee and who seemed to have become as besotted with the crusade as Dr Thom, was skewered by the defence team for representing himself as 'the high priest of justice'.

'Value for money' was a Quaker business principle, and the three former partners for whom Sir John Coleridge spoke, must have felt greatly satisfied with what it cost them in retainers, 'brief fees' and 'refreshers'; according to the *New York Times*, the trial cost $5,000 a day, an estimate hard to convert through the simultaneous equation of currency rates and inflation, but perhaps £50,000 today. He and the phalanx of other defence counsel had clearly mastered the details of their complex briefs and throughout the trial were quickly on their feet, usually with Cockburn's support, to jump on Kenealy's many factual errors and excursions into conspiracy theory, correct ing his law. At one point they even had to correct the judge's own arithmetic.

Coleridge's closing address lasted two days, with a break at the suggestion of a sympathetic jury when he was evidently exhausted. It was a classic of heavyweight Victorian advocacy. In his peroration, Coleridge recalled that Kenealy had quoted Virgil and Lucius Brutus. He would quote from a 'nobler' source: 'Whatever ye would that men should do unto you, so do you even unto them.' He sat down to a burst of applause, smoothly hushed by the judge with the comment that, 'although it is natural that some emotion be excited by such an eloquent speech, I cannot permit such ebullitions of feelings in a court of justice.'

Opening his summing up, Cockburn declared himself 'oppressed' by the 'sense of responsibility I feel at the duty I have now to perform', an introduction which might have given the defendants a momentary shiver. But from then on, despite the cold and dark of a Victorian London December day, inside the courtroom the sun began to shine. In a judgement which ran to sixteen pages, Cockburn told the jury firmly that they were not there to decide whether there had been misrepresentation or concealment, but whether the six men had embarked on 'a deliberate design to deceive and cheat the public'. Cockburn was clear that they had not. Even though the share offering circular – seldom can so relatively brief a document have had so much high-powered legal attention – was 'perhaps the most succinct and jejune a prospectus as one has ever seen', the prospective investors could always have asked to see accounts; none chose to do so. The underlying conventional Bill business was in fact, as had been claimed, one 'with enormous earning power'; and the guarantees of the partners in the old firm had not been a deception, but proof of good faith. The estimates of the value backing them up had been honestly made and the supporting deeds about which there had been so much fuss, were 'regular and proper'. The collapse had been triggered when rumours that the old partners were selling their estates had caused the damaging run on deposits.

He danced delicately through the arguments. The public had taken the prospectus at face value, but what it said was 'something different to the truth'. Nonetheless, the prosecutor had not succeeded in showing that any 'misunderstanding was due to the wording of the prospectus rather than to a popular delusion as to the prosperity of the old firm. Nor had he proved that if the prospectus contained any misrepresentations that they were issued for the purpose of deceiving and defrauding the shareholders.' The directors might have been negligent in disguising facts to which they did not themselves attach much importance, but which they feared would alarm the public. At the same time, they had an 'absolute faith in the recuperative power of Overend & Gurney and they looked forward to immense profits'. They thought that they had done enough by disclosing the real facts to the new Board. 'This was their error and in our opinion a grave error but there is a great gap between such an error and a deliberate intention to defraud.' The old partners had held on to all their shares, as had the new directors who had lost a large amount; hardly what would have happened if the operation had been planned from the outset as a fraud.

Nonetheless, the former partners did not escape Cockburn's lash. 'Through turning aside from the safe and settled path of business, and going astray after vain phantoms and elusive dreams, embarking their capital in the wildest speculations and the rashest enterprises, led away by a spirit of greed and gain, we have seen them reduced to ruin, their lost fortunes scattered in the winds their reputations tattered and impaired', but they were not on trial for that. He was sympathetic to the accused and the 'social degradation into which unfortunately they have fallen'.

Kenealy and Dr Thom were not, one supposes, men inclined to squirm in embarrassment, but even they might have blushed when their turn came to face Cockburn's withering scorn. At least one of Kenealy's claims was 'a most strange hallucination . . . but worse than that I think the prosecution has not been conducted as it ought to have been', and as far as the three new directors were concerned he had never seen a prosecution which 'was less warranted'. They had been put at a special disadvantage since, as the charge was one of conspiracy, they had been denied the opportunity of giving evidence about their 'due diligence' conversations with the selling partners. Cockburn added that the case reinforced his conviction that Britain should follow the example of every other country in Europe and appoint a Director of Public Prosecutions.

It took the jury less than ten minutes to agree about the 'great gap', and its foreman, a tradesman from Bermondsey, announced in 'a firm and loud voice the verdict of Not Guilty'.

The news was greeted by 'the wildest excitement and enthusiasm' inside and outside the courtroom. The audience rose to its feet cheering and applauding, some in tears, and the accused, breaking their habit of stoic reserve, pumped their barristers' hands. The reaction in the City was one of 'intense satisfaction' and Bagehot was not alone in remarking on the way the public mood had changed since the earlier hearing.

The defendants left the court to celebrate their first Christmas in several years not overshadowed by a cloud of apprehension.[41]

The *New York Times*' first report on 24 December was a simple statement of the acquittal. Since the cascading headlines that had announced the terrors of 'Black Friday' three years earlier, the story had clearly almost vanished from the American mind. It was the last of eight items in a foreign news summary headed by a report that the Bishop of Havana, at odds with the Spanish regime, had vanished from Madrid and was thought to be in France. Even a fuller report on 3 January of the atmosphere at the Guildhall when the verdict was announced, gave the news less prominence than events in the still puzzling province of Schleswig-Holstein, a minor financial scandal in Hungary involving a cabal of Counts and a speech by the Pope. The American reports reflect another set of the 'small world' coincidences that are a feature of our story. When news of the collapse hit in 1866, there was still no transatlantic cable, despite heroic and expensive efforts, and the report came by steamship. The capital needed to restart the huge operation, another triumph of Victorian energy, ingenuity and persistence, had finally been committed in a mad scramble just days before 'Black Friday' and by the time the acquittal came, it could be routinely reported along the cable, which had become a commonplace if expensive means of Transatlantic communication. We have already noted that Samuel Gurney Jr was a director of the original promoting company and that the thousands of miles of cable were insulated by the Gutta Percha Company, on whose Board sat Henry Ford Barclay. Rounding things off neatly from our opening page, the final successful laying operation was carried out by Brunel and Scott Russell's *Great Eastern*, which had proved so catastrophically unusable as a liner and had been converted into a huge cable layer, like a once grand London railway hotel demoted to a doss house. Even the shadow of the Galway Line itself hovered over the

Atlantic waves; the *Great Eastern*'s First Officer Robert Halpin had commanded one of the Line's first vessels.

The discount market historian W. T. C. King concludes that the summing up was 'wholly favourable' to the defendants and that 'the moral character of the Gurneys had been vindicated.' (We assume that his reference to 'the Gurneys' in fact covered all six defendants.) Bagehot did not agree, grumbling that while it was the right verdict and

> the public is bound to be just to these unhappy gentlemen, it cannot afford to be generous. They sinned grievously in not putting the public in as good a position as themselves for judging as to the expediency of joining or refusing to join their company. If their reticence has ruined their fortunes and peace of mind it must not be forgotten that it has broken up and wrecked many households besides.

Doctors Thom and Kenealy nursed their wounds, into which Cockburn had rubbed salt by refusing to allow them to recover their costs and fees. In fact, to read his memoirs Kenealy seems to have been unable to acknowledge that there had actually been an acquittal, recording only that the trial had ended 'abortively, no punishment having been inflicted on the offenders despite the losses and suffering they had caused'. Kenealy stoked the grudge he already had against the entire bench. By the time he next appeared before Cockburn in the extraordinary case of the Tichborne claimant, Kenealy had become even further detached from reality. His allegations of Jesuit plots, and that his friend Cockburn had been on intimate terms with London's most infamous 'Madam', led to his being disbarred for having 'insulted the judge and disgusted the jury', though in fairness Kenealy was increasingly weakened by diabetes.

Writing in 1966, Anthony Tuke, who was far closer to the heart of Barclays than King, excellent though the latter's study is, took a more balanced view. It had been 'a story which though tragic enough in its repercussions was, when regarded objectively, considerably less discreditable to some at least of the participants than at first appeared.'

The six defendants lived on in peace and happiness, poorer but not destitute, sadder and wiser – and probably wondering night after night why things had gone so wrong.

28

'Guilty of Our Own Disasters'

The middle-ground verdict provided under Scottish Law, that the charges were 'Not Proven', might have been a more equitable resolution. However, legal niceties aside, we come back to the more pertinent questions of where the blame lies and why did this all happen? We can certainly agree with King that the Gurneys were vindicated in the sense that they did their best to live up to their obligations for the problems they and they alone had caused, and did not resort to exile, bankruptcy or years of expensive lawyer-led evasion and attrition to escape their debts. In so doing, they suffered much financial and social pain.

Nevertheless, each of the historical judgements we have quoted above – King, Bagehot and Tuke – seem to agree that the defendants did serious wrong, even if technically they committed no crime. There were really several interlinked sets of accusations. First, the partners in the old firm had led it into 'unimaginably bad' business and made it worse year by year by a series of bad decisions. They had covered up their misjudgements (which were financed by and at the risk of their depositors, who had trusted implicitly in them), and then in desperation, had foisted on the public an investment whose real nature was concealed and which, because of the ill-thought-out and partly paid structure of the shares, was actually a burden not a benefit. The new directors bore no share of blame for the past, but in the matter of the share offering were clearly culpably naïve.

It is clear that Edwards was not the prime mover. He may have given bad and self-serving advice, and put himself in a position through his financial leverage over David Ward Chapman where his recommendations went through 'on the nod', but he did not start the rot. In a letter to Henry Gurney seeking compensation after he was sacked, Edwards wrote:

> . . . you are well aware that all the accounts I had to deal with were open before I was called to your councils and that they had already reached an amount the announcement of which in the event of bankruptcy or failure of the parties at the critical moment in which these events happened would have had a serious effect upon the credit of your house. Gurney had decided that sacrifices were to be made to save the parties during the crisis hoping of course for better times . . . The greatest labour night and day was bestowed by me to carry out this policy, involving most complicated and extraordinary financial arrangements, during which the most universal confidence was placed in me. Better times did not come and thus from week to week thousands and thousands were added to the now hopeless wrecks but thus and thus only were the great losses brought about.
>
> . . . I frequently spoke to Mr. John Henry Gurney about the increasing amount of some of the accounts, when he told me not to mind, that the House was strong enough to bear it, and that all I had to do was keep the parties from bankruptcies or failure.

His version of events – the last paragraph of which has echoes of the private views of the Bank of England before the débâcle – was not refuted at any of the legal hearings. Lord Chief Justice Cockburn's strictures about the old firm 'going astray after vain phantoms and illusive dreams' were addressed to the partners; there was no evidence at the trial about the supposed malign influence of Edwards.

Regarding the partners in the old firm, King took the view that Henry Gurney was too busy to attend to the details of these deals and had left it to David Ward Chapman to 'check the securities'. The latter had let the firm down by failing to do his job either because he was under Edwards' thumb, or distracted by his own social life, or both. That does not hold much water. Firstly what could have occupied Henry Edmund Gurney more than the escalating problems that threatened the firm's life? Secondly, partnership is a collective concentration of thought and effort, a sharing of ideas, information and above all responsibility, since each partner is personally liable for the consequences of what the others do, or fail to do. All the more so in a banking firm, a risk-filled business, at its nastier moments comparable to running a truck load of dangerously sweating nitro-glycerine over the Sierra Madre.

It is inconceivable that any of the working partners in The Corner House could claim that they did not know the sort of business the firm was taking on, and both Xenos and Edwards quote instances of Henry Gurney's often tough interventions in the day-to-day handling of the problem accounts. The firm balanced its books at the close of each business day, and the partners saw a detailed 'Statistical Summary' each week, in which any problems or aberrations would have been highlighted. It is actually surprising that John Gurney did not spot the rot earlier. He was often in London and, if he did not see the 'Summaries', would certainly have been given a monthly profit-and-loss statement and snapshot of the balance sheet. In any event, the formal legal documents for each major transaction would have been signed by all or most of the partners. The deed which released Xenos from his Greek & Oriental obligations, for example, has the signatures of Samuel Gurney Jr, Henry Gurney, David Ward Chapman, Arthur Chapman, Robert Birkbeck and rather surprisingly the ubiquitous Edwards. None of the partners could have been ignorant of the chaos of which this deed was the expensive result. If David Ward Chapman's extravagance and surreptitious private debt to Edwards had motivated him to slip doubtful deals onto the books, he could never have done so without questioning and support from his partners, and when the deed came to be signed, painful questions cannot fail to have been asked.

It is thus not unduly harsh to conclude that like the Wagon Lits carriage load of suspects in Agatha Christie's *Murder on the Orient Express*, the old firm's partners were collectively to blame for going astray, and that it was the consensus of the firm's active members with at least the tacit concurrence of the non-working partners. But why?

Xenos suggests, in rather hyperbolic style, that the root cause was Henry Gurney's ambition to become what today we might call a 'tycoon'; that he was 'fond of multiplying his money and was ambitious of commanding the commercial world . . . to put his hand upon a vast amount of commercial and maritime property and so in a large measure to control the two chief elements of England's commercial greatness'. But again, even if he was driven in that direction (and reliable though Xenos is generally, it is hard to imagine Gurney condescending to open his mind about his ambitions to a troublesome Greek borrower), he would have to have taken his partners with him. While Gurney probably was as keen as anyone to make money, the second part of Xenos' conclusion is surely overblown.

It becomes more comprehensible if we go back to our overriding theme of change, an age advancing, inventing, adapting, smashing down the old and building the new in ways that were breathtaking. It would be natural for a group of ambitious men to want to be a profitable part of this transformation, a temptation compounded by change at another level, that of generations. After David Barclay Chapman's ambiguous interregnum, Henry Gurney was following in the footsteps of his father; never easy for any son, but especially hard when he was comparing himself to, and knew that the world was measuring him against, 'Samuel Gurney the Great'. He would have been less than human if he had not been determined to show his family and that inquisitive spider's web of Quaker relations that he could do better and move more aggressively, in keeping with the times. Out of The Corner House windows he and his partners could see other firms plunging into 'finance' with apparent success, firms that were less skilled, less well connected, less powerful than Overends.

A short stroll down Lombard Street loomed the one institution that was even more powerful, the Bank of England itself, in its twin roles as a direct business competitor and far more importantly as The Corner House's 'lender of last resort'. Moreover, it was a lender that had made clear when it altered its rules in 1857 that there were limits to its generosity, another change in the accepted landscape which would have served as a sharp spur to find new ways of making money. Why not develop a new source of income, one that admittedly had higher risks but which also offered far higher returns? In those frothily foolhardy times, there was plenty of money seeking a home, so that Overends could attract all the deposits they needed without undue reliance on their overweening neighbour. And as bankers were to reassure themselves in the twentieth-century junk bond market, while there might be losses and aggravations along the way, the heady Victorian Stock Market offered a profitable exit through which the businesses being financed were sold off to the public.

Envy too is another human trait that may have clouded judgements. The Corner House may have relied overmuch on Grant, but being Englishmen they must have shared the City view that he was a shyster. If a man like that could get rich, they as gentlemen of breeding and banking skill could surely get even richer. Like Trollope's weak-kneed hero Alaric Tudor in *The Three Clerks*, 'He had seen that men grew rich around him, men endowed with no talents higher than his own, with no brighter genius, no more enduring energies; he had watched how nameless nobodies had suddenly sprung forth to the world view as possessors of boundless wealth; of boundless wealth and therefore of boundless honour.'

Whatever the mix of motives that led the partners astray, once the problems became too big to ignore, fear too must have been a powerful factor. They must have feared that their mainstream business would vanish in an instant if their depositors knew the truth, and that the contagion would spread to Norwich and threaten an even more valuable business. There was also the natural dread of being publicly scorned as a pack of fools and scoundrels.

Grant may have started as a back-alley money lender but had transformed himself into a powerful if unscrupulous company promoter. He had great flair, the bold 'cheeky chappy' quality and the brazen gall known in Yiddish as *chutzpah*. He was also a man with a nose for weakness. It is not hard to see that in his frequent contacts with The Corner House, which went back to the leather market and the mid-1850s, he would have spotted some or all of these elements in the partners' make-up and made it his business to exploit them. That would have been even easier given what was perhaps their biggest flaw, pride. They were masters of the traditional Bill universe, but knew little about anything else. They would, however, have been too proud to concede the slightest ignorance, even less to admit they made mistakes when these became glaringly apparent. How easy it could be to entice them into blind alleys to have their pockets picked.

Xenos may be hinting at this when, in summing up his own bitter experience, he rather generously concedes that the Gurneys and Robert Birkbeck were 'greater victims than I. They had latterly become tools in the hands of unscrupulous and daring men to whom, in an inauspicious hour, they had granted their confidence – men who at the eleventh hour knew how to avoid the impending catastrophe.' We can note the plural – which may suggest a reference to Grant, Barker, or maybe even Lascaridi – and also remind ourselves that Edwards had been fired several years before that 'eleventh hour'. In a letter to *The Times*, before his book saw the light of day, Xenos said more or less the same of the partners but in tones even more exculpatory. Of Henry Edmund Gurney and Robert Birkbeck he wrote 'I do not believe there are in the City of London more honourable and well meaning men. Their commercial views were large and public spirited but unfortunately in detail they were misled and hurried from precipice to precipice by certain brokers and legal advisors who were, however, prudent enough to shelter themselves from loss and responsibility . . .' Again the plural and again the possibility that 'brokers' was intended as a dig at Grant and Barker.

Though it may be fanciful, it is possible that one of the elements in the explanation can be traced back to the partners' education. To be spiritually nurtured, quietly cocooned in leafy Tottenham from evil and alluvial vices, encouraged to think well of all and surrounded by fellow Quakers, may have made these unworldly men simply unready to appreciate until too late, that Barker and Grant were rogues, and that Edwards' advice was self-serving. Naïveté, in a word. Or in the more prolix phrasing of the Quaker essayist, John Stephenson Rowntree, the risk of a system of 'guarded education' behind 'hedges' and 'external bulwarks', was that 'when children grow to be men and women they must inevitably find that the endeavour of their friends to screen them from evil, is no effectual protection against the allurements to vice with which Satan besets their path.'

Rowntree was addressing a question, the overall decline of Quakerism, that concerned the entire Friends' community and is also relevant for us, since The Corner House story and the apparent abandonment of Quaker principles can be seen as a manifestation of that decline. Rowntree won the first prize of 100 guineas in an essay competition announced in 1858 by an anonymous 'gentleman', 'who laments that notwithstanding the population of the United Kingdom has more than doubled itself in the past fifty years, the Society of Friends is less in number than at the beginning of the century', and that the Quaker 'witness has become more and more feeble'. Writers were invited to explain why. Rowntree took respectful but trenchant issue with almost all the dearly held Quaker tenets, not excluding the 'paralysing effect of an eagerness to be rich' and the 'prevalence of that commercial prosperity to which the profession of Quakerism is specially favourable'. But he found even more fundamental problems. Priest-less quiet worship was un-inspiring; men and women needed to be led and inspired to God. They were too cut off from the world. Quakers' disavowal of baptism and the Lord's Supper made it impossible to associate with other Christians, while on a day-to-day level the 'peculiarities' of Quakers' dress and language created 'an ascetic isolation from the rest of mankind'. The Society was too harsh in its discipline, arrogating to itself the authority to direct the conduct of Quakers in 'eternal matters of secondary importance' even when these regulations were 'destitute of direct scriptural authority'. Young people had been alienated by 'the gloomy, mystical view of religion' often presented to them, coupled with 'unreasonable requirements respecting matters of behaviour and dress'. But the main reason for the numerical decline, in Rowntree's view, was the harsh choice between marriage within the Society or the risk of disownment, a choice women could avoid only by remaining spinsters and thus driving down the Quaker birth rate even more. In the first half of the nineteenth century, Rowntree reported, the Society disowned some 4,000 members under the marriage rule, a policy he rightly characterises as 'suicidal'.[42]

Another reflection of the change in the Quaker moral climate can be seen when we look at the Society's reaction after Overends failed: silence. Silence despite the fact that Quaker country banks and their customers 'from Darlington to Hitchin', including many in Norfolk, had invested in Overends' shares; their losses aside, there was strong evidence of the kind of aberrant behaviour that the community deplored.

Maybe the lack of finger-pointing reflected the standing of the individuals. Maybe it was genuinely felt in the community that by selling up their assets, the partners had done their utmost to make amends, and there was no point in making them suffer humiliation or censure on the scale applied to the unfortunate Joseph Fry and his family.

Maybe The Corner House partners unconsciously saw themselves as somehow above the moral code that bound lesser men. They were, after all, not the Society's rank and file. Rowntree also highlights as another Quaker weakness, the imperceptible evolution in the eighteenth century of what he calls 'birthright' members of the Society – a term which clearly applies to those at The Corner House and their East Anglian partners. As Elizabeth Isichei reminds us, they were part of what the American writer Logan Pearsall Smith, looking back from the twentieth century, saw as 'a world of Barclays and Gurneys and other rich English Quakers which like a Quaker Versailles, holy and yet splendid, shone for us across the Atlantic with a kind of glory'. Among the problems this caused – divisiveness, allowing 'lifeless' members to retain positions of leadership – Rowntree believed that this self-perpetuating group 'increased the tendency which [the Society] already possessed to exclusiveness'.

These comments reinforce the sense of The Corner House partners as aloof and inbred, a dangerous combination of arrogance and innocence, whose 'birthright' membership left them free to pick and choose the rules and disciplines by which they felt bound. In any event, as Victorian England changed, religious choices multiplied. A successful Quaker with a country estate might well have been tempted to 'assimilate' with his neighbours by attending the local Anglican parish church, while the religiously inquisitive could find a home in the plain services and broad reach of the Evangelical movement.

As the world changed, the Gurneys' lifestyle certainly became more worldly. David Ward Chapman was a prime example of a new generation with the familiar urge to dilute or even scrap the discipline, humility and plainness of their parents and grandparents, and to acquire the visible trappings of success; those expensive houses, fashionable paintings, glossy horses and even glossy women their contemporaries enjoyed so much, but which flew in the face of the early Quaker dictum, 'Try to live simply. A simple lifestyle freely chosen is a source of strength.'[43]

The pinnacle on which The Corner House partners stood, even if shakily, made them self-important as well as dangerously self-confident, men who it is hard to imagine ever asking for advice or being called to account by their local Meeting. If an inner voice told them what they were doing was right, they would believe it unreservedly, even though it was no more than self-ventriloquism.

The deceptive voice gradually drowned out everything they had learned at home, at school, in work and in everyday life about the Quaker disciplines of caution and honest dealing. They had been taught to examine their consciences and their business dealings day by day, to make sure they had done the right thing. Yet after at most a year or so in the 'finance' business, it must have been horribly apparent that they had not. Five minutes with Xenos and Lascaridi, a harangue from Father Daly, another set of ledgers in red ink from Millwall, another request to sink more money into a crooked Leprechaun vision of an Irish railway, running across the peat bogs from nowhere to nowhere, were surely each sufficient in themselves to make clear that The Corner House was, in a phrase no Victorian would have used, 'in over its head'.

29

'Memories Are Made of This . . .'

In its old-fashioned working methods, its rigid business and class demarcation lines between merchant and joint stock banks and arriviste Americans, between generally upper class stockbrokers and the rather sharper parvenu jobbers, the City of London I knew even in the 1970s was one the Gurneys would have found familiar. Today, though London is still Europe's financial powerhouse, the remains of the City itself have been transplanted like the fragments of a saint's shinbones; some to the Isle of Dogs, to be venerated in the new-age cathedrals of Canary Wharf, some to areas the Gurneys would never have dreamed of as 'financial', such as Berkeley Square. The Bank of England has been emasculated, stripped of its supervisory authority over the City, the fabled power of a 'raised eyebrow from the Governor' a faded memory. Its marbled halls, centred around a gracious lawn crowned by an ancient mulberry tree, are half empty, the whole place ripe to be converted into a hotel and leisure centre.[44] Gone too are the discount houses themselves: until the 1980s, their top-hatted emissaries fascinated Japanese bankers newly posted to London, as they made their twice-daily rounds of the City banks and the Discount Office of the Bank of England, in a haze of gin, cricket scores and insider-trading tips.

Up in Norwich, the prestigious regional headquarters built by Barclays on the old Gurney site is now 'redundant' and re-branded as the Norwich Youth Venue. Earnest planners are hard at work trying to fit spaces for 'socialising, relaxation and escape' into its echoing voids. Just a few doors down Bank Plain, the Po Na Na night club, with dancing under Marrakech-style tents suspended from the ceiling, offers its own form of escape, a venue past which older Quaker generations would have hurried, tutting, with averted eyes.

We have already explored the industrial archeology of the Millwall shipyards and Grant's mementoes in Leicester Square. Sadly, nothing is left to show the site of the house he built at the southern entrance to Kensington Palace Gardens to mark the high point of his career. Designed in what a contemporary newspaper called 'flamboyant French Château style', it cost Grant, or more precisely the shareholders whose money he had pocketed, £300,000, which multiplied by our Fifty Factor makes it expensive even by the standards of today's polyglot billionaire residents of that tree-lined enclave. For many years the 'Château' had the dubious distinction of being the largest private house built in London, but over the top of each peak lurks a steep down slope, and sometimes a precipice. Increasingly harried by lawsuits and creditors, Grant never actually moved in and the house was eventually demolished, though two relics of his vaulting architectural ambitions survived. In 1884, the magnificent marble staircase, which cost £550,000 in today's values, was sold to Madame Tussauds. Hundreds of thousands of gawping visitors trod its sweeping steps until 1925, when the Tussauds' building burned down and the stairs were damaged beyond repair. The high wrought-iron gates, which today stand at the East Sheen entrance to Richmond Park, are claimed to be those which were expensively forged to impress Grant's hoped-for Kensington visitors. But perhaps the legacy of which Grant would have been most proud was the 258-page speech in the High Court. He was certainly pleased enough with it at the time to have it privately printed; the copy in the British Library has his bold inscription to a Mr. Vernon 'as a souvenir of a hard fight in which his courage was sustained by the services and sympathy of Mr. Vernon'. The fight, known in legal textbooks as 'Twycross vs. Grant and others', was a Victorian business classic, revolving around the failure of the Lisbon Steam Tramways Company. As was typical of so many Grant promotions, when it went out of business before a yard of track had been laid, it had 18s 9d left in the bank out of the £300,000 its shareholders had stumped up. Grant was compelled to pay damages, but crucially was found not to have committed fraud, on the same legal analysis that had saved the Overends' directors.

His well-argued if at times specious declamation is sprinkled with *bons mots* which show Grant's panache under pressure. Of Twycross, who had used three legal firms in turn to pursue his claim, Grant quipped in fine Gilbert & Sullivan style that 'speaking solicitorally . . . he is a trigamist'. In another fine Victorian flourish, Grant claimed that Twycross' counsel had 'covered a rotten case with a large amount of fringe, just as you see ladies with limited incomes freshen up an old dress with plenty of fringe. It looks pretty and fresh, except to a lady who is not to be humbugged and except as I hope to the intelligent jury in this case who I hope are not to be humbugged.'

Grant was not a quitter. When ruin loomed ahead, it would never have crossed his mind to open a bottle of prussic acid à la Melmotte, or, like the real life John Sadleir of the Tipperary Bank, commit suicide with poison and a cut-throat razor as night fell on Hampstead Heath. Nor indeed, to take up the Maxwell comparison, would Grant have slipped ambiguously under the mid-Atlantic waves rather than face public disgrace. Grant was thick-skinned and fought back tenaciously.

So he died peacefully and far from a pauper at his seaside estate, Aldwick Place, near Bognor, in 1890. It could never have crossed his mind that into the twenty-first century the judgement in Twycross vs Grant is still cited in courts up to the House of Lords as a key precedent in establishing the measure of financial damage.

Father Peter Daly died in 1868 having been persuaded on his deathbed, fortunately for Galway, to make over to the Church the deeds of all the schools, churches and other institutions he had built. He still managed to leave a sizeable personal estate. It is a measure of the rise and fall of human reputations that in 2004 a fine portrait of Daly, commissioned in his heyday by the Town Commissioners, was languishing, unframed, dusty and with a nasty tear, in the vaults of Galway's City Hall. He is buried under the flagstones of the church he built at Bushypark (surprisingly unadorned inside and out to the sceptical eye of a Protestant visitor; plainer indeed than many contemporary 'high' Church of England places of worship). In a nicely solipsistic touch, his grave is watched over from a niche alongside the altar by his marble bust, sculpted by John Edwards Jones in 1860.

Dr Thom lived to be eighty-seven, dying in 1890 in the twilight of the Victorian age, in a moral and cultural climate he must have found as abhorrent as the behaviour of the Overends' directors. His home was in Torrington Square, close to the British Museum, where, out-Casauboning Casaubon, he worked on his last book *Emmanuel – Both the Germ and the Outcome of the Scriptural Alphabets, A Pentaglot Miniature*, reviewed rather dismissively as 'the fantastic product of the decline of a vigorous and powerful intellect'.

Henry Edmund Gurney outlasted him and indeed most of our other characters, dying in 1905. His Nuffield Priory estate near Reigate had been sold for £150,000 to meet his Corner House debts but Nutwood House, where he ended his days, was probably comfortable enough. In the best tradition of his family he remained active in good causes, not least the British and Foreign Bible Society, which had worked on a vast scale since 1804 to translate the Bible into every known foreign language; 'Samuel Gurney the Great' had been its Treasurer until his death.

Henry Ford Barclay died in 1893, aged sixty-seven, in the words of the officiating vicar 'in a good old age, full of days, riches and vigour', though the Overends' affair must have taken its toll. As another small sidelight on the impenetrable intertwining of names and relationships that underlies this whole story, when his first wife Richenda Gurney died, he married Hannah, daughter of one Abel Chapman. In 1872 he took over as chairman of Becontree Magistrates from 'a relative', John Gurney Fry.

Robert Birkbeck, a Norwich neighbour wrote, 'may have lost £500,000 but he did not lose his heart'.

Daniel Gurney was financially wounded, the marriage settlements he was so concerned about depleted, but he was not devastated; an allowance from his sister enabled him to go on living on his Runcton Hall estate. Nor was he defeated. Back from a visit to the Lake district and the Quaker stronghold centre of Kendal, the eighty-seven-year-old patriarch wrote to John Gurney, 'I quite enjoyed the music festival. I was determined to throw off all cares and we had a delightful family party to Keswick.'

Samuel Gurney Jr had owned a fine house in Prince's Gate and sat on the Boards of major companies. He had been a solid if undramatic presence in the House of Commons until, in the backwash, he gave it up in 1868. He must have been hard hit: the Quaker memorial after his death in 1875 notes that 'when he lost his riches he bore his lot in cheerful submission to the will of God'. Though the £10,260 he left was hardly a pittance by many standards, it was clearly much less than he had in the days when he hosted a demonstration in his Kensington library of the wonders of the electric telegraph. But even his small non-family bequests are a litany of Gurney and Quaker causes – the Poplar and London Hospitals, the Bible Society, the RSPCA and the Anti-Slavery Society amongst them. We do not know whether he had been among the young men to whom old Samuel Gurney had addressed his memorable injunction. If so, he certainly understood now what his father had meant about 'the uncertainty of riches'.

By 1875, when they presented theatregoers with *Trial By Jury*, Gilbert and Sullivan must have been well aware that the family, as a whole, had not lost its last penny. The judge rivets the audience with his cynical exposé of how marriage to a 'rich attorney's elderly, ugly daughter' had propelled him through a remunerative career at the bar until 'at length I became as rich as the Gurneys'.

Elizabeth Fry is commemorated not just for her reforming zeal, but as the image woven into the British £5 note, an intriguing juxtaposition given her family's edgy relationship with the Bank of England.

Her brother Samuel's more tangible memorial is a 30 inch granite obelisk, as plain and as upright as the man himself, now an incongruous beacon on the edge of the bus terminal at Stratford Broadway, a mile or so from his Upton Park home. To the hurrying twenty-first century traveller the inscription – 'when the ear heard him then it blessed him' – sounds almost mystical. Brought up to know their Bible from Genesis to Revelations, Victorians would have been quicker to recognise the quotation from The Book of Job, and to appreciate that Samuel was blessed 'because I delivered to poor who cried and the fatherless also . . . I was a father to the needy . . .'

We know that David Ward Chapman went bankrupt and eventually moved abroad out of bailiff range. We recall that he had lived in great style in Prince's Gate, a few yards away from the Hyde Park end of Queen's Gate. What we do not know is whether he is the man described in one of Xenos' final tropes about the City as 'Polycrates'. Ever the intellectual snob, Xenos assumes that we know he is referring to the ancient ruler of the Aegean island of Samos, who, according to Herodotus, 'maintained a sumptuous court' and enjoyed years of good fortune, but was 'marked down for destruction'. Xenos is often coy, so when he places Polycrates' address in Queen's Gate, he may be nudging the reader towards Ward Chapman. Certainly Chapman had 'accepted and honoured Bills to the amount of millions of pounds sterling' and had been brought down by a market crash. 'Polycrates' magnificent house and his 'beautiful horses and carriages' – shades again of Chapman – were sold to a tradesman from Tottenham named Briscott, who had made a fortune on the Stock Exchange and in cotton trading. 'Polycrates' and his family moved to an 'obscure house' in the City Road.

There may be hints of Chapman in another of Xenos' anecdotes; an anonymous 'young scamp' who persuades his partners to take their business public after he had lost a fortune 'on the turf and the Stock Exchange', and squandered money he did not have to rent a theatre 'for the convenience of his favourite actresses' and buy a hotel 'for a *ci-devant* mistress'.

John Henry Gurney died in 1890, far less rich than he had briefly been, but far from poor; a stellar-spirited example of the 'person with a well regulated mind', who, in the words of that essay on 'Adversity' in the Grove House magazine half a century before, 'submits with Christian resignation and . . . knows that his life and everything concerning him is intended to fulfil some wise and end of that God, in whom he trusts.'

His obituary in *The Ibis*, the journal of ornithology which Gurney had helped found and finance, wrote of his 'beautiful generosity', unabated in spirit if restricted in scope, after the loss of 'the vast income which he once enjoyed'. It noted that 'a placid temper' was perhaps his most characteristic quality, adding acutely and correctly in the light of what we know that, 'To it may possibly have been due some of his misfortune'.

But fortune, misfortune and how men saw him would have meant less to Gurney than to know that in the twenty-first century, bird fanatics still hack through the forests of Thailand and Myanmar hoping for even a flashing glimpse of one of the world's rarest species, the almost extinct 'Gurney's Pitta'; a tiny kaleidoscopic blur of sky blue yellow and brown feathers named in John Henry's honour by his friend, Allan Octavian Hume.

What of Xenos, that totally contrasting character? In a slang phrase that is not inappropriate, he continued to make waves. Trying unsuccessfully to launch a successor company to Greek & Oriental, he found himself in court, sued by the investors for failing to disclose the inducements he had paid to its proposed directors. In April 1864, a *Times* Law Report headed simply 'Xenos Vs. Xenos' reported a battle over custody of a three-year-old daughter; it may be unfair to leap to the conclusion that this refers to Xenos himself, since he had a brother, but from what we know of the fragility of his marriage, it almost certainly was.[45] The judgement is just as interesting for what it reflects of Victorian mores. Though he thought neither parent was fit to take charge, the judge declared: 'Nothing could be clearer than that according to English law, the parental power [over children] is vested in the father alone . . . he is entitled to control of their persons during their minority.' The case was settled out of court and, from what we know of Xenos' later life, his daughter Ariadne stayed with him after her parents separated.

Xenos went back to Greece in 1877, where, in contrast to the debonair image of his early photograph, he is remembered as 'a man with the style of a retired English general, with a long grey overcoat and a tall top hat . . . a man who talked too much and seemed constantly angry. But [his tirades] always ended with a reassuring smile.' He skirmished in local and Levant politics, dabbled as ever unsuccessfully in business, crusaded for the building of aqueducts and the creation of the Vouliagmeni district of Athens, all the while wielding his polemic pen. Echoing his involvement with the *British Star*, journalism landed him in hot water yet again in a story as bizarre as anything in the entire Overends' saga. 'Merchant of Death', 'The High Priest of War' and 'Millions Died So He Could Live' were the sort of headlines European newspapers liked to splash over stories about the shadowy, early twentieth-century arms dealer and power broker who became Sir Basil Zaharoff. The name is Russian – his family had fled from Constantinople to Odessa to escape Turkish pogroms – but he was born a Greek, Zacharias Basileos Zacharides. In the 1880s, his reputation was as a rather shady thirty-something wheeler dealer with a conviction in London for obtaining money by false pretences. A man who shuttled across Europe and around the Mediterranean, and even to America, in search of his fortune, often under the alias Z. Z. Williamson; in his first marriage, he had used the more exotic 'Zacharias Basilius Gortzacoff, General of Kiev'. In 1884, Xenos published a story in an Athens newspaper that 'the convict Zaharias Basilius Zaharoff [*sic*]' had been shot dead trying to escape from Athens' Garbola jail. The story was false; the dead man was an unknown Canadian and Zaharoff was in Cyprus. Quite what prompted Xenos to do this is, like everything else to do with Zaharoff, murky. Some claimed it was revenge for a quarrel over a woman, won by Zaharoff, though there may also have been a business argument. We now know from a recent Greek biography of Xenos, that for a brief period he worked as a salesman for Armstrong's, the British arms manufacturer for whom Zaharoff came to play a key role. Whatever the motive, the story understandably came as a nasty shock when it reached Zaharoff's sisters in Constantinople, and something of a surprise to the very much alive Zaharoff in Cyprus. The plot then becomes truly macabre since family members prevailed on his political 'patron', Stefanos Skouloudis, later a prime minister of Greece, to get an exhumation warrant. Faces wrapped in carbolic-soaked cloths to deaden the stench, he and Zaharoff's dentist Dr Agaley watched as the rotting cadaver was dug up. Skouloudis immediately declared that the hair was not Zaharoff's and, after prying open the jaws,

Dr Agaley – surely acting above and beyond the call of dental duty – confirmed that the teeth did not match a mould he had recently taken. Zaharoff hastened back to Athens to confront Xenos, threatening physical harm if the story was not retracted: 'I am not a man to be trifled with.' But after he stormed into Xenos' house and found the one-time proud proprietor of Greek & Oriental Shipping grovelling behind the sofa, no more than harsh words were exchanged and Xenos published a correction.

Xenos died penniless in 1894, a reckless charmer several times larger than life, who would have been proud to know that his great grandson, Oliver Moxon, wrote three books about his experiences as a Second World War Hurricane pilot in the Far East. He would likely have been equally proud that a scholarly study of his own life and work was published in Athens in 1998, and that his own publishing initiatives are the centrepiece of the chapter on Greek printing in London, in a volume of essays issued by the British Library.

Even those with only a small role in our story are remembered. Though his business career ended badly, the blockade-runner Zachariah Pearson is commemorated in Hull by the 23-acre Pearson Park, on a site he gave to the town to mark his term as mayor; and for some reason, there is also a rather drab pub which bears his name.

Also appropriately for a man whose Theory of the Wave of Translation was developed on a Scottish waterway, John Scott Russell's name has been given to the aqueduct which carries the Union Canal over the Edinburgh City Bypass.

Charles Mare died in 1898. As probably the most enterprising of the Thames shipbuilders, he deserved his own memorial, which his wife 'and friends' loyally commissioned from the Thames Yard's naval architect. As Mare died in poverty the Yard itself may have been the major 'friend'. The imposing marble plinth, surmounted by a bronze bust stood for many years in the hallway of the Technical Institute in Stratford, a mile or so from Upton Park. Sadly, it too has long since vanished.

Even the American artist Asher Durand, who captured for us the fuggy tensions of the trial, has emerged with fame and a high price on his head. In 2005, his *Kindred Spirits*, a portrait of Thomas Cole, founder of the 'Hudson Valley School' of painting, posed against a Catskills' background with the poet William Cullen Bryan, was sold by the New York Public Library for a reported $35 million to a supermarket heiress.

If only we had more of a sense of what the enigmatic Edwards was like, and of what became of him. Xenos' verbal sketches and the press accounts of his second, self-assured defence against allegations of improper dealing, conjure up the image of Dennis Price as Louis Mazzini in the Ealing Studios' comedy *Kind Hearts and Coronets* smoothly defending himself in the House of Lords, charged with the one murder he did not commit. Risking a Xenos-like trope, we can wonder how the entire Overends' story might have been cast in the halcyon days of cinema; a black-and-white Hitchcock classic or even as a romp, with Alastair Sim as John Gurney, John Laurie as Dr Thom, James Robertson Justice as the lawyer Kenealy, Cyril Cusack as Father Daly, George Sanders as Albert Grant and Anthony Quinn as Xenos.

When all is said and done, the simplest explanation for what happened is the 'human factor'. Basically good men led themselves further and further astray, and they paid a heavy price. It has happened many times since; in the years to come the cast will change but the basic plot will be the same.

When Trollope reflected in his autobiography on the Overends' era, he clearly had Grant's corruption and extravagance much in mind. But he could as well have been writing about the 1970s or the 1990s, as a time

in which a certain class of dishonesty, dishonesty magnificent in its proportions and climbing into high places, has become at the same time so rampant and splendid that there seems to be reason for fearing that men and women will be taught to feel that dishonesty if it can become splendid will cease to be abominable. If dishonesty can live in a gorgeous palace with pictures on all its walls and gems in all its cupboards with marble and ivory in all its corners and can give Apician dinners and get into parliament and deal in millions then dishonesty is not disgraceful and the man dishonest after such a fashion is not a low scoundrel.

Sadly, his words (which take for granted his readers' familiarity with the name of the Roman epicure Apicus) are likely to prove equally true of the 2010s. As the cycles come and go, and the scars of the last trauma fade under the Barbados suntan of a new era of 'folly and euphoria', history will repeat itself. Maybe it will be in the ever-expanding universe of the so called 'private equity' firms; the buyout kings, who use brimming pools of international private capital to buy businesses at a good price, load them with debt and sell them on, usually to the public at an even better one. Maybe, in its way, this is what The Corner House would have thought of as its strategy, had it had one. The problem, as Henry R. Kravis, legendary doyen of the buyout game, recently told a conference, according to the *New York Times*, is that 'Unfortunately there is a flip side to having access to plentiful capital. It means that too many people without experience in building businesses have too much capital.' 'Amen,' Overends' shareholders would have chorused. Maybe the problem will come from the shrouded computer screens of 'hedge funds', maybe in the arcane byways of 'futures', options and other 'derivative securities' whose real risks few understand. As this book was being completed, the financial press trumpeted the shamefaced bankruptcy of a giant US 'futures broker' (an almost metaphysical trade description) after questionable dealings by its boss; dealings which went undetected by its Board, its auditors, its regulators and the Securities and Exchange Commission and which may well have been aimed at hiding losses made years earlier by an imploding hedge fund. The affair under-scores the sad truth that it does not matter how many envious bureaucrats are recruited into the regulators' ranks, how many exemplary sentences meted out, or how many billions are lost, fraud and deceit are always with us.

Indeed, some of the scandals which have rocked the markets in recent times can actually be traced back to the feverish zeal of politicians of all stripes to be seen to be 'doing something' and gaining headlines. Looking back to the 1970s, we can see that the

Crown Agents were themselves victims, caught up in a maelstrom that was the direct result of a government policy styled 'Competition and Credit Control'. Trumpeted as a consumer benefit, to unfetter the clearing banks' lock on the UK lending market, it achieved only the folly, pain and loss of the secondary banking crisis. Some of the wilder modern excesses of corporate America can likewise be traced back to the 1980s' decision of the Securities and Exchange Commission, to loosen the stranglehold major investment banks supposedly had on major corporate clients by a mechanism known as 'shelf registration'. In a few short years, the relationship between companies and trusted advisors was replaced by an adversarial free-for-all in which banks competed against each other to present ever more outré schemes for money raising and profit enhancement, to any corporation prepared to listen. Corporations ceased to trust their advisors and Wall Street's 'fee and bonus' culture led the advisors to regard their 'clients' merely as a source of transactions, sheep to be fleeced, rather than in the context of a relationship and responsibility.

Back in London a good case can be made that Barings would not have failed through a 'rogue trader's' horrific misjudgements, if the structure and profitability of the London merchant banking market had not itself been destabilised by the government-inspired 'Big Bang'. Yet again, conceived in a 'do-gooding, do something' spirit to break down cartels, stimulate competition and wipe away market inefficiencies, all it actually achieved was to drive smaller banks to seek profits in uncharted territory. Some died in the process, while many simply surrendered to invading foreign battalions, succumbing, in the words of a pre-Euro *Monty Python* chorus, to 'the feel of the French Franc, the heel of the Deutschmark, the cool antiseptic sting of the Swiss Franc'.

Life offers some valuable maxims. 'Never play cards with a man called Doc', 'Never eat in a restaurant called Mom's', 'Never lend money to a man who wears his overcoat draped over his shoulders'. To these we can add, 'Never trust a banker with a great new way to make money'. There's no such thing. Let a pillar of the post-Second World War money market, Arthur Trinder of Union Discount, have the last word: 'Honesty is the best policy. We've tried both.'

Postscript

Not every cloud has a silver lining. The saddened shareholders, many of whom may individually have paid a relatively heavier price than The Corner House families, certainly never saw even the glimpse of one. The liquidators did in a small way, since it was not until 1893, twenty-six happy, fee-generating years after 'Black Friday', that the final entries were made and the books closed on the long dead Overends.

The partners of the group of Gurney firms which made up the Norwich bank, and their extended families, as tightly woven as the Quaker Tapestry, did in fact see a fair amount of silver; gold too.

Quiet, steady, not too obviously diverted by ambition, greed, or the lure of London life – much, one imagines, in the mould of John Henry Gurney, who worried about lending too much to farmers in Fakenham – the Norfolk partners steered their bank profitably forwards. In 1896, the bank was one of the main constituents in the amalgamation of a large group of private firms under the corporate umbrella of what had now been truncated to Barclay & Co. Limited, and which later became Barclays Bank.

The first Barclays Board is a roll call of names now familiar to us, hardly a surprise since the 1926 *History* tells us that every single one of the partners in the Gurney group of banks, when it amalgamated, was descended from the two sisters of Bartlett Gurney, who had died in 1803. Among the serious men with polished boots, spats, watch-chains and high stiff collars, seated round the baize-covered Board table, were Samuel Gurney Buxton as vice chairman, a pair of Birkbecks and two Barclays, one of them Hugh Gurney Barclay.

The Corner House partners had done almost everything wrong, except the initiative to 'rearrange' the holdings in the Norwich bank.

A shrewd decision. So shrewd that in the commercial weighing scales it might be said to have more than cancelled out the bushel baskets brimming with failure and loss, at least from the families' point of view. Any arithmetical judgements can only be superficial at best. We do not know the profit contributions of the component parts, nor what basis was used to allocate shares in the new company. But taking the assets and liabilities of the Norwich bank and its affiliates in its own audited accounts as a percentage of the amounts shown in the first combined Barclays balance sheet drawn up on 1 July 1896, the Norwich bank contributed some 30 per cent of shareholders' funds and 25 per cent of the deposit and current accounts. Barclay's most recent historians Margaret Ackrill and Leslie Hannah found that under the 'initial' merger agreements, the partners in the Gurney and Barclay groupings were each to be allocated three sevenths, or some 42 per cent, of the new company's shares; but as a slew of other smaller firms then entered the pooling, this initial allocation will have been adjusted. Whatever the exact figures, the broad measures show that in the long term, the founding families benefited handsomely from the canny caution of their forebears. When a later John Gurney died in 2000, aged ninety-four, he was portrayed in his obituary as 'a fascinating blend of workaholic, benefactor, quiet eccentric and private individual' (many of the same attributes, we can note, also applied to Samuel Gurney the Great, to John Henry Gurney and no doubt to many others in this remarkable family). He was also said to have been 'for a long time the largest shareholder in Barclays Bank'.

'A firebrand plucked out of the burning,' old Dr Thom might have quoted from the Book of Amos. Or, as Berthold Brecht put it rather more cynically, '*Was ist ein Einbruch in eine Bank gegen die Gründung einer Bank?*' – 'What is robbing a bank compared to founding one?'

Notes

Introduction

1. The euphoria of an earlier landing, in 1858, had proved premature – the cable soon snapped.
2. The Garraway link may have had its roots in the Gurney's commitment to the anti-slavery movement. Originally from Scotland, the Garraway family had established itself and intermarried on Dominica to the point where in the 1860's James Garraway, owner of the Morne Prosper Estate, had become its President: 'the first man of African blood who ever reached this high honour in any of the former slave-holding dependencies of the British crown.' The name remains prominent on the island today.

Chapter One: *History Repeats Itself*

3. In contrast to Overends and other 1970's banking casualties however the Agents were briskly restored to stability after their near fatal giddy spell and thrive today as 'an international development company delivering capacity building and institutional development services in public sector transformation'.

Chapter Two: *Paper Promises*

4. In the Overends' era and for many socially stratified years thereafter, when the partners and directors of banks and stockbrokers gathered in their dining rooms or The City Club at 1 p.m., they were unquestionably having 'lunch'; if asked, they would have said equally firmly that what their clerks were munching in the pubs, chophouses and cafes around them was their 'dinner'.

Chapter Three: *Halcyon Days*

5. It fits uncomfortably with modern sensitivities to recall that much British sympathy, even from Mr Gladstone himself, lay with the rebellious South, most pragmatically because Lancashire mills depended on Southern cotton but more generally among the ruling 'upper class' because America's espousal of the principles of equality evoked nasty echoes of the not-long-distant

French revolutionary resolve to wipe out the monarchy, the aristocracy and the Church.

6. Another contemporary project, the building of the Suez Canal, completed in 1869, probably merits a similar accolade.

Chapter Four: *The Smoke, the Wealth, the Din*

7. He also had a penchant for late night prowls around Piccadilly in search of ladies of the night to 'rescue', but that was between him and his guilt-gouged conscience.

Chapter Five: *Men Only*

8. His pseudonym and his tone suggest that 'Monadnock' could not wait to get back to the Puritan values of the granite mountains of New Hampshire; in another dispatch, he fulminated that while 'life, liberty and the pursuit of happiness' worked as a doctrine in America, what Britain needed was 'intelligent despotism, well laid on'. To be fair, though, he did find two aspects of London life worthy of praise. One was the new underground railway, which he felt New York should quickly copy. The other was Britain as a place where 'genius could find expression'. He hailed the arrival in London of the 'coloured tragedian' Morgan Smith to star as 'Othello', with the strong implication that this would not have happened in America.

9. It was a long week, that is, by the standards of 1970s banking. The wheel has now turned full circle and today's traders, dealers and support staff often arrive at their desks around 7 a.m. and don't leave till the last pizza crust has curled up and died on top of their computer perhaps twelve hours later.

Chapter Six: *'Not Slothful in Business'*

10. And not just in Britain. Quakers, especially the Bristol community, were much involved in Atlantic trade and Quaker-owned ships in Boston Harbour were the scene of the Tea Party, which sparked the War of Independence. America is as good an example as any of how hard work bred material success. One hundred years after William Penn founded Pennsylvania, his 'Holy Experiment' as a home for Free Thinkers and Dissenters in 1682, Friends made up only 15 per cent of its population, but accounted for twelve of its seventeen wealthiest men.

11. Now PricewaterhouseCoopers and still auditors to, among many other giants, Barclays Bank and that vast offspring of the Hanbury pharmaceutical business, GlaxoSmithKline.

Chapter Seven: *The House That Samuel Built*

12. The breed died out in the 1970s; Siegmund Warburg, and his fellow founding partners in the once pre-eminent banking house which used to bear his name, epitomised it; none of them were born in Britain.

13. It is a reflection of the relative standing of those quiet towns at that time that in the scale of its business ranked by the banknotes it was allowed to issue, Wisbech was second to Norwich; Yarmouth came a close third.

14. 'Plain' is another stereotype. William Penn had advised his fellow Quakers, 'Chuse thy clothes by thine own eyes and not another's. The more simple and plain they are the better. Neither unshapely; not fantastical and for Use and Decency and not for Pride.' That conjures up images of women uniformly and drably clad in grey. This was not actually the case, although the colours were hardly vibrant, soft brown, chocolate, sage green and even cream were commonly worn.

Chapter Eight: *A New Generation*

15. We have already highlighted the impenetrable interrelationships, which are a defining part of our story. The Chapman family tree, which includes a Joseph Gurney Chapman and an Edmund Henry Chapman, and in all probability yet another Chapman who was in unsuccessful partnership with Elizabeth Fry's husband, is another of many examples.

16. This reference to a four-volume, seventeenth-century French romance is characteristic of Xenos' habit of flaunting his learning on every page, larding the text with references to literary characters, Greek mythology and philosophy, as well as nautical metaphors; some of his more florid paragraphs come across as a blend of *The Oxford Companion to Classical Literature* and a Patrick O'Brian novel.

17. In recent years the address has quietly lost its apostrophe and Chapman's former home has now been swallowed up by the western end of Kingston House, an equally expensive modern apartment building, but some sense of the grand style can be seen in the remaining houses, one of which served as the home of Joseph Kennedy and his rambunctious and extensive family in the Second World War; another was the London home of J.P. Morgan. Yet another became the Iranian Embassy, site of the siege and bloody shootout in 1980.

18. The earliest auditors spent as much if not more time sorting out bankrupt businesses as they did actually drawing up balance sheets and the first official recognition of accounting as a profession had come in the 1830s, when they were thought to be good candidates for the Assignees' positions.

19. Quakers had no monopoly on archaic dating systems; the printed copy of the transcript is headed 'Lunae 60 die Junii 1864'

Chapter Nine: *A Powerful Neighbour*

20. With hindsight, an ironic metaphor. In 1830 Husskison entered the history books as the first person in Britain to be killed in a railway accident, when he fell under the wheels of George Stephenson's 'Rocket' while on a VIP voyage inaugurating the Liverpool to Manchester railway.

21. Though Samuel Gurney told a parliamentary committee that as a matter of principle – and no doubt of pride too – The Corner House 'dress ourselves' so as to avoid having recourse to the Bank, the records show that even in his day they were forced to go cap in hand to ask for sizeable short-term loans when a crisis drained liquid funds from the money markets; on one awkward afternoon they needed the equivalent of £35 million.

22. Despite Monadnock's conviction that America did things better, the New York of that period was just as heavily intoxicated by the heady fumes of money. The chapter headings in William Fowler's *Ten Years on Wall Street*, published in 1870, tell of 'The Gold Room', 'the Speculation in Stocks, Gold, Governments, Pork, Petroleum, Grain, etc.' 'The Great Rises and Panics', 'The Famous Pools, Rings, Cliques and Corners' and 'The Gold Ring of 1869', even 'The Women Who Speculate'.

Chapter Eleven: *When Greek Meets Greek*

23. He also told Xenos that he was having some unspecified 'domestic difficulty' at the time; we can guess that his problems were also becoming known to the watchful and protective Ionides family, who being London based were hard-wired into the community's 'early-warning' system.

24. However badly The Corner House behaved, it is hard not to have a sneaking sympathy with the intemperate comment of Henry Gurney after being on the receiving end of another Hellenic diatribe, that Xenos was his own worst enemy: 'You always have something to complain of.' It has also to be said that the two balance sheets drawn up by Xenos, and included in his book to demonstrate his solvency, show to most modern eyes that he was heavily over-borrowed, his surplus 'capital' entirely a function of hull values.

25. Again, if only Overends had been able to learn from Medici history. One of the main reasons for the failure of the Florentine bankers' London firm was a disastrous foray into the operation of two galleys, originally built for Phillip the Good to use, in a crusade against the Turks, a mission Xenos would have applauded. In a foretaste of what would happen to Pearson, the galleys were attacked off the Dutch coast by privateers from Danzig. One was captured, along with Memling's *Last Judgement*, which was part of its valuable cargo; the other escaped, only to be wrecked in a storm.

Chapter Twelve: *'Those in Peril on the Sea'*

26. As Adjutant of the Galway Militia, another clerical Clancarty, the Honourable and Venerable Charles le Poer Trench, Archdeacon of Ardagh, had become infamous for his eagerness to have soldiers and their wives flogged; on one occasion in Ballinasloe he volunteered to wield the whip himself when no soldier could be found for the task. He became known as 'Skin Them Alive' Trench.

27. Characteristically this led to a series of bitter disputes, including an allegation by the Sisters that he had helped himself to some of the money earmarked for the new chapel he had himself encouraged them to build, to buy himself another estate; to adapt the biblical words of St John, the Father's house indeed had many mansions.

28. Whether he used his friend Anthony Trollope to open London doors, especially the doors of the Post Office department which dealt with overseas mail contracts, we do not know, but, given Daly's skills, he probably did. Trollope's biographer, Richard Mullen, suggests that the two men met when the author was in Ireland in the early 1840s as a Post Office supervisor and that much of Daly comes through in the main character of his story 'Father Giles of Ballymoy', although it is hard to imagine the quick-tempered Peter Daly being quite so amiable after being pushed down a flight of stairs.

29. Yet another illustration of Ireland's submerged wealth is Roy Fitzroy Foster's observation in his history of modern Ireland that when in the 1850s Irish estates worth £20 million changed hands, 'they were not broken up by native tenants raising themselves to the level of proprietors, nor did English capitalists enter the market on a large scale. The purchasers were local speculators and solvent members of the landed class; as usual Irish capital was available when the object in question was the purchase of land.' The observation is as true today as it was then.

Chapter Thirteen: *That Sinking Feeling*

30. Daly in the flesh was nothing like the *Punch* cartoon. Even making allowances for the understandable tendency of portrait painters and sculptors to flatter those who commission them, he was a man of some physical distinction, giving an impression of intellectual weight. Early in his career another local newspaper, the *Connaught Journal*, had caught this aspect of him, noting that he was well versed in literature and theology, 'possessing a mind highly cultivated and accomplished'.

Chapter Fourteen: *Going to the Dogs*

31. Mare's original yard, reborn as the Thames Ironworks, should now pass from our story; like the Overend name and the *Great Eastern* it does not. It reappears much later in a new and curious context.

Chapter Fifteen: *The Baron*

32. In later years when what was perhaps Grant's most notorious promotion, the Emma Silver Mine in Utah, failed at a huge cost to its shareholders because there was no silver and the company's ownership of the mine was in some doubt, the wags added two more lines:

> Yes, but you're in an even worse dilemma
> If you can't get a title to your Emma.

33. Reflecting on the South Sea Bubble, a scam on a scale even Grant never matched, Newton had observed ruefully that, 'It is impossible to measure the limits of the madness of a people', words which would have given Grant some comfort as he went on coaxing millions out of the pockets of his gullible 'investors'.

Chapter Sixteen: *Millwall's Last Hurrah*

34. Imperial Mercantile's expensively engraved share certificates, now sold as collectors' items for far more than they were ever worth as shares, reflect what might be called The Corner House *leitmotif* – on the left, a train puffs busily away to some unseen industrial heartland, loaded with bales from a cargo ship moored at a quayside, sails furled, on the right-hand side. In a rather mixed piece of symbolism, a statuesque woman in the foreground holds a set of weighing scales, a cornucopia of fruit overflowing at her feet.

Chapter Seventeen: *East Enders*

35. An earlier nickname from the 1890s, when Peter Rolt's successor, the vegetarian, non-smoking, non-drinking chairman Arnold Hills, picked the team from men prepared to follow his abstemious example, is no longer used; it is hard to imagine today's fans roaring, 'Go, Teetotallers' with any conviction.

36. Plashet Park just to the north was the married home of Elizabeth Fry until her husband's painful bankruptcy, and the nearby St Stephen's Church, built in 1887, was dedicated to her memory.

37. The parcel that is now West Ham Park, is another example of Gurney generosity. When as part of the break up a local group offered £25,000 for a tract on which to build, the local corporation stepped in to buy the land as a park; John Gurney himself donated £10,000 of the price and the City of London, no doubt in honour of old Samuel, gave another £10,000.

Chapter Twenty-one: *'Fictitious Capital'*

38. One of them, Robert Bevan, was a partner in Barclays; wrapped in a gossamer web of banking and family threads, his mission must have been especially delicate and fraught with conflicts, though clearly hard-nosed Quaker business values prevailed.

Chapter Twenty-two: *Shipwreck*

39. It is tempting to think that Clarendon's well-deserved reputation as a scandalmonger and gossip may not have helped the reception of his message; it was he who did much to create and spread the rumours of a closer than healthy relationship between Queen Victoria and her devoted Highland ghillie John Brown, gossip which did little to endear him to his Sovereign, all the more when word inevitably reached her that Clarendon had taken to referring to her as 'The Missus'.

Chapter Twenty-three: *Truth and Consequences*

40. The buyer may well have been part of the 'extended family'; to track the genealogy would be too diverting, but the full name of the 1930s' politician nicknamed 'Slippery Sam' Hoare was Joseph Samuel Gurney Hoare.

Chapter Twenty-seven: *In the Dock*

41. Though the comparison is unfair, something of the spirit of Disraeli's 'Two Nations' is caught by the almost contemporary London Magistrates Court's reports that a barman, Samuel Bell, had been sentenced to two years' hard labour for stealing a shilling from the pub where he worked, while three boys aged thirteen, twelve and eleven were punished by 'seven days and whipping' for stealing a dozen books and 11s from the North London British Schools.

Chapter Twenty-eight: *'Guilty of Our Own Disasters'*

42. The Society responded and the rules were relaxed. However, although Quakers took some pride in the fact that after 1861 membership began to grow again, as Elizabeth Isichei has pointed out, the British population was also growing rapidly, so that relatively, and also compared to other denominations, the real picture was less positive.

43. It is outside our time frame and an extreme example, but nonetheless Alfred Pease, *rentier* descendant of the staunch and steady Quakers whose family fortune was built on railways, iron, banking and Middlesborough, nicely particularises the general point. Educated at Eton and Trinity College, Cambridge, he was an early member of the Shikar Club, founded in 1905 to celebrate 'the virility of British Imperial big game hunting', whose aspirant members had to prove they had killed game on three continents. In a neat closing of the circle of family history, many of Pease's trophies are now on display at the Dorman Museum in Middlesborough.

Chapter Twenty-nine: *'Memories Are Made of This . . .'*

44. This speculative whimsy was written just a few months before the announcement that a later celebration of banking triumphalism, the headquarters of the former Midland Bank just a few yards down the road, were indeed slated to be turned in to a hotel. Why, one wonders, would anyone want to spend a holiday in an area that by 5 p.m. is the London equivalent of *Arabia Deserta*?

45. An indication of the frosty relationship is a letter Xenos wrote to his wife on 7 March 1865. Addressing her icily as 'Madam', he tells her that if she continues to write her 'insulting and slanderous letters', he will 'start at once with the children for Greece', where she would be free to visit them 'as much as you like . . . But [they] will never come out to stay with you'.

Bibliography

It is invidious to single out one book or another in the list below, but it would be equally unfair not to express deep appreciation for W. T. C. King's history of the discount market (he coined the phrase 'irrational exuberance' some sixty-five years before it was relaunched by Alan Greenspan), the pioneering work done on the Thames shipyards by Tony Arnold, and by Tim Collins on the Galway Line, Elizabeth Isichei's fine study of the Quakers, and of course Xenos' own contribution. Anyone who ventures into the City's past also owes a considerable debt to David Kynaston, the master of the art, while K. Theodore Hoppen's study is invaluable for anyone seeking to understand the England of Overend & Gurney. Nostalgia even more than the rules of copyright compels me also to acknowledge the song title used for Chapter 28. Sung by Dean Martin and written by Terry Gilkeysen, Richard Dehr and Frank Muller, it gave me and many thousands of duffle-coated teenage boys much pleasure as it hung for six weeks at the top of Radio Luxembourg's Sunday evening hit parade at 208 metres on the Medium Wave.

Ackrill, M., and Hannah, L., *Barclays: The Business of Banking 1690–1996* (Cambridge University Press, Cambridge, 2001)

Allfrey, A., *Man of Arms* (Weidenfeld & Nicolson, London, 1989)

Almon, H., 'Utopia Ltd: The Crystal Palace and Joint Stock Politics', in *The Journal of Victorian Culture* (Edinburgh University Press, Edinburgh, Autumn 2004)

Anon., *Collingridge's City of London Directory* (n.p., London, 1871)

Anon., *Overend Gurney & Company, or The Saddle on the Right Horse* (Effingham Wilson, London, 1866)

Anon., *Overend, Gurney & Co. Limited, List of Shareholders* (Digby Atherton, London, n.d. [?1866])

Anon., *A Selected List of Companies, Foreign Loans and Miscellaneous Projects, Many of Which Were Issued under the Auspices of A. Grant* (Grobecker and Sons, London, 1872)

Anon.('TS'), *Dictionary of National Biography*, 1st Supplement, Vol. 2 (London, 1901) entry for 'Grant, Albert', pp. 338–9.

Anon., *Remarks on the Colonization of the Western Coast of Africa by the Freed Negroes of the United States* (W. L. Burn, New York, 1850) cited on American Colonization Society website

Anon., 'Glyns and The Overend and Gurney Crisis', in *The Three Banks Review*, (London, December 1972), pp 47–59

Anon., *The Grove House School Magazine, 1851–2* (G. Coverly, Tottenham, n.d.)

Archer, M., and Huggard, J. T. (eds), 'Recorder Adam Thom', in *The Western Law Times*, Vol. 1, p. 43, and Vol. 2, p. 71, (The Stovel Company and Western Law Times Publishing, Winnipeg, 1890–91)

Arnold, A. J., *Iron Shipbuilding on the Thames 1832–1915: An Economic and Business History* (Ashgate, Aldershot, 2000)

Aspey, M., *Nathan Rothschild's Company: Jews, Quakers and Catholics* (The Rothschild Foundation, London, 2004)

Balen, M., *A Very English Deceit: The Secret History of the South Sea Bubble and the First Great Financial Scandal* (Fourth Estate, London, 2002)

Ballantine, W. H., *Some Experiences of a Barrister's Life* (Richard Bentley, London, 1882)

Bidwell, W. H., *Annals of an East Anglian Bank* (Agas H.Goose, Norwich, 1900)

Brinton, H., *Friends for 300 Years* (Allen & Unwin, London, 1953)

Carswell, J., *The South Sea Bubble* (revised edition) (Alan Sutton, Stroud, 1993)

Chambers, J., *Palmerston: 'The People's Darling'* (John Murray, London, 2004)

Clapham, J., *The Bank of England, a History* (Cambridge University Press, London, 1944)

Collins, T., *Transatlantic Triumph and Heroic Failure: The Story of the Galway Line* (The Collins Press, Cork, 2002)

Cookson, G., *The Cable: The Wire that Changed the World* (Tempus, Stroud, 2003)

Davis, P., *The Oxford English Literary History*, Vol. 8, 1830–1880: The Victorians (Oxford University Press, Oxford, 2004)

De Roover, R., *The Rise and Decline of the Medici Bank, 1397–1494* (Harvard University Press, Cambridge, Mass., 1963)

Diamond, M., *Victorian Sensation or The Spectacular, the Shocking and the Scandalous in Nineteenth-Century Britain* (Anthem Press, London, 2003)

Eddington, A. (collator), *A Synopsis of the Gurney Manuscripts* (Society of Friends Library, London, 1933 *et seq*)

Elliott, N., Odgers, J., and Phillips, J. M. (eds), *Byles on Bills of Exchange and Cheques*, (27th edition) (Sweet & Maxwell, London, 2002)

Emden, P. M., *Money Powers of Europe in the Nineteenth and Twentieth Centuries* (Sampson Low, London, 1937)

Emmerson, G. S., *John Scott Russell: A Great Victorian Engineer and Naval Architect* (John Murray, London, 1977)

Emmott, E. B., *A Quaker History* (The Swarthmore Press, London, 1923)

Fairbairn, W., *History and Progress of Iron Shipbuilding* (Longmans, London, 1865)

Fay, His Hon. Judge E. S., QC (chairman), et al., *Report by the Committee of Inquiry Appointed by the Minister of Overseas Development into the Circumstances Which Led to the Crown Agents Requesting Financial Assistance from the Government in 1974*, 3 vols (HMSO, London, 1977)

Fildes, C., 'City and Suburban' in the *Spectator* (January 2005)

Flanders, J., *The Victorian House: Domestic Life from Childbirth to Deathbed* (HarperCollins, London, 2003)

Floud, R., *Height, Weight and Body Mass of the British Population Since 1820* (National Bureau of Economic Research, Cambridge, Mass., 1998)

Forrest, D., *St James's Square: People, Houses, Happenings* (Quiller

Press, London, 1986)

Foster, R. F., *Modern Ireland 1600–1972* (Allen Lane, London, 1988)

Fowler, W. W., *Ten Years In Wall Street* (Worthington, Dustin & Co., Hartford USA, 1870)

Fulford, R., *Glyns, 1753–1953. Six Generations in Lombard Street* (Macmillan, London, 1953)

Geldhart, Mrs T., *Memorials of Samuel Gurney* (W. & F.G. Cash, London, 1857)

Grant, A., 'Speech of Albert Grant', in *Twycross vs. Grant and Others* (Waterlow, London, 1876)

Grubb, E., *What is Quakerism?* (Allen & Unwin, London, 1949)

Gurney, J. J., *Observations on the Distinguishing Views and Practices of The Society of Friends* (J. Fletcher, Norwich, 1842)

(Gurney, John), Obituary, *The Eastern Daily News*, (Norwich, 3 March 2000) cited by RootsWeb.com.

Hancock, T., *The Peculium: An Endeavor to Throw Light on Some of the Causes of the Decline of the Society of Friends, Especially in Regard to its Original Claim of Being the Peculiar People of God* (Smith Elder, London, 1859)

Hare, A. J. C., *The Gurneys of Earlham* (George Allen, London, 1895)

Hibbert, C., *Disraeli: A Personal History* (HarperCollins, London, 2004)

Hilton, B., *A Mad, Bad and Dangerous People? England 1783–1846* (Clarendon Press, Oxford, 2006)

Hoppen, K. Theodore, *The Mid-Victorian Generation, 1846–1886* (Clarendon Press, Oxford, 1998)

Howarth, S., *Henry Poole: Founder of Savile Row – The Making of a Legend* (Bene Factum, London, 2003)

Howatson, M. C. (ed.), *The Oxford Companion to Classical Literature* (Oxford University Press, Oxford, 1997)

Hyde, R. (intro.), *Stanford's Library Map of London and its Suburbs* (Harry Margary and The Guildhall Library, [1862] 1980)

Isichei, Elizabeth, *Victorian Quakers* (Oxford University Press, Oxford, 1970)

Kaukalides, Z., *Stefanos Xenos* (Ekodseis Kastanioti, Athens, 1998)

Kenealy, A. (ed.), *Memories of E. V. Kenealy* (John Long, London, 1908)

Kindleberger, C., *A Financial History of Europe* (Allen & Unwin, London, 1984)

King, W. T. C., *History of the London Discount Market* (Routledge, London, 1936)

Kynaston, D., *The City of London: A World of Its Own, 1815–1890,* Vol. 1 (Chatto, London, 1998)

Jessel, Sir George, 'Master of The Rolls', in *All England Law Reports,* 1879, Vol. X1, pp. 918–41

Langford, P., *A Polite and Commercial People: England 1727–1783* (Oxford University Press, Oxford, 1989)

Marsden, G. (ed.), *Victorian Values: Personalities and Perspectives in Nineteenth-Century Society* (Longman, London, 1990)

Marx, Karl, *Das Kapital,* Vol. 3 (Charles H. Kerr, Chicago, 1909)

Marx, Karl, Correspondence with Friedrich Engels at www.marxists.org

Mathews, P. W. and Tuke, A. W. (ed.), *History of Barclays Bank Limited* (Blades East & Blades, London, 1926)

Mayhew, H., & Binny, J., *The Criminal Prisons of London and Scenes of Prison Life* (Griffin Bohn, London, 1862)

McCormick, D., *Pedlar of Death: The Life of Sir Basil Zaharoff* (Macdonald, London, 1965)

McKenzie, C., 'The British Big Game Hunting Tradition', in *The Sports Historian,* No. 1 (London, May 2000)

McKie, D., 'Monument to a Crook', in the *Guardian* (24 October 2002)

Michaelides, C., 'Greek Printing in England', in Taylor, B. (ed.), *Foreign Language Printing in London 1500–1900* (The British Library, London, 2002)

Milligan, E. H., *Quaker Marriage* (Quaker Tapestry Booklets, Kendal, 1994)

Mitchell, Father J., 'Father Peter Daly', in *Journal of the Galway Archaeological and Historical Society,* Vol. 39, 1983–4, pp. 27–114.

Mullen, R., *Anthony Trollope: A Victorian in his World* (Duckworth, London, 1990)

Munday, J., *E. W. Cook, R.A., F.R.S.: His Life and Work* (Antique Collectors Club, London, 1999)

Nead, L., *Victorian Babylon: People, Streets and Images in Nineteenth-Century London* (Yale University Press, New Haven and London, 2000)

Neumann, R., *Zaharoff: The Armaments King* (Allen & Unwin, London, 1936)

O'Donoghue, J., Goulding, L., and Allen, G., *Consumer Price Inflation since 1750* (Office for National Statistics, London, 2004)

Reid, M., *The Secondary Banking Crisis 1973–5: Its Causes and Course* (Macmillan, London, 1982)

Reitlinger, G., *The Economics of Taste* (Barrie and Rockliffe, London, 1961)

Rowntree, J. S., *Quakerism Past and Present: Being an Inquiry into the Causes of its Decline in Great Britain and Ireland* (Smith Elder, London, 1859)

Russell, J., *London* (Harry N. Abrams, New York, 1994)

St John Stevas, N. (ed.), *The Collected Works of Walter Bagehot*, Vols 9–11, The Economic Essays (The Economist, London, 1978)

Sclater, P. L. (ed.), *The Ibis, A Quarterly Journal of Ornithology*, Vol. 2, No. 7 (Gurney & Jackson, London, 1890)

Shorthouse, C. C., *'Grove House', Tottenham School*, 1828–1878 (n.p., 1913)

Smith, C. M., *Curiosities of London Life, or, Phases Physiological and Social, of the Great Metropolis* (London, 1853) cited in www.victorianlondon.org

Stamp, G., and Amery, C., *Victorian Buildings of London, 1837–1887: An Illustrated Guide* (The Architectural Press, London, 1980)

Standage, T., *The Victorian Internet* (Phoenix, London, 2000)

Taylor, J., 'Light Fittings in Georgian and Early Victorian Interiors', in *The Building Conservation Directory* (Cathedral Communications, Tisbury, 1998)

Thom, A., *Overend and Gurney Prosecution: In Its Relation to the*

Public as Distinguished from the Defendants (Effingham Wilson, London, 1869)

Thompson, F. M. L. (ed.), *The Cambridge Economic History of Modern Britain* (Cambridge University Press, Cambridge, 2004)

Trollope, A., *An Autobiography* (Oxford University Press, Oxford, 1923)

Trollope, A., *The Complete Short Stories*, Vol. 5 (Texas Christian University Press, Forth Worth, 1983)

Trollope, A., *The Way We Live Now* (Trollope Society, London, 1992)

Tuke, A. F., 'The Story of Overend and Gurney', in *The Times* (May 1966)

Vincent, J. (ed.), *Disraeli, Derby and the Conservative Party: Journals and Memoirs of Edward Henry, Lord Stanley, 1849–1869* (Harvester Press, Hassocks, 1978)

Vincent, J. (ed.), *A Selection from the Diaries of Edward Henry Stanley, 15th Earl of Derby (1826–93), September 1869–March 1878* (Royal Historical Society, London, 1994)

Walvin, J., *The Quakers: Money and Morals* (John Murray, London, 1997)

Watson, S., *The Reign of George III 1760–1815* (Oxford University Press, Oxford, 1960)

William, M., QC, *Round London: Down East and Up West* (n.p., London, 1894)

Wilson, A. N., *The Victorians* (Hutchinson, London, 2002)

Windsor, D. B., *The Quaker Enterprise: Friends in Business* (Muller, London, 1980)

Woodward, L., *The Age of Reform, 1815–1870* (2nd edition) (Oxford University Press, Oxford, 1962)

Young, G. M. (ed.), *Early Victorian England 1830–1865* (Oxford University Press, London, 1934)

Xenos, S., *Depredations, or Overend, Gurney & Co. and the Greek and Oriental Steam Navigation Company* ('Published by the Author', London, 1869)

Zeigler, P., *The Sixth Great Power: Barings 1762–1929* (Collins, London, 1988)

Index